THE SON
of the
MADAM OF MUSTANG RANCH

Published by BookLocker.com, Inc., Bradenton, Florida.

Printed on acid-free paper.

BookLocker.com, Inc.
2016

First Edition

Editor's Note: "Joe Leonard is a man who spent his first five years living in the Idaho back country in his grandparent's cabin. From that point, his life just got more interesting each year. He was behind many "first" accomplishments in Idaho, including the first winter ascent of Mount Regan the first back country skiing guide service in the United States, the first Kayaking school in the country. It is our good fortune that Joe has agreed to share some of his Idaho adventures with us. He is an enthralling writer and you will find the following account of his early Idaho adventures uplifting and rewarding. This account, including success and failures on Regan and early stories of life in Stanley and Clayton, a smashing good read."

IDAHO: A CLIMBING GUIDE, Tom Lopez

"I remember looking carefully at Joe. I suppose I envied him, at least in the way we envy those who represent something we know we can never become and whose lives are of a completely different cut from our own. Joe, above all was living his life assertively. He was asserting he was an individual, that he renounced the urban jungles of his past, that he disputed mankind's rape of the earth, that he was one with nature. Utterly unpretentious, totally practical, completely absorbed in what he does and who he is, Joe has gone beyond competing with other human beings. He gives them space to do what they do and be what they are, those very tenants of his own life, but beyond that, he has come to a finely tuned appreciation of what matters and what doesn't. This is best characterized, I believe, by a story he told me about himself. Some years ago he had occasion to come to Los Angeles on business. He made it as far as the San Fernando Valley, took a good look around, decided his business wasn't that important, and made a u-turn. He never got to Los Angeles; his business, whatever it was, is still waiting.

In a way, Joe typifies the person one might meet in the mountains. It isn't fair to believe that he is out of touch with things, because he isn't. But he is the sort of person who discriminates between different orders of the same simple thing. He sees a mountain adventure as being exactly what it is; he doesn't elevate the experience to a life and death struggle against hostile elements (even when it is), nor does he downgrade it to a nuisance better accomplished by helicopter. Walking or skiing across mountains is not so much a "trip" as it is a pilgrimage, even though a pilgrimage is supposed to lead somewhere. Joe's pilgrimages, for him, lead to a heightened spirit, an intangible perception of self that is neither egocentric nor analytical. It is always a spiritual adventure for Joe. Even though he doesn't compete with other humans, he does compete with himself, and that is altogether different. He tries steep slopes, seeks extreme altitudes, forever testing how fast he can go. In a way he looks the part: eyes steely blue, hair prematurely gray, a long mustache, medium build – on the wiry side – and a deliberateness of action that makes for few false moves. He conjures up a vision of Hollywood's strong silent types. But he has a sense of humor and can be drawn out."

ZEN AND THE CROSS COUNTRY SKIER, Dan Blackburn

"You are the one that has the unbelievably interesting life story, including the story about your mother being the Madam of Mustang Ranch. My continued deep affection to you Joe Leonard and for the privilege of knowing you."

Ed Gellert

Great retrospective of the Mt. Regan climbs and near-death experiences. You and John had the balls to explore and the will to survive and learned a great deal about yourselves and "deep" survival in the process. The Robinson Bar years taught me a great deal about wilderness travel and central Idaho's unique traits - life changing!

Clark Wurzburger

Are you kidding me? I thought I was reading Hemingway. You have a ton of talent my man. This is something you should have started years ago. I've always said anything you put your mind to is top drawer. Why in the hell haven't you run for President yet? Better yet why haven't you written six top selling novels? You have the knack. There's nothing that I can tell you that you can't do ten times better. The best thing for me to do is keep my mouth shut and let you do your thing. Keep up the good work!

OVER THE EDGE, Terry Taylor

THE SON
of the
MADAM OF MUSTANG RANCH

JOE LEONARD

For my sons
Joe, Richard, Jesse, John,
and Conrad David, my grandson.

Life is a drop of dew on the tip of a blade of grass ...
evaporating with the suns first rays. Not dead, but reborn.

TABLE OF CONTENTS

Until one is committed, there is hesitancy, the chance to draw back, always ineffectiveness, concerning all acts of initiative (and creation). There is one elementary truth the ignorance of which kills countless ideas and splendid plans: that the moment one definitely commits oneself, providence moves too. All sorts of things occur to help one that would never otherwise have occurred. A whole stream of events issues forth from the decision, raised in ones favour all manner of unforeseen incidents and meetings and material assistance which no man could have dreamed would have come his way. Whatever you can do or dream you can, begin it. Boldness has genius, power and magic in it. Begin it now."

GOETHE

FORWARD

"I prefer to understand rare human beings of an age as suddenly emerging late ghosts of past cultures and their powers... Now they seem strange, rare, and extraordinary; and whoever feels these powers in himself must nurse, defend, honor, and cultivate them against another world that resists them, until he becomes either a great human being or a mad and eccentric one – or perishes early."

What the reader holds in his hands is no book, it is a life – and, as the reader will discover, it is a life of no small scope, given to no frivolous dreams, and always somehow living in a sphere greater than itself. It is not a life that has been simply *led;* it is a life that has been lived, in all the ebb and flow of existence, in the storms and springs of passion, in both tragedy and bliss. It is a life that has scaled mountains and lived atop mountains, at a height that most of us do not dream. It is a life that was driven back from many mountains, too, by foul weather or avalanche or injury; but it did not perish nor lose its way in these misfortunes, neither in body nor spirit, and always tried once more to summit, and once more again, until it stood above them.

I have long thought of my father as a man who might have been happier in the time of explorers, when there were still unseen worlds to conquer and unknown mountains to climb. To that extent, it has sometimes seemed to me that he was born several hundred years too late. What does a man do who is born into the wrong time? He makes his time his own – or he lives or dies in resentment of it. Without hesitation, my father chose the first of these paths; I do not believe he ever even suspected the existence of the alternative. His soul beckoned him to places where no human had set foot nor eye; and so he set out for such places. There were no new continents for him to discover in this modern age, no virgin forests, no uncharted lands; and so, he sought to traverse new continents *within* himself. Africa, Costa Rica, Mexico, the Arctic – he followed the wilderness and its primordial beauty wherever he could, as the precondition for a deeper kind of exploration. He climbed the mountains of the world, that he might climb the mountains of his own soul. And most of all, he found what he was seeking in the Sawtooth Mountains of Idaho, one of the most pristine wildernesses remaining in our country – and one of the fiercest.

Many men go to the mountains to escape themselves or their lives or their deeds, only to learn that "you can't cheat the mountain," and that in the end flight is a fantasy. My father was never among this company. He went to the mountains to *find* himself, his *true* self, in the fullness of love, and with a courage that sometimes courted recklessness, and a faith that did not shrink before the mysteries of this world. The wilderness is a mirror, as anyone knows who has passed some true hour in its company, and one must have the strength in those silent and profound spaces to gaze honestly also upon oneself. But when one can do this, and for even a few minutes rend asunder the veils of falsity that so commonly enshroud our lives, one perchance sees *through* to a richer vein of life and a truer mode of being. It was this that my father sought in every mountain he ever looked to climb – including in this book itself. And I need not remark, to anyone who knows my father, that he has pursued this purpose with a resolve, a clarity, and an intensity that is at once admirable and daunting. For there are human beings who as it were rebuke us, not through their speech nor through any intention, but through their very existences; *because* they live fully, their lives demand to know of us, why we live only halfway.

Joe Leonard has pulled so many souls into the orbit of a fuller existence; when he could not bring them there in person, he has brought them there in spirit, through a photography that seems to live and breathe, and captures the essence of those places, as much as anything ever could; and through his stories, the stories of seventy years of life, stories of joy and laughter, and misery and defeat, and growth and triumph and love. And though most of the people that my father has one way or another guided finally returned from the mountains, went back to the civilization that they knew and loved, and in which they might live safely, I do not doubt that the majority of them never forget the touch of their experiences in the company of a distant wilderness; I do not doubt that some part of them went back to the city basically *changed* after sharing in my father's world, and beholding the majesty of those ancient lands through *his* eyes. And when they find their moments of silence, when their eye turns still and inward, I do not doubt that their minds must wander back to days they once spent under the clear gaze of the open sky, to experiences that were in some fundamental way unequivocal, to a time in which they learned, once again, what it means to live truly.

What the reader holds in his hands is not a book, it is a life; it is not to be read, it is to be experienced. It is a life of some seventy years, a life that never once, in all that time, stopped feeling deeply and learning whatever secrets the world had to teach. It is a life that has seen and done marvelous things, and has brought others to the same. It is a life lived in the way that one wishes, in one's youth, to live forever: without compromise, with-out falsity, and most fundamentally, most importantly – without fear.

John Bruce Leonard

PROLOGUE

I believe that out of life's myriad possibilities and choices, the hand of destiny is always at play. It will forever be the silent pulse that compels one to grow beyond limitations, however acquired, and to find true meaning in life. All of us struggle with limitations and overcoming them can at times seem impossible. I have learned that it is all in how one looks at a thing, through dark shadow, or in light. This book is but part of my life story. It is a record of how I have struggled with my own limitations and how I found the strength to grow beyond them; how my own silent destiny has guided me in my quest for understanding the gift we have been given: *Life*.

My journey has taken me from an isolated childhood, into a crazed world filled with danger, violence, lust and regret. I have grown, through God's good grace, beyond the dark realms of my youth into a brighter world filled with challenge, adventure, and silent memories of times past. Life has beckoned me, carried me irresistibly as a river, toward spiritual enlightenment, and the wilderness with its mountains, rivers, skies and everlasting beauty, has been my sanctuary and place for reflection, forever my life's beacon and savior.

The stories that follow are but a few of those I shared with the people I was fortunate enough to guide into the mountains and rivers in my younger years. Some stories in this book are told simply for the humor or adventure they hold, some to share the colorful character of the people I have encountered over the years and the imprint they made on me. Then there are stories in this book I have never told before, some not to be proud of and many of them I never thought I would tell, those ancient secrets that we all keep buried in hopes they will never see the light. I have discovered that such secrets are no more than a millstone, capable of dragging one to despair and creeping depression. The correction is to reach into the dark closet where they lurk, grab them by the neck, ignore their protests, their whimpering, and drag them out kicking and screaming into the light where they will, like morning fog on a river, fade away with the light and be forgotten.

In the historical sense none of my adventures would qualify as epic. Even though the tales about kayaking dangerous rivers, climbing remote mountains, and back-country skiing in uncharted wilderness are filled with unexpected and extraordinary moments, they are not the same as discovering that the world is round or attempting the first ascent of Mt. Everest. But I have found that through a life of seeking, life itself can become an epic journey, leading to the discovery of love, compassion, courage; discovering the power of the mind, the power of faith, the way to joy and happiness. And, most importantly for me, learning the simple truth that my path has been, and continues to be, a journey home.

PART 1

SOWING THE SEED AND REAPING THE WHIRLWIND

ALL THE DEMONS IN HELL
WERE TURNED LOOSE

Struggling with
personal demons
is hard enough.

We hadn't gone more than a couple of miles when we saw a man in uniform standing on the bank of the river frantically waving at us. Like a covey of quail we started paddling in his direction and got close enough to identify his uniform - he was the Forest Ranger in this neck of the woods.

"Where the hell do you think you're going?" he yelled.

We paddled into a small eddy in front of him, "We're floating to Riggins."

In those days there were no permits required to float the Main Salmon River in Idaho – although, it was required that you sign in at the Forest Service office before beginning your river trip, something we neglected to do.

"The hell you say, are you crazy? This river is flowing at over 100,000 cfs - that's more than 100,000 cubic feet of water flowing every second out there, it is the highest level in recorded history! It's a monster and it'll get much bigger downstream, it'll swallow you up and never spit you out! Four people on a commercial guided trip drowned in this canyon yesterday, and they were in tandem rubber rafts. Two rafts tied together, twenty feet wide and thirty feet long. They use them on the Grand Canyon for Christ sake - they even had motors to steer and propel them. The people in that boat didn't live to tell about it - what chance do you think you boys have in those piddly-ass little boats? Looks to me like they'd do just fine on some small lake somewhere!"

That got my dander up and I couldn't stop myself from responding, "These 'piddly-ass little boats' as you call them stand a much better chance of getting down this river than any raft, even if you tied a hundred of them together. I have a kayak school on the Salmon River below Stanley, I know what I'm talking about!"

"Look, I don't have the authority to stop you," the ranger replied in resigned anger. "If I did I would haul your asses out of that river in a heartbeat and send you up to the madhouse. But if you insist on this insanity then all I can do is have you sign a paper saying that you understand that this trip is *suicidal* and you're going anyway."

His words were not reassuring and the word suicidal put me on edge. "We'll be fine," I said, my damaged ego rebelling. "We know what we're doing."

"I sure as a hell hope so. Wait here." He went to his truck and retrieved a form the Forest Service used to count the number of people floating the river each year. "What are your names?" he asked.

"John Ward, Vane Jones, Bob Richardson, and I'm Joe Leonard."

When he finished filling out his form he handed it to me. "Read that carefully and sign it," he said. On the form he had scrawled the following paragraph: "The people whose signatures appear below have been informed of the danger of this river at this time. The Salmon River is in flood stage flowing at over 100,000 cfs. I have explained that four people I know of drowned yesterday and the river is still rising. The signers understand that to attempt to float the Salmon River at this water level is <u>suicidal</u>."

With not a little trepidation I signed his form, and so did the rest of the group.

"Don't think for a moment that *when* you get in trouble we'll come looking for you. Good luck and God help you." He shook his head, walked back to his truck, climbed in and drove away, too disgusted to even look back.

I looked at my companions. "Sounds horrifying. I have no idea what we're getting ourselves into. What do you think?"

It's very easy to talk yourself *into* something, but very difficult to talk yourself *out* of something. It's human nature to believe we are more skilled than we actually are. "Let's do it." they all replied.

I learned recently that the high water in June of 1974 holds the record high water on the Salmon River to this day.

I paddled into the current and let my bow lead me downstream ahead of the others. It was only fair that I go first - I had been the one that had suggested this folly, after all. It wasn't long before the canyon started to narrow, the river was running fast and we were already facing heavy turbulence and huge waves. I could already read the signs, at this level the river was a Goliath and we were its toys. Before long the river would be *very* dangerous, *very* wicked and *extremely* violent - it would not forgive the least mistake. I was no stranger to peril. I had hazarded my life on the back of ice-bound mountains and water-gorged rivers. I had tangled with the dark underworld of illegal gambling and had risked my skin with the mafia itself. By all rights I ought to have been dead already. But this river was infinitely beyond anything I had confronted before and it was already too late to turn back.

As the river narrowed, we all heard the sound at the same time. As if someone were beating a huge drum in a cave - a deep *boom, boom, boom.* It was without rhythm and it came from everywhere, rattling our nerves like the Forest Ranger had, only worse. I could feel muffled vibrations in the boat hull beneath me. I looked around, nervously, and the others did the same – what in the devil was making that noise?

I was thinking about the ominous sound when a giant diagonal wave rose up out of nowhere in the boiling water to my left, and flipped me upside down so fast that I didn't have time to react. When I finally gathered my wits and brought my paddle to the surface readying myself to roll up, I heard the drums again, incessant in their *boom, boom, boom.* In big whitewater when you are upside down you can hear a roaring sound made by crashing waves and turbulent water, but this sound was short and abrupt - a hard thud, like a giant was beating stones together. I rolled back up and was instantly wrestling with the first difficult rapid - prelude to what we would be facing farther down the river.

All of us managed the first whitewater well. With our confidence boosted somewhat we entered a reasonably quiet stretch of water once again. We floated on, each of us trying to imagine what we might be facing ahead, seeking uneasily to ignore the eerie unaccustomed noises around us. I realized at last what we were hearing, and the realization sent a chill through my blood: the force of the water was so strong it was rolling boulders in its turbulent depth, moving and crashing them along the bottom of the river. We were riding on top of forces too great to imagine. We drifted on in silence, disquieted and apprehensive about what we would be encountering in the canyon below.

Our ignorance and our huge egos were making us very foolish, indeed. We hadn't thought that there would be no possible way to scout the rapids, therefore we wouldn't be able to portage a rapid that we felt was too dangerous to run. We were constrained now to pass through every gauntlet set before us, from here to the end of the line.

We had all kayaked the Main Salmon River before and were anticipating some of the harder rapids, with not a little dread: Salmon Falls had a rocky waterfall with a drop of about fifteen feet; and Whiplash and Chittam were the two most difficult rapids in high water, at least as far as we knew. Already the rapids in the steeper sections of the river were more violent than any we had encountered before. The waves were massive, many were looming ten to twenty-feet high, staggering in their size. The angry eddies were boiling and frothing along the sides of the river. Whirlpools would appear near the eddy lines, some of which looked big enough to swallow a kayak or a rubber raft, and some were so fierce and deep that if you were caught in one you would never get out.

All the important rapids had names. We had run them all in moderate water, but at this water level we had moved into a new dimension - the river was transformed. Time and distance had distorted our sense of where we were, even the landscape seemed foreign. Whether we would admit it or not we were in way over our heads. But, there was no turning back, there was no choice, we were embarked.

We were so lost on this river that we had no idea when we floated over Salmon Falls, a drop that we feared as much as any. The river was so high the falls had been completely washed out.

We were floating down a long straight section of the river when we saw a strange wave appear downstream. We watched it grow out of the river, hovering ominously twenty-feet above the water, with whitewater crashing at its crest. As we drifted closer to the enormous wave it suddenly collapsed and disappeared, leaving us stunned. I wondered if Salmon Falls could have created a pressure wave of this magnitude. Not only were we were floating down a monstrous river, but it also felt like we were caught up in some kind of a science fiction epic in which the laws of physics had been utterly suspended. There was no way of predicting what we would be facing next.

We found a small eddy that looked calm enough to venture into, and we took due advantage, all of us needing a moment to gather our strength for whatever was laying ahead. With great relief we climbed out of our kayaks and stood on t*erra firma.* I bent down on my knees and kissed mother earth and then dug our lunch out of my dry bag. We ate quietly, each of us at a loss for words. At length we broke our silence and started talking about our fears and our chances of survival. We were much wiser and more realistic about the magnitude of our undertaking than we had been when we put our boats in the river, just a few hours ago.

"If it doesn't get any worse than this I think we'll make it." I was trying to reassure myself as much as my mates.

Vane gave me a startled look, "What the hell are you talking about - worse than what we've been through? If memory serves me well, which I think it does, there are much bigger rapids ahead and when the confluence of the Middle Fork of the Salmon joins up, the volume of this river will almost double."

John mentioned the eddies and how dangerous they were, adding that without an accessible eddy there would be no way of exiting the river except bailing out of your boats and clinging to a rock or a bush - if you could find one. "We'll be in big trouble if one of us swims," he observed quietly. "A swimmer will drown, or at best be left sitting on the bank in a wetsuit with no food, no boat, no paddle, while the rest of us disappear downstream."

"That's what I've been thinking." agreed Vane. "If you swim you're dead. If the rapids don't get you, the eddies will. Worse yet are the holes. They're ferocious, I've never seen anything like 'em. If you drop into one, a big one, I can't imagine what it would be like - something like being trapped in a tornado that's lying on its back.

I agreed. "You're both right, but the most important thing to remember is if you swim you'll be sorry - really sorry. Even if by some stroke of luck you're able to swim out of the river, your boat will be lost."

"Roll up or die trying? Is that what you're saying?" asked Bob, glancing at me nervously.

"That's the way of it," I nodded. "We're all doing what we can to live through this, but we're in it together. If someone swims the rest of us have to do everything we can to save him. If you *do* swim remember to keep a good grip on your paddle. The rest of us might be able to keep track of your boat but the paddle is a different matter. Do *not* lose your paddle."

Trying again to lighten up what in reality was a horrifying situation, I added, "Then you never know, you might need it to fend off a cougar if by chance you make it to the shore alive. The others laughed nervously. After a moment, I added, firmly, "So this is what we've got to remember: *Don't swim.*

Everyone nodded in silence. As we carried our boats back to the river I couldn't help but think about Walt Blackadar.

In the nineteen seventies we were on the cutting edge of big-water kayaking. Walt Blackadar lived in Salmon, Idaho. He was the first of the new breed of big-water boaters, risking his life exploring the limits that a thirteen-foot long kayak could survive. From him I bought two boats and in exchange he taught me how to kayak. He was a bear in the river, he had powerful arms and he was fearless. His exploration ended on the South Fork of the Payette River when his kayak buried its bow under a log that was wedged between rocks, blocking the river. He told me once that he wanted to die in his kayak, and he did.

How did *I* want to die?

After our short reprieve we climbed back into our kayaks and headed once again down the river. We hadn't gone far when ahead of us we saw a giant wall of granite, blocking more than half of the river. On the right side of the wall the water was extremely violent and dropped out of sight, there was no telling what waited back there - on the far left side there was a dangerous eddy, a death trap, where the devil himself lurked.

The powerful river careened into the wall above the eddy, climbing almost to the top where it curled into an angry diagonal wave. At times the wave would break back, spewing massive amounts of water down its face. The force and violence of the diagonal wave was not continuous, there were moments that it would relax, and in that moment you could pass through. Chances were high that the wave would throw your kayak off its face and straight into the eddy below, but I foolishly thought I could make it.

"Which way are you going, Joe?" Bob asked me.

* * *

While researching for this book, I learned that this rapid was most likely Whiplash. If so, the dangerous eddy on the left was responsible for the deaths of the four people the Forest Ranger told us about. The guide of that unfortunate raft chose to sneak by the vicious wave by motoring into the eddy. He must have thought that his 35-foot long rubber raft would make it through the eddy line, but it didn't. The steep eddy line and the whirlpools were too much, even for that large craft - the big rig was flipped upside down and four people were drowned.

* * *

I looked at the wall of water that we had to skirt, and back-paddled slowly, contemplating. "I've never seen a wave that vicious," I said at last. "But I think it's runnable. I'm taking the wave. I'd rather face the devil I see then the one who might be hiding behind that wall of rocks."

With that, taking courage, I paddled out in front of the others and headed for the center of the wave. As I neared the bottom of the wave I was shocked at how steep it was - it was, at least, a forty-five degree climb to the crest of the wave. I started up the face paddling hard. The fast moving current was helping me climb, but soon I started sliding backwards. I dug my paddle deep into the back of the wave, which stopped me from backsliding and I looked back to see where my mates were. They were nowhere to be seen.

I slowly continued climbing the steep slope of glass like water. Just as I reached the crown of the wave, it rose high above me and exploded, tons of water slammed into me sending backwards off the crest. I was sliding backwards, totally out of control and there was nothing I could do. In an instant and before I even knew where in the hell my boat was going, I was hurled into the eddy - a swirling mass of an angry hell.

I was upside down in the devil's playground. The raging, frothing eddy was sucking me out of my kayak. I was fighting against tons of turbulent water, struggling to wedge myself in my boat and attempting to push my paddle to the surface, desperate to roll up and breathe again. Time and again I would try to get my paddle up and out of the water so I could roll my boat upright, only to have it sucked back down again, and again. I was running out of oxygen and told myself to focus. There were only two options – *roll up now, or drown*. To be sucked out of my kayak, or abandoning it, would mean certain death.

I struggled to keep my eyes open, trying to get a sense of direction. The water was so turbulent it was almost impossible to tell down from up. Suddenly I felt a strong upward surge on the paddle, and I could sense the flow of the water. Knowing it would be my last chance, I forced my paddle through the water toward the light, skimming the surface. I snapped my hips and found myself upright, gasping, coughing, and puking water - all the while frantically bracing with my paddle, slapping the boiling water on both sides of my kayak, first on the left then back to the right, left, right, left, left, right, trying desperately to stay upright.

The eddy was worse than a nightmare, it was alive. It was about sixty-feet long and thirty-feet wide. The center of the eddy was moving downstream, upstream, cross-ways, side-ways, up and down. Everywhere I looked there were whirlpools forcing the water down into black grottoes, giant boils exploding, throwing tons of water into the sky. The eddy was dead set, determined to pitch me over.

The turbulence was continuous. I was battling to maintain my equilibrium, but the eddy never let up. The water would grab an edge of my boat sinking it, trying to flip it over. I would brace with my paddle, fighting to stabilize my boat, only to find the currents sneaking round to grab the other side. I had no time to paddle or turn - I could do nothing but slap and slash the water frantically, attempting to keep from flipping over again.

It was outrageous. I was bordering on exhaustion and terror was setting in. My kayak was still floating backwards, slowly making its way downstream. Looking over my shoulder I saw tree upon tree jammed against a huge boulder at the end of the eddy, with water flushing through the logs like a sieve - if I tipped over here I would be sucked into the log jam.

It must have been divine intervention that helped me force my way toward the center of the eddy, and away from the eddy line. The treacherous whirlpools once more started dragging me down and releasing me, again and again. I couldn't do this forever, I had to keep moving forward. I took a deep breath and with tremendous effort, combined with luck and determination, slowly pulled my kayak forward through the brutal water in the center of the eddy.

With indescribable relief I entered the fast flowing current heading back upstream and away from the log jam. The upstream current forcing the water back to the river was not violent but was moving fast, tearing away rocks and eroding the bank bordering the eddy. There was nothing for me to grab hold of on the eroded bank. It would have been impossible to climb the steep, muddy, slippery bank and get the hell out of the river and onto dry land, so I focused my attention on punching the eddy line at the very top end. I didn't have to worry about getting there, the current was carrying me much faster than I wanted to go.

At the top of the eddy, where the upstream current was trying to return to the river, it was crashing into the wall of the river, it was at least four feet higher than the level of the eddy. I had only to follow the upstream current and punch through that wall of water and I would once again be back in the river, which would seem like a return to paradise. I paddled with all the strength I had left, knowing that if I didn't get far enough out into the river I would once again be caught in the eddy line and have to start all over again. The prospect of that was horrifying.

But that is exactly what happened.

The instant the bow of my kayak hit the wall, it slammed the front of the boat around and back into the eddy. The only difference this time was that my kayak was pointed downstream and I could see where I was going, even if I had no control over the process. I was, once again back in the wild terrifying unreality of the eddy's immensity. I was in a wrestling match with a diabolical force.

As fast as this thought went through my mind, a whirlpool caught me from behind and sucked the tail of my kayak down. It felt as if my kayak had taken on water – the back of my boat was pulled deep below the water and my bow was pointing straight to the sky, and I was sinking deeper into the darkness, the wall of spinning water was rising around me and I was spinning like a top, sinking, spinning, time slowing down, spinning - memories of my life flashing back, like a movie, through my mind, spinning through the echoes of time...

ECHOES OF AN ANCIENT PAST

*In the darkness of night lay a newborn babe and his
mother. The chill of coming winter was broken in the
warmth of their soft feather bed. The souls of mother
and son had been together on thousands of journeys,
experiencing life in the past, none of which would be
brought to conscious mind in this one. And so it began
again...*

My mother, Dorlene, was 16 years old - not too young to
bear a child in 1939 at the tail-end of the Great Depression. She
was a beautiful young woman, gifted with eyes blue as the
Mediterranean Sea and long, soft curling dark hair. Her body
was perfectly proportioned, lovely and graceful, a body that
would serve her well as her life unfolded. The only fault she
could find in her well-sculptured countenance was a slightly
oversized nose, a flaw she could not abide, which she would
correct in the future during the years when reconstructive
surgery held that a perfect face would somehow bring on a
perfect life. She had an independent streak and instinct for
survival that would take her to the top of her profession; she
would become a fine example of entrepreneurship. She would
become the most famous of madams, the Madam of Mustang
Ranch.

But all that lay still and dormant, awaiting its proper time.

In this moment, with a newborn babe lying in her arms,
she was still a mother; she was still a wife. She still had a
husband who, she still believed, would play the part of a
responsible family man and look after her and their son. Life
had yet to deal her the harder blows, and she had yet to respond
in kind.

Perhaps, with a keen enough eye, one could have seen the cracks on the surface even from the start, all those parts that seemed to join together, but wouldn't quite; all those individual pieces that promised one day to break apart.

My mother met my father, Dick Leonard, a dashing 20-year old, one golden fall day in Boise. He lost no time in convincing her that their love was meant to be, a match made in heaven, and that by marrying him she would discover all the goodness life could hold. They married soon after and my mother found herself, after a memorable New Year's Eve celebration in 1939, a pregnant woman. My mother wanted to name me Dorian, but my father insisted that I was no Dorian and named me Joe. It was the best, the *only* gift, aside from that of my life, he ever gave me.

My mother's father, Bill, was an original Idaho cowboy. His whole life was about cows and horses. He grew up while sitting in the saddle of his favorite horse. His education was hard-gained and his mentors and heroes were the rough and tumble cowboys of the Idaho range whose lives were as wild and free as the land they rode. He could break a green horse and lasso a calf off its back and hog tie him before he was old enough to grow hair on his face. He loved the rowdy life. He learned to drink at an early age and soon became a favorite amongst the boys, on account of his stories. He could keep his cowboy friends laughing, slapping their knees and drinking their whiskey dry until the lights went out.

My mother's mother, Nellie, was crafted of different clay. A pioneer before she was ten years old, she had left her home in Oklahoma with her mother and father in the late 1800's in a covered wagon, and headed northwest to Idaho. They had heard of an exquisite place called Indian Valley there, a paradise where the weather was perfect and the Indians were friendly. The soil was as black as coal and so fertile that you could raise vegetables from early spring to the verge of winter. The warmth from the low mountains surrounding prevented the killing frosts that visited much of Idaho so unexpectedly at almost all times of the year. The land was perfect for apple trees, plum trees, pear trees, peach and cherry trees, and mulberry trees. It was claimed that the climate and land were so perfect you could even grow grapes. Water was abundant, flowing everywhere, and rainfall was dependable. Grass was as high as a horse's withers and your livestock would never grow hungry.

That was the story they were told, in any case, and in full faith they headed for the land of opportunity where plenty awaited.

My grandmother, Nellie, walked almost the whole of the distance from Oklahoma to Idaho, as I remember hearing the tale. It was her responsibility to carry the heavy flat-iron, and she fulfilled her promise to see that it arrive safely in her new home. She was the picture-perfect farm girl. Her eyes were as blue as the Idaho sky, and she would pass that gene on down through the generations, to her daughter and hence to me. Her hair tended towards blond, bleached by the sun, witness to all the time she had spent out of doors. When Nellie met Bill for the first time she found him irresistible.

He was the perfect cowboy, and a young woman's dream. She married him without looking back and stood by her vows - until death do us part, through thick and through thin.

My father, on the other hand, was no cowboy, and Bill had no use for him. He let him know in no uncertain terms just how worthless he thought he was, each time they had occasion to meet. To avoid the pain my grandfather inflicted upon him, my father joined the Merchant Marines. It would be the last I would see of him for decades. His absence, or so I later heard, would force my mother to prostitution.

I was born at home with the help of Nellie in September of 1939. Home was 160 acres of Idaho ranch located on Deer Creek, nestled into the foothills of the Sawtooth Mountains – a mystical setting that has carried me throughout my life. It lay in my heart like fallow land through the dark times that were to follow.

BROKEN BEGINNINGS

Some say that life
begins
with
your first memory.

There are memories that break through the hidden recesses of mind, as though a camera shutter had opened and seized upon the moment, capturing not only the visible, but everything that created the world of that instant – the things you smelled, the way you felt and the sounds that surrounded you. You know that for as long as you live you will remember every detail, in the same way and for the same reason as you remember who you are. My first memories of the ranch at Deer Creek began when I was about four. To this day at times I still catch scent of a fragrance or hear a sound that carries me back to that vanished life. Living in such a quiet and secluded environment one was hard-pressed to acquire much in the way of social skills, a deficit that plagued me in my early years. The only other child my age that I met was a cousin who infrequently visited the ranch.

So I grew up alone, but I don't remember being lonely. To the contrary, without playmates I had become self-sufficient and self-reliant, absorbing the peace from the forests that surrounded the ranch and drinking the tranquility of the crystal clear stream that flowed endlessly by our log house, seeming to arrest time in its very constancy. Even the minnows and insects that inhabited its cold waters could rob my attention for endless hours.

I remember the early morning light that visited my home, I remember walking to the barn with my grandmother to help her milk our cow. As I write I can smell the hay and the sweetness of warm milk, I can hear the lowing of the cow being relieved of her abundance and the sound of the stream striking the sides of the pail. I remember the vision of grandmother's strong but gentle hands pulling on the pink udders. Looking back on those precious moments I wonder what life would have been if I had never departed.

The ranch-house was built of logs harvested from the pine trees that shadowed the foothills of the mountains like the beard of a great sleeping giant. They were cut by hand and hauled from the forest by Bertha, an old Clydesdale work horse. Bertha was a wedding gift, as the ranch itself had been, to Nellie, from her father. Little did my great grandfather suspect at the time how this heritage would be menaced by his own son-in-law.

My grandfather Bill suffered from alcoholism his whole life. I don't think he struggled with it, it wasn't self deception. He accepted that he was an alcoholic. Alcohol was the fuel that fed his identity. When the urge was strong on him he would drive his old Model T Pickup to Boise, spending their hard-earned money, buying drinks and spinning yarns for his cowboy friends. He would come home when he ran out of money and stay a few days until being sober was more than he could stand. Then he would back the pickup to the corral once more and load up a calf, to be sold for cash money, and he would head yet again to town, as Nellie watched with her hands on her hips and helpless consternation on her face.

As a child, I was generally exempt from the consequences of my grandfather's dereliction, but sometimes it touched me, too. Late one afternoon Grandfather returned from one of his excursions to town with a man sitting next to him in the passenger seat. We didn't get many visitors and in great excitement I ran down the narrow dirt path, traveled by so few, to greet them. Grandfather opened his truck door and slid easily to the ground. Then the passenger's door opened. I watched the stranger make a curious wobbling descent out of the truck. His body was partially hidden behind the truck door so all I could see were three legs resting on the ground, two of them small as a stick. I stopped short, dumbfounded.

He was slow to move and his face looked tight. He grimaced each time he took a step towards me. I had never seen such a thing. My mouth hung open, my eyes grew wild with shock. I wanted to flee back to the safety of the cabin but fear permitted no escape. He stared at me with his hard eyes and without saying a word slowly lifted one of his bizarre legs, touching me in the stomach with its foot. It felt as if I had been struck by lightning. Horrified, I turned at last and fled to refuge. But the stranger pursued.

My small bed was made up in the corner of the kitchen next to the wood-cook stove. It took me no time to slide under it. Hidden in its shadow I watched as the three-legged man walked into the cabin with his inexplicable lurching gait and sat down at the pine table. Grandfather took two mugs from the cupboard. He pulled a brown bag from his coat pocket and unscrewed the cap from a bottle of whiskey. I watched as he poured the amber stuff, set the bottle on the table between them, and the mugs before them. Grandfather and his friend talked on endlessly as they drank their whiskey, while Nellie sat quietly in the background. By and by she became disgusted with their conversation, which I remember not a word of, and rescued me. She took me to the barn to help with the evening chores.

My excitement for future visitors was subdued to say the least, and my young years were spent alone in the vastness of the ranch. On occasion, in summer months, Nellie would take me with her into the mountain forests where she would gather blueberries and choke cherries and huckleberries along Deer Creek with me by her side, beating off the occasional rattlesnake with a long stick.

It didn't take Bill many years to sell off what remained of the cattle, as he sought to appease his unappeasable thirst for liquor. The day came when he loaded the last calf they owned into the bed of the old pickup. Standing on the porch of the cabin, with arms folded across her breast, Nellie called out to him as he opened the door of the truck. "I can't take this anymore, Bill. I've had enough and don't want you to return until you've been sober for a year." Grandfather removed his hat, held it tightly in his fist, and reached his arms towards the Idaho sky, as if he could pull the clouds down to hide his helplessness. But those beseeching arms fell at last, and he set his hat back on his head. He checked the halter rope that secured the calf, climbed in the truck and drove away.

At the age of 83 he would return to Nellie, cowboy hat in hand, arms open once more. "Nellie, I haven't had a drink for nigh onto a year and am asking if your offer to take me back still holds true."

Looking at him with eyes filled with the weariness of the hard spent years, she opened the door of her little house and replied simply, "Welcome home Bill." All that time Nellie waited for his return. Home he had come, and at home, three months later, he died in her arms.

DESERTED

Childhood is a struggle
without
 the tenderness of a loving mother,
without
 the guidance of an understanding father.

In my earliest memories I find a conspicuous absence, which in the end was as important to my development as anything that actually surrounded me. I look back on the past, on my past, my distant childhood, and I see no father's guiding hand, no mother's tender smile.

I often wondered about my parents as I grew up on the ranch with Nellie. It was not something that was discussed openly. The story I heard many years later was that my father had disappeared to some unknown land across the ocean. My mother had moved to Boise and worked as a waitress at one of the local cafes until Grandfather left the ranch. Her income as a waitress was not sufficient to cover the expenses of the ranch, and so she made the decision that would change her life forever.

That, at least, is what I was told, long after the decisions had been made and their true motivations lost to the past.

I didn't meet my father until I was fifty years old. Plenty of time to create an imaginary life for him, a life filled with mystery and intrigue. I think it is normal for children whose fathers abandon them to try to invent fantasies that might substitute the glaring and agonizing omission of a real father. But not everyone in such a situation is given the possibility, as I was, of seeing how that fantasy compares to the truth.

I had been invited to a party in Boise when a well dressed man about my age approached me and asked, "Joe Leonard?"

"I am."

"I'm your cousin. My father is your father's brother."

It was a stunning moment. I was bewildered, and sputtered, "I didn't know I had any relatives from that side of my family."

"In the flesh," he smiled. We have read about your adventures in newspaper articles. So, you are a mountain climber, a skier, and a kayaker? Heck, there was a film of you kayaking Shotgun Rapids on the Salmon River on the television recently. It looked like a wild ride."

Still trying to get my arms around the fact that I not only had a cousin, but one that might know what had become of my father, I replied rather hastily, "You must know something about my father – is he alive? All I know about him is that he left my mother soon after I was born."

"Alive and well, living in Sacramento with his wife and son."

It seemed almost impossible after all these years to hear of him. If my father's brother knew who I was and where I lived, I thought my father must have known too. Why had he never written or tried to find me?

I asked my cousin if he had my father's address and he assured me he would send it, along with a short version of my family tree, as soon as he could.

The proof that my father was alive unearthed emotions that I had carried since childhood. I had been abandoned and felt profoundly unloved. When my cousin finally sent me my father's address, I wrote him a scathing letter asking for answers, not really expecting a reply, merely to express my frustration, anger, and pain; but reply he did and his answer was simple, "I have been waiting for you to find me."

Casting aside my anger, I drove to Sacramento to meet him determined to understand why he had chosen to desert his wife and his son.

His life was far from the mystery and intrigue I had created for him. He was nothing like I had imagined at all. He was not a tall man, but handsome, and he looked to be in good shape for a man over seventy. Most astonishing of all, he had spent his life working in a mortuary, of all things. The reality of his life was almost an insult to me. He had abandoned me, had abandoned my mother – for *this?*

I also met his wife, an angry old woman, bitterness permanently etched on her face. She treated my father without respect and gave me the impression that she thought she had married beneath herself, that her life had not turned out to her satisfaction. She was plainly resentful. Her words were full of self pity for her wasted life, and contempt for him. She seemed haunted with suspicion of my motives for being there, and my forty-year-old half-brother, who still lived with them, wasn't much happier than she was, and was less than enthusiastic about meeting me. It was an odd and uncomfortable reunion and I found in the end that my initial resentment was disappearing into an unexpected emotion: I felt sorrier for my father than for myself.

After visiting him and his second family, I was finally able to realize – though this realization too would take time to grow in me - just how lucky I was that he had stepped out of my life. We continued writing letters to each other over the years until he died. His life had passed without a hint of passion, and he could neither boast of success nor accomplishment. His existence had no obvious merit. He died an unhappy man and there was nothing I could do to help him, but accept what had passed between us without judgment, and most importantly, without guilt. I didn't praise him or hold him in high regard but I had forgiven him, and in doing so my anger died with him.

My mother's absence, even to hindsight, was harder to understand. It was sporadic. She never missed a Christmas when I was a boy. Like clockwork, every Christmas day morning, she would drive up in her beautiful Cadillac and open the trunk, laden with presents, which she would unload for me to open. I made the unwrapping of them fill as much time as I could, thinking if she would sit with me for awhile she might find some magic in it and decide to stay, or maybe take me with her. But it was as if she was just a figment of my imagination. She would flit in and out of my life before I could even take a breath. By Christmas day lunch she would be gone, and I would not see her for months, as she lived her secret life – a life that I was too young then to even begin to understand.

It has not been easy to peel back the layers and the feelings of rejection and lack of self-worth that have haunted me for most of my life. I have learned to replace them with what I now know to be truth. Yet I struggle with it to this day and have to be wary of falling into the trap of self indulgence and judgment. I have had to learn how to live at a higher level of understanding and constantly remind myself what levels I want to reach in this lifetime. Then, and only then, has this difficult lesson become something worthwhile, something I can teach and live by. I can love my parents for all they have taught me about anger, judgment and guilt.

In hindsight, the best thing my mother ever did for me was to give me up to Nellie to raise in my young years. She knew Nellie would give me the best home she could, something my mother could not do, or would not do. I believe she also wanted to protect me from the ugliness and the demons she had welcomed into her own life. For the duration of my childhood, she did. But I would find my way there, one way or another.

EDUCATION

Learning to talk
to walk
is essential -
everything else
can wait.

When I was old enough for it Nelly decided to move to Boise so I could attend school. She sold the ranch for one-thousand dollars and bought a small house within walking distance of Garfield Elementary. At the time I did not appreciate the gravity of her sacrifice, but I can see now that there was nothing she wouldn't have done for me. As difficult as her memories were of the ranch, she loved it and would probably have lived all her life there had it not been for her determination to provide me with a good home and life.

My first day of school was terrifying and traumatic. Two hundred or more children spanning the first through the fifth grades had gathered in front of Garfield Elementary, some lined up in rows, waiting to go inside others were rowdy, wrestling, laughing, running here and there. More children than I had ever seen or thought about, more children than my young mind could comprehend. I stood in their midst, paralyzed with timidity. I was blessed in the moment to be standing in line behind a little girl just about my size who confessed she was starting school for the first time too. She seemed as frightened and out of place as I, and we at once shared our fears.

I remember her eyes, enormous and perfectly round. She wore a pink dress that looked as if it hadn't been washed for several days, and she had no shoes. Time passed as the never-ending line of children crawled forward. We continued talking and stuttering about our anxiety and our excitement, wondering what adventures lay before us. I was comforted in the thought that I had made my first friend and was grateful that I was not alone. As we slowly approached the door of the school my terror abated. I was filled even with a glimmer of hope that I could make it in this new undertaking, had in me the sense of some great new beginning.

When finally we arrived at the door we found our way blocked by a huge woman, as wide as she was tall, filling its whole expanse. She was asking questions of the young boy in line just ahead of us. "What grade are you in? What is your name?" As her interrogations filled the air we timidly started up the steps. When we reached the door the woman looked down at my new friend with her hard eyes and commanded, "Where are your shoes?"

"I don't have any." my friend responded, so quietly I could barely hear her voice.

"No *shoes?* You *can't* come to school without *shoes!*" cried the woman, utterly appalled. I stood in bewilderment, yearning to tell this enormous and unfriendly woman that my friend could have *my* shoes, but my thoughts were frozen in my mind, no words could be spoken. My little friend turned and looked at me with tears streaming down her innocent face, and she ran down the staircase and away without a word the more. Disappearing with her was the confidence she had given me. The suffocating fog of fear returned. I never saw that girl again and her absence marked the darkness of my early education. I was alone once more, lonelier than I could conceive of or ever imagined possible. I had lost my first and only friend and was about to discover that new friends would be hard to come by.

As my first year of school progressed, I would think about that girl and wonder what kind of people her parents were, parents who would not even provide her with shoes for her first day of school. I wondered over the lack of feeling they must have had, unaware and careless of her needs. And I wondered over her future. It was my first conscious thought of the suffering that some must endure in life. It was a suffering many times greater, so much more tragic than my own.

I hated school and feared teachers from the first moment. I am the only person that I know who flunked the first grade. Many days I vividly remember sitting in the corner with my back to the class with a dunce hat on my head – more times than I care to recall. It was humiliating and demeaning. I was lost to shame and remained convinced of my basic lack of intelligence for many long years afterward.

I had trouble making friends, but it seemed as if I had my share of enemies. Just a few blocks away from my house lived two young boys, twins, whose names were Vicky and Dicky, names I am incapable of forgetting. Each day they would chase me home from school hungering for a fight. They were filled with a hatred I just couldn't understand. I was no fighter and would end up at home crushed by their aggression, showing the bruises of abuse. Nellie never said much and silently tended to my cuts and sores, washing the dirt and blood off my face.

During the summer months Nellie would hire out as a cook in logging camps. Thus I joyfully returned to the mountains with her, feeling relieved to be away from my dreaded school teachers and the bullies who tormented me. My days were once more filled fishing the streams and pools of nearby creeks, wrapped once again in the sensuous pleasure of the natural world. Nellie warned me each morning, as I left the logging camp with my can of worms and fishing pole, to watch out for bears and rattlesnakes. Those were meager threats to me, compared to what I faced at Garfield Elementary.

But the summer months would end too soon and I would find myself back there again, full of dread of teachers and threatening classmates, filled with longing for the streams and mountains, the bears and rattlesnakes.

* * *

Out of school at least my life was beginning to take a normal shape. I was energetic and filled with adventurous spirit, and I was starting to dream of a bright future, as children will and should do. I had recently found baseball, and more than that, found that I had some promise in it. This was a great discovery for me, for it was one of the first times in my life I felt I had any worth. My head was filled with dizzy fantasies of becoming a professional baseball player, and leaving behind the painful reality of school and abandonment that was already pressing round me.

I was eight years old and was becoming quite bold in the manner of young boys. But, even more than most young boys, I was prone to hurt myself.

I had an injury which demolished any dream I ever had of becoming a professional baseball player; indeed, an injury which made it seem unlikely I would ever be capable of doing anything that required much physical strength.

As most boys are wont to do, I had climbed onto the roof of an old barn near our house and was straddling its peak, savoring my accomplishment. I was wearing my cowboy boots, the worst climbing footwear one could choose. Their smooth soles slipped on the mossy shingles of the old roof and I flailed helplessly, trying to stop my downward descent, to no avail. I fell off the roof landing on the frozen ground head first. I was fading in and out of consciousness and was having a hard time breathing. I struggled to get up, but fell back to the ground, a sheering pain piercing my muddled consciousness. In my foggy stupor I saw that my arm had been bent backward and was lying at a horrible angle. My arm had been snapped at the elbow.

Nellie found me writhing in pain on the ground. She helped me to stand and held me tight as I clutched my dangling arm. We ran to the house to find my uncle who was visiting that day. Not being of a particularly compassionate or tenderhearted disposition, he told Nellie my arm was just fine. He grabbed it and bent it backwards; through my scream of agony I watched his mirthful face turn to one filled with revulsion. We raced to the hospital where the doctor set my arm and left us with instructions on how to care for it. I had a compound fracture at the elbow and it would take a long time to heal.

The months went by slowly; the cast that bound my arm was an impediment to all my usual activity and games, prohibiting me from entering the only world in which I was still a normal young boy. I had already shown I was irremediably slow, and now I was physically handicapped as well.

But time did pass, and finally the day came to remove my cast. Nellie took me back the doctor who had set my arm, only to find the he had left on vacation. So we awaited his return. It was a whole month more before the doctor would cut my cast; and when he did, he found that my arm had become a mass of blisters and putrefied skin. I stared down in dumbfounded fear at this appendage attached to my body. It was immovable, frozen in the same position it had been held in all those months, and of a color and a form that were almost alien to me.

I couldn't move my arm, from the tip of my fingers to my shoulder. My fingers were rolled into a ball, sitting shrunken and white on the palm of my hand, stiff and unmovable. The doctor, on the spur of the moment, came up with the most unbelievable remedy; God only knows what he had been thinking at the time. He straightened my fingers one at a time, then my wrist, forcing each digit with agonizing pain, and taped the whole miserable mess onto a board. I remember screaming with each straightened finger, and the terror that had filled me at the sight of my wretched arm was compounded by the excruciating pain of the doctor's maneuvers.

When we left his office my arm had already started swelling. The skin was bulging between the layers of tape. Sleep did not come to me that night and by morning my arm had grown to gigantic proportions, its colors dark blue, almost black. If character is destiny, pain must certainly be one of its creators.

The next day Nellie, utterly distraught at what was happening, took me to another doctor. When he saw the work that had been done by his colleague, he became so enraged that he took the board off my broken member and broke it over his knee.

I spent the next three months in Elks Rehabilitation Center for daily therapy. There were children of all ages in the center, most suffering from polio. My broken arm seemed nothing compared to the suffering of most of the other boys and girls. Many of them were in iron lungs, and several would never leave the center. My sympathy and compassion had been stirred and I made an effort to get to know them. They were kindred spirits, each trying to find a place in life, each suffering from a malady which marked them out from the other, healthy children of the world, and separated us in some basic way from a normal life.

I returned home three months later and Nellie took over my therapy. Each and every day she sat with me and straightened each finger, moving each joint, and my arm – not as the first doctor had done, with gruff brute force, but rather gently, slowly pushing the limitations of my injury, seeking out some kind of normalcy in the shrunken and twisted remnant of a human arm. It took one year of her devoted efforts before I was able to move my little finger.

I had memories of my grandfather looking down on me before he left the ranch, after I made this or that mistake, and saying to me, "Boy, what's *wrong* with you?" The question stuck: and I had no good response. I was not bright, and to boot one of my limbs was next to useless. My life was shaping up to be a great disappointment for anyone who might care. And I was certain at least of this: that there really was at bottom something *wrong* with me.

It might have been much worse. Without Nellie, I would never have regained the use of my hand, nor arm, and my life would have been a wholly different thing. I never regained full use of my arm, but over the years it improved, until it became almost fifty-percent of normal. It was in the end a blessing, though at the time I could not possibly have known it. I had to learn how to compensate for the loss of mobility and strength, and in that necessity, I became more resourceful, and finally began to develop my intelligence, without even knowing what I was doing. My perceived limitations worked on me for the better part of my youth as obstructions to my growth, insuperable walls to my progress. But when I finally learned to surpass them, the tension I had built within them served to cast me far ahead.

It was not long before I was to meet another kindred spirit, one whose situation in life was even more extreme than the children in the polio ward, and many times more severe than my own; she would make an everlasting and profound difference in my life.

* * *

Nellie was not a particularly religious woman, but fulfilling the requirement she perceived as essential in any good upbringing, come Sunday each week she would dress me in my finest and send me to church. The nearest church was a small parish within walking distance of our new home. Its congregation believed that illness was a sin - that the only way to be healed was through prayer and that God alone was the healer. Doctors and hospitals were no more than false substitutes for true faith. In one and the same breath they preached a benevolent God who would send a person to eternal fire for the least transgression. But they were unanimous in this: that God would defend the innocent.

Next door to us lived a family, poor like we were, who had a daughter my age. She had cerebral palsy and was unable to communicate in any way. Her body was out of her control, in constant motion. Her arms, shoulders, torso, legs and head moved wildly, never ceasing their spastic frenzy. She couldn't feed herself, nor so much as scratch an itch. I remember feeling almost paralyzed when I was with her, not knowing quite how to behave.

Her parents were sorrowful people. They could never leave their daughter, had no time for just one day to themselves to go fishing or just to sit and relax in the sun. I was their neighbor, and they had known me long enough to trust me, so they would hire me to sit with her when they just couldn't take it anymore, or if occasion arose that they were both required to be gone at once. They asked that I watch over their daughter and make certain she didn't come to harm. Tentative and timid, I would do as they asked, and would do my best with it.

One day when I was watching over her, I remember turning to her, looking into her eyes as she looked into mine. In that fleeting instant I perceived horrible pain. There was awareness in that tortured body, someone who was intelligent and alive, needing to be loved, incapable of communicating her need. In her eyes I saw her hopeless longing for a life of hope and happiness. I sensed her longing to be given respect for an intelligence that no one could perceive. She was a miserable and helpless slave, imprisoned in a body that would do nothing her mind asked from it.

It was at that moment I truly understood the torment she was living with. She was trapped in a nightmare, and worse yet, she was conscious of it. And I knew suddenly I would rather be dead than to suffer a burning craving for a life denied. Indeed, death was her only possible release. Those were my thoughts at the time.

The next Sunday morning during church lessons I described to my teacher the suffering I had witnessed in the little girl who lived next door to me, and I asked, "Why did God do this? She's never hurt anyone."

"God works in mysterious ways," my teacher answered enigmatically, and at once changed the subject.

I soon left that church. I tried another, and another, and another, and for five more years searched for the answer to that simple, urgent question: why does God punish innocent children? Every time the answer was exactly the same: "God works in mysterious ways." Exactly the same, and every bit as unsatisfying.

At last I found a church where it seemed I might fit in. I did not care much for the congregation, but they let me play the steel guitar to accompany their hymns. I liked the steel guitar, it did not make great demands on my meek left arm and I liked playing for the congregation. The music was an inspiration to me. However, I was burning out on religion, and the final blow came soon.

One Sunday the minister ascended to his pulpit and looked out over his flock for a moment, smiling down on us. The crowd below gazed up at him in silent anticipation. He raised his arms triumphantly and announced in a booming voice, "Brothers and sisters, I have *great* news! I have learned that *we are all going to heaven!"* - Here he paused for effect - "And we are the *only* ones going to heaven!" He beamed down on all of us benevolently.

I looked around at all the church members, all chattering excitedly and smiling at each other in righteous anticipation, and I thought to myself, "I don't want to go..."

I could not believe in a heaven that my beloved grandmother was not allowed to enter. I could not believe in a God who would permit the suffering of the pure and the innocent. If he existed, I decided, he must be either crazed or cruel. That was the last Sunday I went to church. Nellie wasn't happy with my decision but accepted my choice, with undisguised regret.

I was eleven years old when I came to these conclusions. None of the churches I had attended agreed about the nature of God, and none of them could afford me a vision that could answer the questions that burned in me. I still remember a picture I saw hanging in one of these churches – a bearded God sitting on his throne, a man the size of a mouse writhing piteously at his feet. The bearded old God was pointing his finger at him in divine wrath. The meaning was clear: this sinner was on his way to hell. God was unforgiving, a cranky old man on a throne, damning everyone for the smallest of sins. Not once, in any of the churches that I visited, did I hear the preacher mention the self-righteous, insensitive teachers in my school, nor the bullies who tormented me, who were the only people that seemed to my childish mind deserving of any punishment. It did not seem to me that I was leaving the church; I felt rather that the church in its arrogance was abandoning me.

I was eleven years old, and I no longer believed in God.

In 1955, I was a sixteen-year-old having a hard time staying out of trouble. My mother, seeing all the mischief I was getting up to, decided at last it was time to try her hand as a mother.

Mom had just married husband number three, Bill Smith, who turned out to be much the same as her own father Bill. The only difference between the two was that my mother's new husband was a city boy and didn't have to sell his cattle to buy his liquor. His pockets were deep. I was suddenly brought into their lives, with no preparation whatsoever and almost no warning. Overnight, it seemed, I found myself living in a whole new world.

Mom and Bill moved to Boise and bought a huge two-story house with a basement, a swimming pool, and seven bathrooms, a far cry from the tiny house I lived in with my grandmother. It was strange living with my mother after all the years spent apart. I wasn't sure what she expected of me so I kept my distance, which wasn't hard to do in her large house. I sensed that she was as uncomfortable with her new life as I was with mine, but she at least seemed determined to overcome our tentative relationship, even if she did not know how to.

Occasionally she would invite me to dine with her and Bill at one of the better restaurants in Boise. She was adamant that I have good manners, and our restaurant sojourns became our classroom; forks, knives, napkins, behavior, a time and a place for each. She was patient and unremitting. I learned quickly and soon could have eaten at the same table as the Queen of England without turning a head.

It did not take long for me to learn that my mother also had a temper. I was intimidated by it and took extra care to avoid its arousal. Yet, over time we both felt more confident in our relationship and had grown comfortable with each other, but still, it was not the same as my life had been in my grandmother's home. There was far less warmth, far less human contact. Everything followed rules that I could never quite grasp nor see with much clarity, and the people I lived with were almost strangers to me in everything but title. Her attempts to bridge the gap always seemed to miss the point.

I awoke one morning to find my mother in a state of ecstasy, unusual for a woman who kept always a demeanor of quiet self-control. She ushered me to the door of the house and opened it with aplomb. Sitting in the driveway was a sparkling new fire-engine-red 1954 MG TD. She handed me the keys, kissed me on the cheek and whisked back into the house.

It was not the love I needed or secretly craved, but I was still a sixteen-year-old boy. If I had any hesitation or question about why my life had taken such an extreme turn, they were laid to rest – for the moment anyway. That beautiful new MG and the mansion with a swimming pool rocketed me to new heights of respectability. For the first time I had friends, girls waiting in line for a ride in my little red car, and a growing ego to accompany them.

But nothing lasts forever.

Soon my mother tired of Bill's drinking and their marriage fell into chaos. In hope of repairing a broken relationship, Bill took my mother and me on a road trip to Yellowstone National Park. The smell of the mountain air awakened fond memories of where I had grown up. One afternoon while warming myself at the huge fireplace in the Old Faithful Lodge, a young mountain guide introduced himself to me. He was an impressive figure – a strapping, handsome young man, filled with vitality and abundant healthy strength. He impressed me beyond words. I had found my hero, and I knew for the first time what I wanted to do with my life. Though it seemed impossible – me, with my stupid head and my ruined arm – I wanted to become a mountain guide, like the young man I had just met.

Not long after we returned home everything in my life changed abruptly. My mother and Bill began fighting, constantly. She was hard and unhappy, and Bill became a tyrant and took all his frustrations out on me. I could do no right and became the target of his verbal rampages. I couldn't live with the turmoil in our home and on a cold winter's day my best friend Tom and I decided to run away.

Our plan was to head for the mountains and become ski instructors, perhaps even get a job with the mountain guide I met at Yellowstone. We were only 16 years old, and delusional as most boys of that age, but that is the beauty of youth –it can always replace darkness with a brighter fantasy and can sometimes even make that fantasy become real. Tom liberated five-hundred dollars and a car from his parents. We packed our ski equipment and were off on a wild ride to the North, chasing our dreams of guiding glory.

There came a bitter cold the farther north we drove, and by the time we reached McCall, Idaho, the temperatures had become frigid. Night had descended as we drove into town and we parked the car on a side street where we planned to spend the night. The snow on the side of the road was deep and it was extremely cold outside, well below zero. Tom curled up on the front seat and I got as comfortable as I could in the back seat. We had nothing to cover ourselves with so we decided to keep the car running for what little warmth it would offer.

I awoke groggily to the distant sound of hammering and voices from a long way off. The banging got so loud I couldn't ignore it. Managing to open one eye I looked up to the window to see the barrel of a pistol resting against the glass. Reasoning power was beyond my ability. In groggy stupor I watched my hand rise above my face and unlock the door. Everything seemed far away and I slowly became conscious there was someone rubbing snow on my face. I began struggling to clear it away. When I finally opened my eyes I was laying in the snow, the only thing in my line of vision was a badge. As I sat up I saw another police officer rubbing snow on Tom's face. When Tom finally came around the police officers threw us, unceremoniously, into their police car.

On the way to the county offices the officers explained how close we had come to being asphyxiated. If it hadn't been for a neighbor calling the police when he noticed our car idling endlessly away, we would not have survived. After an excruciating night spent in the jailhouse, the only accommodations available for such as us, Tom's father and my mother came from Boise to find their wayward children. After listening to the story of how the officers had saved our lives, they loaded their two humiliated boys into separate cars and headed them for home. My dreams of guiding had been crushed – forever, it seemed. I was hauled back home just in time to watch the collapse of my mother's latest marriage.

An abusive husband and an erring son – not quite what my mother had pictured in her fantasy, and at last she caved. She left Bill and sold the Boise mansion, along with my beautiful MG. She packed our bags and without so much as a word drove us to Seattle, Washington, where she promptly handed me the keys to an apartment – not the one she would be living in. She gave me enough money that I could eat breakfast, lunch and dinner out, relieved to have me out of her day-to-day life again. It was but the latest in a long list of rejections I had suffered, and I was getting used to the idea that I would never be accepted by anyone I loved. In a way I was relieved, too; I had no one to answer to, no one to please. It was my first step into a life of independence.

My mother, ever the entrepreneur, acquired a cigar store in Seattle's Washington Hotel. I learned, a few years later, that its primary function was to provide call girls for the guests who stayed there. At the time, as inexperienced and naive as I was, I suspected nothing of this shadowy underworld, and took everything at face value. Not giving up her responsibility as a mother completely, Mom hired a private tutor to complete my high school education. This woman's name was Olive Suprell, with the accent falling aristocratically on the last syllable. Miss Sup*rell* had a home in the heart of town within walking distance from my apartment and was as trustworthy as the day is long. She was a calm, settled, virtuous woman, and utterly without arrogance. Six days a week I would be tutored by Miss Suprell. She was the first teacher that I ever learned anything of value from.

I saw little of my mother during those months, and was left mostly to my own devices. My grandmother was miles away and I had no contact with her, although I thought about her often. Miss Suprell was my only contact with the adult world.

Miss Suprell and I talked a lot about life and how to live it. Her lessons were the first that ever stuck with me. One of the pieces of wisdom Olive shared with me was through a question.

"Joe, do you daydream?" Olive asked.

"Sometimes I do" I replied, my eyebrows rising.

"There is only one justification for daydreaming, Joe, and that is to bring your daydreaming into reality."

I took Olive's words to heart.

And here was another piece of wisdom: "Joe never sleep in your underwear. Either sleep in pajamas, or naked."

And most importantly: "You make your own movie, Joe. If you don't like the movie you are in, you change it. You are the producer, script writer and the actor."

The wonderful Miss Suprell could sense a need, and had the gift of a born teacher to explain clearly what she saw. The lessons she taught me were set in motion by her wisdom and she intuitively knew where to ring my bell. She had lived a solitary life and was willing to share with me her joy and pain. I learned a lot from Miss Suprell. She was an angel.

But not angel enough to satisfy my mother, who was soon looking for a private school, someplace she could send me where she would no longer worry about what I was up to, living alone in the bustling and vice-ridden city of Seattle. I think being a part-time mother was more than she could handle. I can only surmise what she thought back then, but giving her the benefit of the doubt, I can see that she was probably worried that I might discover the world she lived in, and I don't think she wanted to face the image of her chosen life as it might be reflected in her only son's eyes.

The first private all-boys school we visited was in Vancouver, Canada. While Mom was talking to the administration, I walked around the campus asking questions of some of the students. What I quickly learned from them was that discipline was harsh and unruly students were not tolerated. That didn't bode well for a boy like me. As we drove away from the school, I asked Mom if there were any other choices.

There was. Hopkins Military School in Redmond, Washington. It was, of course, an all-boys school. This time Mom took me with her while we visited Colonel Hopkins. He seemed like a sensible man - a chain smoker with fingers browned from tobacco stains. How bad could he be? I thought to myself. Mom was also reassured when the Colonel informed her he would make a man out of me. I watched her face fill with radiance - making a man of me was *exactly* what she wanted.

Two days later I was well on my way to manhood.

It didn't take long for me to realize that making a man out of me entailed all the techniques that the American army used to make soldiers out of their recruits. The first class was instruction on how to make your bed properly. During inspection the Colonel's First Sargent would drop a quarter on it, and that quarter had better bounce. The bugle blew well before dawn. We had fifteen minutes to make our beds, wash in a cold shower (mandatory), get dressed in full uniform, and wait for inspection outside in the dark, standing at attention with our rifles in hand (not our *guns;* a *gun* was used for something else). After inspection we would return to our barracks, replace our uniform for gym clothes, and return outside for calisthenics and a two-mile run off campus, up a dirt road that ended at the highway, where we turned around and ran back to the mess hall for a long-awaited breakfast.

All disputes between students were settled in the boxing ring. Difference in weight was not a consideration, the Colonel was not a cautious man. Punishment for small infractions required a student to stand at attention on the parade ground until a Sargent gave permission to stand at ease, followed by a lecture. More serious infractions required the student to suffer the bull ring, carrying a heavy pack full of rocks with a rope tied to a pole and looped around his neck. This could go on for several hours before you were lectured, and asked if you understood what you were being told. "Yes, sir," was the smart answer. If further discipline was necessary the Colonel would be notified, to determine whether or not you were a *troublemaker.* In the unfortunate event that title was ascribed to you, you would be locked in the guard house, to live on bread and water for twenty-four hours straight.

Once every month or so the Colonel would order that we have training exercises in scenes of a mock war. The cadets were divided into two groups - one the enemy, the other the defender. In the middle of the night the Colonel would play his recording of a bugle calling us to arms. Five minutes later we would be on the parade ground dressed for battle, rifle in hand. One student in my barracks was a young man who just couldn't wake up in the middle of the night. He could never make it to the parade ground fully prepared to stand at ready in the required five minutes. On one occasion he arrived naked, his only adornment his rifle. This was preferable to the alternative. If you were late you were considered AWOL, and the penalty was twenty-four hours in the guardhouse.

The guardhouse was a four foot square box with a cold concrete floor, not even a chair to sit on. The only light came from a small opening near the ceiling. It was unbearable. If you didn't learn your lesson after a stay in the guardhouse, God help you. Expulsion was not an option as the school needed the revenue it received from its students. I had done my share of standing at attention, until my legs felt like rubber and wouldn't hold me, and I had run the bull ring several times. I felt destined for the agonies of the guard house. As I pondered my options, I thought I had two ways to freedom. I could talk my mother into taking me out of the school, which wasn't in the cards, because I had not yet proved myself a man. That left only one possibility – *run like hell*.

And that is just what I did.

I stuffed my uniform into my rucksack after returning from the morning ritual of inspection, dressed in my gym shorts, and grabbed my rucksack, hoping it wouldn't be noticed in the frail light before dawn. Luckily no one saw my pack during calisthenics. I dropped to the back of the line and I ran up the road following my fellow students. When we arrived at the highway, I turned and watched as all the students headed back to that Godforsaken school. I turned in the opposite direction, and fled for my life.

Thinking that I might have a better chance of finding a ride in my school uniform, which was a copy of the US army uniform, I hurriedly pulled it on over my gym clothes and started walking down the highway, determined to be picked up before the Colonel realized I was gone. It was early in the morning and there was not much traffic on the highway. It did not take but fifteen minutes before I heard a car approaching. I stuck out my thumb and held my breath. The driver stopped and I looked into the car. In the passenger seat sat an elderly woman with a warm smile on her face, so I opened the back door and climbed in.

The woman turned and introduced herself and her elderly husband, "My dear young man, it is *terribly* early to out on the highway looking for a ride!"

I didn't think it smart to inform them I had just run away from the military school down the road, so I told them the first thing that came to mind, "I've been on leave and was visiting some friends. I have to get an early start to get back to my unit before I am AWOL."

The elderly gentleman said, "You look quite young for a military man."

"Just unlucky I guess. It runs in the family."

The uniform had served me well. Two days later, hungry and tired, I was back in Boise standing at my grandmother's door.

"We have been so worried about you, Joe," she said with tears in her eyes.

My mother, on the other hand, wouldn't speak a word to me for the next two years.

* * *

Not looking forward to returning to school, but with no way of being able to provide for myself, I enrolled in Boise High School as a sophomore. On the first day I almost managed to get through three classes. The third class was gym. The coach's curriculum for the day was a contest to see who could do the most sit-ups. I was confident that I would be a contestant, as daily sit-ups had been one of the numerous exercises required in military school. The coach paired us up and I found myself coupled with a skinny kid. I was lean myself, and surely the coach wanted to match us up evenly. We weren't considered to be in league with the meaty jocks of the class. I started first, while the skinny kid sat on my feet. I felt strong and my mate started counting. When I reached fifty I noticed that a lot of the starters had switched places with their mates. I had reached over 300 sit-ups when the coach came over and asked my mate, "How many sit-ups did you do?"

"I haven't done any yet," he replied, nodding to me. "He is still doing his turn." I continued on with my sit-ups while they were talking.

"How many have *you* done?" he asked me. The coach had that over-aged ex-football champion look. He was overweight and red in the face, and he had an expression that revealed an unpleasant mixture of ignorance and pride. This was a man who had never descended into the valley of humility. As I proceeded with my sit-ups I thought to myself that he probably had high blood pressure.

Continuing on I said, "By his count I was at 330 when you arrived but I lost count while listening to your conversation."

He looked incredulous. He asked me to repeat what I had said, and I did. "Bullshit!" he shouted. And he turned and walked back to his jocks.

I stood up, went back to the dressing room, put on my clothes, leaving my gym clothes on the bench, and left the building. School wasn't for me, and never had been. That was my last day of formal education. In later years I passed my GED and took classes at Boise State University in Political Science, which did naught but titillate a life-long interest in politics and history.

I found a job at a nursery balling out trees for fifty cents an hour, figuring at least that way I would stay in shape. Fifty cents an hour doesn't sound like much these days, but it adds up – ten hours a day, six days a week. It was enough for a seventeen-year old in 1956. I saved enough to buy a used car, my transportation down the dark road that lay ahead.

YOUNG LOVE

Makes all
else
irrelevant.

I lived with my grandmother after leaving military school and kept my job at the nursery. My nights were spent cruising the streets of Boise, my days balling trees. I had a few run-ins with the local authorities and spent a few nights in jail. Nothing extraordinary for a young man with no direction and no family. Nothing extraordinary until I met Bonnie.

I don't remember when or where I was when I met her, but I will never forget looking into her striking sapphire blue eyes for the first time. It was like looking into a pool of crystal blue water, and brought to mind stories I had read about ancient Egypt. She was 16-years old and her parents had recently divorced; I was 17 and my mother was living with husband number four. Bonnie and I were both floundering and we both had a longing for our own home, one filled with family, love and happiness. We were young, unafraid, and as happens in life, had fallen hopelessly in love.

We married in the fall of 1957 and moved into our first house, not quite the dream we had envisioned, but good enough for us. In the blink of an eye our bruised lives had found brilliance. Our new-found freedom and sense of belonging gave us the courage to break away from past and burdened memories. We knew we could face anything life could throw at us, as long as we were together. We were malleable and adaptable enough to be shaped by the world we lived in, characteristics we would need for the challenges we would be faced with in the future.

I left my job at the nursery and became an apprentice plumber, making three times as much as I had balling out trees, $1.50 an hour. Ten months after our wedding, our first child was born, a son that we named Joey. One year later our son Richard followed. I was a proud father and Bonnie and I were ecstatic. I had been given a raise, a whopping $2.50 an hour. Everything we had dreamed of was coming true and life was getting better and better each day.

Then the recession hit like a bolt of lightning and the building trade disappeared overnight.

I was laid off and found myself all at once spending my days hopelessly looking for work. In the manner of improvident youth, we hadn't saved any money and were living off of my last paycheck, which was dwindling rapidly. Almost overnight our ecstasy transformed to panic. Bonnie found a part-time job at a 5 and 10 cent store, making just enough to put food on the table, but it was not enough to tide us, and we knew it. In the sleepless nights we tossed and turned in our beds, fretting over the present, worrying over the future, and without a clue as to how we might turn everything around.

Don and Lee Gibson, two acquaintances and fellow job seekers, told me they had heard that the Hells Canyon Dam was under construction and was hiring. All three of us were dead broke so we decided to pool our money and drive to the construction site together. Our money would buy just enough gas to get us there, but not enough to get back. If we didn't get a job we would be hard pressed to get home.

There was a lot going on at the construction site when we arrived and it looked promising. There were massive trucks barreling down compacted roadways, cement trucks lined up waiting to drop their loads, workers thick in every direction. It took some searching to find the man who did the hiring and in less than one minute we were politely informed that they were not taking on new workers at the present time. Dispirited, we walked to our car wondering how in the hell we were going to make it home on the remaining gas in the car.

That night we stopped in Baker, Oregon, at the Salvation Army. Don and Lee were familiar with the organization, having used their services in the past. Their pet name for the Salvation Army was Sally Ann. Sally Ann fed us a sturdy meal and gave us each a bed for the night. In the morning, after a night of fighting bed bugs, we were given a bowl of warm oatmeal and were sent on our way.

A few miles out of town Don noticed a car parked out in the desert. He turned off the highway, drove through the sagebrush, and pulled up behind it. The car had obviously been abandoned, for it was covered with dust and detritus, and tumble weeds had almost buried it. Don walked up to the car, lifted the hood and smiled. "It has a radiator!" he called. "Lee, break the tools out of the trunk. Let's see if we can't salvage this." They were worldly and experienced young men, prepared to survive off anything the land would hold out to them, the sort of men who could scratch through the dust and come back up with gold. Thirty minutes later Don had dislodged the radiator from the deserted car and we were on our way back to Baker. We found a junkyard and sold the radiator for twenty dollars, went to the nearest gas station and headed home.

Determined and persistent I kept searching for work. I heard rumor of a construction company that was hiring laborers in Idaho Falls. It was the same old story. I scrounged up enough money for gas to get there but not enough to get back.

This time I went alone and Bonnie wished me luck, watching as I drove off. I arrived at the construction site before eight in the morning, and found the foreman. Another wild goose chase, no jobs available. Where were Lee and Don when you needed them? At the time I had a 1950 Mercury. It was my pride and joy - there was no way I was going to abandon it and hitch-hike home.

While driving to the construction site I had passed by a field filled with farm equipment – tractors, wagons, trailers and lots of people just waiting to go to work. Idaho Falls was farming country and Mexicans did the heavy work of harvesting the crops. On my way back home I could see the workers in the field, bent over, chopping tops off of sugar beets and loading them in the wagons. I parked my car off the highway, climbed the barbed wire fence, and walked toward the laborers. They were following a wide plow as it slowly moved through the rich soil. With one hand they would pick up a sugar beet, and with the other they would chop off the top of the beet with a machete, shucking the green stalks. They would then throw the beet into the bed of a trailer pulled by a moving tractor, never stopping the whole while, they were in constant motion.

There were only three white men and they were driving the equipment. All the laborers were Mexican. Chopping the tops off the large beets didn't look too difficult and as I was young and strong enough I reckoned it was something I would have no trouble with. Heck, it was only a half day's work, after all. At a fast walk I caught up with the farmer who was driving a tractor that pulled one of the wagons. I jumped up on the step of the tractor, while it was moving, and asked if he would hire me.

He peered at me hard. "You're the first white boy who has ever asked me for a job topping sugar beets," he said as he wiped the sweat off his forehead with the back of his sleeve. "As a matter of fact it has been years since I saw a white *man* topping sugar beets."

"I am a hard worker and I need gas money to get home."

He nodded, shrugged, and spat off the tractor. "Well. The pay is four dollars a ton. A Mexican can top two tons of sugar beets in a day. If that suits you you're hired. We stop work when the light fails or when this field has been cleared."

"Sounds great," I said. I stepped off the tractor.

"Hold on there, boy," he called to me as I was setting out. "You'll need one of these." He rummaged for a moment in a compartment in the tractor, then threw a machete out the open door. It landed at my feet and slid in the dust.

Soon I was bent over with the Mexicans topping beets. I had an inkling that I was into some real hard work with the first beet I picked up. An inkling, but no idea yet.

The hardest job I had ever had before was child's play compared to this. Dragging heavy cast iron pipes under the floor of a house, carrying molten pots of lead to fill each joint, or balling out big trees with two-hundred-pounds of dirt wrapped in burlap and dragging them out of a hole didn't compare with topping sugar beets. There was no let up - the tractor pulling the trailer didn't slow down for stragglers.

I had never dreamed how much a beet could weigh. Holding one in my left hand and swinging the machete with my right hand to remove the stalk required concentration. A slight misjudgment with the machete could mean the loss of several fingers. For a while my technique improved. I wasn't working as fast as the Mexicans but I hadn't fallen too far behind either. As the day progressed my left hand had wasn't holding up and my back became so stiff that I feared I might never be able to stand upright again.

Then the fatigue set in. I found I could no longer pick up a fifteen-pound sugar beet with my left hand. I had to lay the beet on the ground to chop off the top, then lay down the machete and use both hands to throw the beet into the trailer. Hours later I was wrestling with the beets, like a man struggling to manipulate cannonballs. I couldn't lift one anymore and had to roll them up my legs just to get them in my hands. My left arm had given out and I no longer had the strength to throw them in the trailer. I would stagger to the trailer and toil to lift my beet over the sideboards, and then I would stumble back to the row I was working, drop to my knees, drag a sugar beet out of its hole, swing the machete – sometimes two or three strokes were necessary – cut the top off, and do it all over again.

Late in the day a young Mexican girl walked to me where I was working. She was very young, perhaps seven or eight years old. Without a word she picked up the sugar beet that I had just topped, and carried it to the trailer. In silence she helped me through the rest of the evening.

At last the machinery came to a halt and I looked around at all the people I had worked beside that day. Their faces glistened with sweat and were black from the dark soil. Even after a day of hard toil, their eyes still sparked with life.

The farmer climbed down from his tractor and held out his hand. Humbly I took it in mine, and could not even afford the strength to give a good firm grasp. He shook my hand. "I doubt like hell if you managed to top even one ton of sugar beets, son. But it wasn't for lack of trying, I'll give you that." He removed his hand from mine, reached into his pocket and counted one dollar bills as he placed them in my hand.

"That's four dollars for the ton you didn't top and four dollars for sticking with it. If you ever need work again all you have to do is ask me. I can appreciate a hard worker. I'll find something for you to do."

"Thank you," I said with sincerity, and then added, "And please tell these people that it was an honor working with them."

"Adios white boy," he said loud enough that several picked it up and repeated it as I walked from the field. As I passed the little girl who helped me get through my excruciating day, I handed her one of my dollar bills and thanked her.

As I slowly walked towards my car, I turned and looked back. Many of the workers were watching me leave, and as I waved goodbye, several hats waved back. A white-faced American boy had labored beside them for a few hours this day. Perhaps he would understand how hard they worked to feed their families.

Perhaps I did. I had learned a lot from those Mexican laborers and because of this experience they hold a special place in my heart to this day. I had always considered myself a worker, but I knew now what real work was. And I knew I would do just about anything to stay out of it.

ANOTHER LIFE

It takes many lifetimes
to reap
the benefits the
soul cries out
for.

I was caught up in the worst recession since the great depression, with two boys to feed and no work. Day after day I checked the job listings in the Idaho Statesman. The only openings were for salesman. Out of desperation I answered one of the ads for selling encyclopedias door-to-door, with no guaranteed salary. The management were all high-powered and confident. Their job was to sell selling – to convince applicants that selling encyclopedias was simple, anybody could do it, and that all it took was determination and confidence. But I wasn't confident that I could sell a dollar for a dime.

When I knocked on my first door my knees were weak. I was sweating and it wasn't even warm. I was terrified before I had spoken a word. People generally were too polite to slam the door on my innocent face and would allow me into their homes where I could at least practice my sales pitch. As time went on I grew confident, unafraid, and actually got quite good at it. Selling wasn't as bad as I had imagined, and somehow, impossibly, I started closing sales. I was finally supporting my family again.

I traveled a lot in those days – small towns in Idaho, Montana, Nevada, Utah, any small town where people were receptive to a newcomer with a sales pitch. On road trips we usually traveled in pairs, taking turns knocking on doors. Rick Records, a fellow salesman, was planning a trip to Wells,

Nevada, and asked if I was interested in going along. I liked Rick. Bonnie and I had been invited to his home several times and Bonnie liked his wife Sherry, a lovely, lively woman, and a good cook. We had started up a kind of friendship.

Rick and I drove nonstop to Wells passing by small towns along the way where I expected we would stop and try our sales pitch, but Rick was determined to make it to Wells. We arrived there around 10 at night, grabbed a motel room, washed up and walked to a restaurant next door for a hamburger. While we were eating Rick said, "I need a drink to calm me down after that long drive. I won't sleep at all if I don't relax with a few drinks."

"You should have let me spell you," I chided. "I was getting bored looking at this scrub desert. I wouldn't have minded driving for a while."

Rick grinned. "Sorry, but driving keeps me sane. Anyway, I know just the place. They not only serve good drinks but the entertainment is beyond your wildest dreams." That sounded good to me, if a little vague. We drove a short distance out of town and turned off the highway onto a dirt road. In the distance I could see a well lit two-story house.

"It must be a good bar for people to drive all the way out here for a drink," I said. "I bet they don't get much walk-in business."

There were several cars in the parking area, even a shiny new black Cadillac, but plenty of spaces left over for us. We parked and walked in the bar, and I was stunned; I had never seen the like. The place was filled with scantily dressed women, at least a dozen. *This must be the entertainment*, I thought to myself. There were five or six men standing at the bar, each with a woman at his side. The bartender was a middle-aged woman neatly dressed in black slacks and a white blouse. She had the face of someone who had lived a tough life. We sat down at the bar as she walked to us, laughing as she came.

"Hello, Rick! Long time no see. How's Sherry getting along?"

I was surprised that they were acquainted and thought that Rick certainly knew his way around the country.

"She's all right Patty. She's the reason I'm here."

Patty nodded with a knowing expression, but she said, "That's fine. Excuse me a minute, there are some dry throats just waiting for a drink, starting with this young stud you came in with. What can I get you, love?"

I was only nineteen years old, underage, and expecting her to ask for my ID. This was the first time someone standing behind a bar had posed that question. With a guilty frog in my throat, I said, "A whiskey with 7 Up please."

"Holly shit, a real gentleman!" she goggled "Now that's a rare event in *this* establishment." She moved with elaborate elegance as she walked to the other end of the bar to her waiting customers. She returned with my whiskey. I spun around on the whirl-around stool, acting like the gentleman that she had called me. I watched the scantily dressed ladies entertaining the customers. Some were reclining on overstuffed couches toying with men who sat beside them, others were sitting on their laps. One was gently caressing the hair on a man's head, another was looking into a man's eyes as if he were the most adorable thing she had ever seen.

Entertainment, hell! I was in a whore house!

This wasn't the first house of prostitution I had been in. When I had turned thirteen my mother's brother, Uncle Arlen, cornered me one afternoon. "Now-a, now-a, now-a, now-a get in the, now-a, now-a, c-c-car I have something to now-a, now-a, talk to you, now-a, now-a, about," he stuttered. Arlen had been given the nickname Jiggs because of his stuttering. Early on in life he discovered that if he drank enough alcohol he could control his impediment, so he drank from first light to first light.

We drove up into the foothills of Boise, and Jiggs parked the car on a dirt road overlooking the city. He reached into the glove compartment, brought out a bottle of cheap Tokay wine and unscrewed the cap. He threw his head back and drank what seemed to be half the bottle before handing it to me.

"Now-a, now-a, Joe, I am going to get you *bred*."

"Bread?" I asked, startled.

"Yeah, now-a, now-a by a woman, one who will take good care of you, now-a, now-a, show you the ropes. But first drink some of this, it will now-a, relax you."

I wondered if this woman was a baker.

What the heck I thought, as I took a swallow of the cheap, fake wine. "This tastes pretty good, Jiggs." I passed the bottle back to him and he took another big slug, handing it back to me once again. He started the car and drove back towards town. We finished our bottle of Tokay and by the time we reached our destination I was feeling no pain. Uncle Jiggs parked the car in front of an old gray clapboard house.

"Follow me." he said as he climbed out of the car and headed to the house. I staggered along behind him feeling relaxed and a bit breathless, not totally conscious.

Jiggs knocked on the door and a large black lady opened it, "Jiggs!" Looking down at me she said, "Who's the boy?"

"He's my nephew and it's time for him to get bred." The Tokay had worked its magic. Jiggs was speaking perfectly.

"What does his mother have to say about this Jiggs, huh?" she asked, looking at me dubiously. "He looks like a baby. Just how old is he?"

"Yeah, he sure *looks* young. But he's not. Hell, he's a teenager!"

I don't remember much after that, but I do remember lying on my back on a bed, violently ill and vomiting, explosively. I can remember the vomit, laden with Tokay wine, hitting the low ceiling of the room, slowly falling off the ceiling and dripping in my face. I was helpless. I couldn't even roll out of the way. I was in no condition for anything – not for bread or breeding.

These memories came back to me as I sat looking around the room. But this was a far cry from the seedy little shack that Jiggs had dragged me into. Rick and Patty were sitting next to me discussing business, but I wasn't paying much attention. I was enthralled with what was happening in the room. I noticed occasionally a couple would head up the stairs, always the lady leading the way and sometimes holding the hand of the man following her. It was all a bit too much for a nineteen-year-old head. I didn't drink much in those days, and I was already sot at my third drink. It was time to stop or *this* gentleman might have to be carried – to the car.

I turned back to the bar where I found that Patty and Rick were still in deep conversation, often interrupted by customers. The ladies in the room were dressed to stimulate the sex drive - long legs, thighs luring the eye, exposed breasts lurking behind finely spun cloth. I was experiencing lust on a scale that the future president of the United States, Jimmy Carter, couldn't possibly have fathomed.

On the back bar sat a punch board. They were common at bars during the fifties and sixties. Most bars used them to entertain customers trying to win a few bucks or a free drink. This one was different. They called it a pussy board. For one dollar a punch you might get lucky and win the services of a lady of the night.

The alcohol I had consumed was leading me down the road, with no return in sight. No matter how rational or responsible a person I was, my sex drive combined with liquor had turned me into an animal with the mind of a reptile, in pursuit of raw sexual gratification. Attributes such as faithfulness, sense of responsibility, breaking trust, fell out of my mind like I was flushing a toilet. I hadn't asked how much it cost for one of the girls, and I knew I probably couldn't afford one – but I could afford a few bucks for a few punches on the punch board.

"Patty," I said, catching her as she broke away from her conversation with Rick for a moment. "I want to buy a punch on that pussy board if you don't mind."

She went behind the bar, picked up the board and placed it in front of me, and I laid three dollars on the bar. She handed me the metal punch key and I randomly punched three of the paper tabs out of the board and handed her the key.

"Good luck." She smiled as she returned the board to the back bar.

"Sounds like you've finally come alive, Joe. Good luck." Rick laughed.

The first punch tab I unfolded was a winner. I had won a free drink, but that wasn't what I was looking for. The second said "Sorry, Better Luck Next Time." The third tab unfolded like an accordion and sent a chill up my spine. I was flirting with disaster, and that was part of the thrill. As I read the words, I blushed violently, feeling myself stirred, my senses running amok. "Pussy Winner." The power of self-deception was so deep, that I had no resistance to the moment. I sensed I was being tested by some profound power and tried to talk myself into sanity, but the serpent lurking inside of me was burning and the flame was in absolute control.

I looked at Patty and handed her the winning ticket. She smiled, "Take your pick of any girl not attached to a customer."

My eyes roamed the room. There seemed to be several women without partners, but one had caught my eye earlier and my eyes focused on her. She was young and extremely attractive in her white virgin negligee. She noticed me staring at her and with an innocent smile on her face walked to me and took my hand. I was flushed with guilt and seized with shame, disgusted with my lack of willpower – none of which stopped me as she led me up the stairs.

My demons had taken control and shoved me plummeting off a cliff with no one to save me but myself. There was no escape once the boulder of lust started its descent into the unspeakable emptiness that awaited in the abyss. The empty fire burning inside my body would only be extinguished when my lust had turned to ashes. The road to building character sometimes hands one a moral crisis.

Once in her room I made a heartfelt attempt at conversation. I was moved by an inner desire to know something about this young woman. I wanted to know why she had chosen to earn a living in such manner. "Do you like your profession?" I asked quietly.

"What better way than through intimacy is there to get to know someone? I enjoy my work, it's fulfilling, I'm providing a service, and I see happiness and joy reflected in the eyes of the men I entertain."

"Don't you get tired of it? Don't you want a normal life, a husband, a family?"

"I have a family, a big family. All the women who work here are my family. I couldn't ask for more, and even if I did my life would most likely hold little hope for the future. Here I have a roof over my head, good food on the table, and I get a week's vacation every month. If I were a waitress, which I was before I got this job, I would be lucky to get a week off in a year and wouldn't have enough money to buy anything or go anywhere. I would probably sit alone in my cheap apartment watching TV."

I was impressed with her candid answer and could think of nothing to say in return.

"My monthly vacation starts next week," she added after a moment. "We don't work when we're having our monthlies. My boyfriend will pick me up early in the morning and we'll drive to Reno. He treats me like a queen. He'll buy me a pretty new dress and we'll do the town up like royalty. I'll be treated with respect because everyone will think I'm sophisticated and wealthy, and at the end of my vacation he'll bring me home to my family.""What about marriage?" I ventured. "Don't you feel a need for a life companion?"

She laughed. "Marry some slob that couldn't make a decent living even if he wanted to? Or a couch potato, demanding beer and potato chips? No thanks, I don't think so. It's not the life *I* dream of."

In a few years I would hear many ladies of the night express the exact same sentiments.

Rick stood when he saw me coming back down the stairs. As I walked to the bar I overheard Patty ask him, "When will you be bringing Sherry?"

"Is Friday of next week soon enough?"

"The sooner the better. I need a new face. Sherry's a pro and I'll keep her busy. It'll be nice to have her around."

"All right then, we'll see you on Friday." Rick said, waving as he turned for the door.

"Thanks for the hospitality, Patty," I said. I was flushed, satiated and relaxed. Yet worn out, weak, burned out, full of guilt. And I needed some sleep.

"Come back any time," she laughed. "I need to get my money back."

"Soon, I hope to see you soon," I muttered. I followed Rick to the car. As we drove out of the parking lot I looked at him, filled with curiosity.

"Sounds like you found a job for Sherry?" "Sure did," he nodded, smiling. "She loves her work and she's one of the best. Now I can quit this stinking job of pounding on doors trying to cram a set of encyclopedias down some sucker's throat. This is the best day I have had in a long time. If Patty hadn't hired her I was going to talk you into going on to Fernley, Nevada. The bordello in Fernley is where Sherry worked before we left for Boise. The madam there was sorry to see her go and would hire her back for certain."

I learned much later that the madam of the bordello in Fernley was my mother. I had missed her by a hair's breadth. What a shock it would have been for both of us if I had walked through that door.

Soon after, Rick and Sherry moved back to Nevada for Sherry's new job in the Wells bordello. They would live comfortably off of Sherry's income. We were sorry to see them go.

In the meantime, I kept on keeping on.

Confident that I was on my way to a successful career in sales, I started looking for a better product, with bigger commissions. I found it: a startup Life Insurance Company. The product I was selling was a combination of stock in the company combined with a life insurance policy. It was a great product and the commissions were fantastic.

Bonnie and I bought a newer used car and rented a bigger house. I felt like I was on top of the world and Bonnie was happy. How good could it get?

The question should have been, how *bad* can it get.

We soon sold all of the stock issue, and all that was left was selling life insurance. It became too boring for a hot-shot salesman like me. Through the grapevine I heard of another start up life insurance company in Cheyenne, Wyoming. It sounded like another gravy train and I convinced Bonnie that we should move, get on that train while it was hot and moving fast. We packed up our 1954 pink Lincoln, the perfect automobile for a successful salesman. We loaded Joe and Rich into the back seat, I opened the door for Bonnie, patted the soft white leather seat, and away we went. A few days later we drove into Cheyenne and rented a motel room by the week. When we arrived it was windy, cold, and snowing.

"Don't worry honey," I told her. "We won't be here long. We should be able to start looking for a nice house real soon." I looked out the window of the motel room as the snow fell heavily to the ground, hoping my words would come true. Bonnie smiled. She had the ability to accept life without complaint. She never doubted that we would be provided for and took each day as it came, without question. Yet she was concerned for the boys and was wondering how she could keep them entertained while I was working.

Cheyenne is the most miserable place on the planet in the winter. It snows a lot and when it isn't snowing the wind blows the existing snow around. One way or another you are constantly fighting a blizzard. And it turned out that the weather matched my situation. It didn't take long to realize that this job was no gravy train. The local salesmen were given all the new leads and had all the contacts. I was new, and the only help I received was a pat "good luck" from the sales manager, accompanied by a nasty smile.

I was twenty years old, back to selling door-to-door, and rapidly losing my confidence. Doors started slamming in my face. Most people opened only a crack, worried about the cold air and the snow blowing in. I would begin with the biggest smile I could work up and say, with faked enthusiasm, "Sorry to bother you, I just wanted to make certain that you didn't miss this wonderful new opportunity to---" SLAM – SLAM - SLAM.

Hardships often prepare ordinary people for an extraordinary life.

The answer to how bad it can get began dawning on us much faster than the wind blowing a Cheyenne snowball off a cliff. The rent for our motel room was bleeding us dry and we were left eating canned beans, warmed by a candle, for breakfast, lunch and dinner. As time passed and nothing appeared on the horizon to help us in these desperate straits, I broke down. I called Nellie and explained our situation. She replied piteously that she was sorry, she didn't have enough money to make a difference. She suggested I call my mother. I thought the matter over, but I could see there was no alternative.

It was the first time I had heard Mom's voice in two years, and I was worried that the phone, too, would slam shut on me. But it did not.

"Mom, how are you?"

"I'm well, Joe. Where are you? Nellie told me you left Boise on some kind of get-rich-quick scheme."

I blushed. "I'm in Cheyenne, Wyoming," I managed. "Things aren't panning out like I had hoped. We're broke and hungry, the boys are living on canned beans. I was wondering... that is, can you loan me a few bucks so we can get out of the hole we're in?"

"Well, I'm not about to let my grandchildren starve to death, that's for sure."

Swallowing my pride, I said, "Thanks Mom. Bonnie and I would be grateful for any help you can give us."

"What are your plans?" she asked.

"I guess we'll go back to Boise. We can't take the miserable weather here anymore."

"Would you be willing to work for me?"

The question came frankly and without hesitation. This was something I hadn't expected. Our relationship had most always been carried on at arm's length. When I called to borrow money I hadn't been confident that she would help me. I wouldn't have asked her for money if my children weren't on the verge of starvation. I had hardly expected a job offer, and did not have the time to think of all that such an offer might entail. I had to respond fast – and desperation was speaking for me.

"That would be wonderful," I said. "I've been at a total loss... You have no idea what this means to me."

"Good. The timing couldn't be better. I have a motel near the Seattle Tacoma Airport and I need someone to manage it. Would you be willing to do that?"

"You bet," I affirmed. "We'll head your way as soon as we have the money to travel."

"I'll wire you the money today."

So my mother took us under her wings. The idea of running a motel seemed to me innocent enough at the time. I probably even thought it was cleaner work than what I had lately had my hands in. I thought I had seen something of the world and knew a little about life. But I was still a naive young fool who had never guessed what his mother did for a living, and didn't have the slightest notion what he was in for.

LONG NIGHTS, A REVELATION, WHISKEY AND CARDS

Life is a gamble,
in the dark
of nightmares,
whiskey dulls
the pain.

I called my mother from a pay phone near the airport. "We made it Mom," I said after her hello. She gave me directions to the Palms Motel, which was located on the Seattle Tacoma highway across from the airport. It was a windy, rainy March day when the four of us arrived. We parked under the canopy and entered the next year of our lives, a year that would change our course dramatically.

It had been a few years since the last time Mom and I had been together. She was thirty-six years old and more beautiful than ever. She seemed very happy to see us. She hugged us one at a time starting with Bonnie, then moved on to her grandchildren, Joey and Rich. Last she gave me a very loving hug. It had been several years since I had run away from Hopkins Military School, and it had been just as long since we had spoken at any length. I had thought during that time that she was furious with me, and would not ever want to see me again. But it seemed that all was well, and she had finally forgiven me.

Mom turned around and took the hand of a tall good-looking man who had been standing watching us during this reunion. She introduced us to my new stepfather – stepfather number four. His name was Jim Bennett, and I would soon learn that he was a well known professional gambler.

I had never had much to do with my mother's brief husbands, but this one was destined to be different. Jim had a marvelous sense of humor; it was one of his better qualities, and one of the first to come to view. He came off as a fine fellow, a real good guy. Later, Jim, born as Richard Bennett, would be accused of being involved with the mafia. He would be subpoenaed to Washington DC during the mafia investigations held by Bobby Kennedy, the attorney General of the United States. At the time, looking into the face of this friendly, composed, handsome man, I would have laughed had anyone told me anything of the sort.

Even in retrospect there is something about the idea that just doesn't hit the mark. Jim was the kind of man who held his past close to the vest, and it is difficult to say what he was or was not involved in during his life. Yet I don't believe he was closely involved with the mafia. He probably knew people who were, but he didn't altogether fit the mold although he seemed to follow a similar code of ethics. He was a man of honor and defiant pride and he would go to great lengths to defend his honor. But he was always fiercely his own man, and I think he lacked the element of submissive obedience necessary to be a good mob man.

Although he was a professional gambler, he never gambled. When he played, the game was in his hands. He also kept firm rein on his habits. He didn't touch alcohol or chase woman – neither fit into his code of ethics. He was loyal to my mother. He honored her and loved her, for she brought him prestige.

His friends called him Big Jim. The name was earned, and it had more to do than with his size. His unbounded pride showed in his ego, in the way he talked, and in the way he carried himself. I felt he liked me and would provide assistance if he was asked, but there was a distance between us, and the distance was blood. I was not of his blood, and that was a barrier that could never be broken.

Bonnie and I settled into motel life, renting and cleaning the rooms and washing the tons of laundry that the customers used each day. We could never leave the motel together, because it was always open for business, twenty-four hours a day and seven days a week. The hardest part of the job was attending to the frequent late night guests. Three or four times a night a man would come to the registration desk asking for our special rate. These rooms were available for those who only needed the room for an hour or so. The regular room charge was $6 for the night but only $4 for the rooms at the special rate.

I was informed by Jim that if the motel was full we would have to clean a room immediately after it was vacated, no matter what the time of day or night, in case another guest arrived. Young and naive, we accepted this as normal, asked no questions of Jim or my mother, or really even of ourselves. We did as we were told and did our best to adapt to this new life, as we had always done. It wasn't easy. It was constant, dull work, and the airport just down the way sent planes roaring over our bedroom at all hours of the night. Bonnie and I weren't getting much sleep. The best I could do was to tell her that it wouldn't last forever, and I would eventually find a better job. Those words were beginning to wear thin.

We managed to make it through the summer. It was all work and no play. Occasionally, Jim would stop in to see how we were doing and retrieve the money the motel had taken in. Sometimes he would stay long enough to watch a football game. It was the only social interaction we had and we were tiring of it. I was twenty years old, Bonnie was nineteen. We were too young to waste our lives being captive to a motel. I had to find a better way to make a living. Door-to-door selling had lost its appeal and I wasn't willing to start again as an apprentice plumber. So what could I do? Bartending had crossed my mind, but I couldn't do that until I turned 21. There was nothing else to be done, then, but sit tight and wait.

My twenty-first birthday arrived in September of 1959. That very morning I headed across the highway to the Hyatt Hotel at the airport and sat down at the bar to celebrate my first *legal* glass of whiskey. "You look kind of young," said the bartender. "Let me see your ID." I handed it to him, he looked at it for a few seconds, smiled, and said, "Happy birthday."

After my drink I screwed up enough courage to ask. "Say, how does one become a bartender?"

He looked at me with a gleam in his eye and a grin on his face and said, "Son, bartending is not as pleasant a job as you might think."

"I have come to realize that *most* jobs aren't as pleasant as you might think, but the job I have now is a nightmare compared to bartending."

"Yeah, what job is that?"

"I'm manager of the Palms Motel across the highway. I'm also the maid. I do the laundry and I clean the rooms. I'm pried out of bed three or four times a night, and if the wind is out of the north jet airplanes are roaring about hundred feet above the roof every twenty minutes. I haven't slept a whole night in six months."

He laughed and shrugged. "Well, you got me. Bartending beats the hell out of that. I guess it isn't the worst job in the world, after all. Heck, I should be more grateful."

I looked at him. "My guess is that you aren't just a bartender. My guess is that you're the bar manager."

He smiled a self-satisfied smile. "Good guess."

"Can I buy you a drink?" I asked.

He chuckled and shook his head. "I don't drink on the job, friend. Tell you what, you lay a tip on the bar, I'll drink to your health after my shift."

"Sounds good to me. Since I'm on this side of the bar I'll have another whiskey. Take enough out of this to buy one for yourself, later." I shoved five dollars to his side of the bar. I had warmed him up, but a third drink would be in order to get me ready, if I was going to tell him what I had in mind. When he returned with my whiskey I raised the glass, "To your health."

Thankfully it was early and I was the only customer sitting at the bar. I took another healthy swallow of my third drink, breathed deep, and started my sales pitch.

"I have a proposition for you," I said, looking him in the eye.

He crossed his arms, all at once defensive. I saw it. "And what would that be?" he asked, suddenly suspicious.

"I want to learn how to tend bar, and to show you how much I want to learn to tend bar I'm willing to work as your bar boy for as long as it takes. I'm also willing to work for nothing but your teaching."

He hesitated for a few seconds, considering, and looked keenly at me. Finally, he said, "If you have a white shirt and black pants show up at nine tomorrow morning."

And so I did.

Fortunately the bar was not at all busy in the mornings and there was plenty of time for Vern, the manager, to teach me the trade. First lesson, he handed me a black bow tie and said "You have to dress for the job." He then proceeded to teach me the correct way to wash a glass, which was much easier than washing laundry. Next on the list was how to pour whiskey out of a bottle with a spout in it, and how to measure it by pouring from the bottle into a shot glass as you spilled it into the customer's glass. So far so good.

Three weeks later I had memorized 40 or 50 mixed drinks, and I was well on my way to developing a bartender's persona. Door-to-door selling had taught me the importance of selling myself first. If people liked you, and better yet if they trusted you, selling the product would be that much easier.

I scanned the newspapers every day looking for a job. It didn't take long, and a few days later I was working as a full on bartender at a neighborhood bar in downtown Seattle. They started me on the morning shift. I told Mom and Jim about my new career and explained that we would stay on until they found someone suitable to take our place. Mom knew what the motel was like and she was happy for us. I do not know if there was an element of relief in her happiness, as well. Needless to say, Bonnie was thrilled.

When I arrived at my new job at 6:45 in the morning there was crowd hovering at the door, all men between the age of fifty and seventy. They opened up for me as I came. I unlocked the door, trying to smile at them, and as I walked into the bar the crowd followed me in like a herd of ragged black sheep. I walked behind the bar and set it up for the morning crowd. Some of the men grabbed bar stools and some stood leaning against the bar while I opened the cash register. I turned around to take my first order, and did not even know where to begin. They were all gazing at me with dull desperation in their eyes and they all had money under their shaking hands. It looked like a line of beggars as long as the bar itself.

I chose the one directly across from me and with a smile asked, "What would you like?"

"Shot of whiskey," he grumbled. I had been taught that a shot of whiskey was served in a small shot glass. I slid the shot glass in front of him and filled it to the proper level and moved on to the next customer. "How about you?"

"The same," he replied with a shaky voice. This went on as I served a couple of more customers.

"And you?" I asked yet again.

"You dumb ass!" came a sudden yell from the end of the bar. "Wha'd'ya think? You think any of us want a Daiquiri? We *all* want whiskey and for Christ sake pour it in a glass that has some room in it! Those guys you served are spilling it all over themselves! And hurry up for Christ sake, some of us got to go to work!"

I got the message. These men were desperately in need of a drink. I grabbed a tray from under the counter and as many drinking glasses it could hold and, without paying much attention, poured a generous amount of whiskey in each glass and walked down the bar sliding glasses at each one. I then went back to the men I had served with a shot glass and gave each one a drink on the house, in a big glass. It was a rough start.

Two weeks later my boss told me he was moving me to the night shift. "Better tips," he explained laconically. He was right. The tips were much better. But I earned them. I not only serviced the bar, but the restaurant as well. The cocktail waitresses were lined up at their stations screaming their orders. It seemed the dinner guests all wanted something exotic. Every table in the bar was full of costumers and I was busier than a one-armed paperhanger. The bar itself was filled with locals who liked their whiskey straight, tough guys from a tough neighborhood.

A week later I was getting up to speed and starting to feel confident in my abilities. The barmaid was a young attractive woman and I could tell she liked me. One Monday night when the bar was slower than normal I caught her staring at me, licking her lips.

"Hey, Joe, why don't you and I go in the back room behind the bar and enjoy a quickie?"

I stood speechless. It was the first time I had ever been propositioned. "Nothing I can think of would be more fun – but I'm a married man."

"What difference does that make? I'm a married woman."

Now I was really stunned. The only thing I could get out of my sorry mouth was a pitiful, "Sorry." I saw her eyes darken. I knew I had angered her, but I could hardly dream at the moment what that anger was going to cost me.

The following Friday night was challenging. I was running from one end of the bar to the other scrambling to fill the orders. In the background I could hear someone's voice getting louder and louder, it was impossible to ignore, and was getting on my nerves. The barmaid whom I had so abruptly rejected was obviously no longer enamored with me and yelled in a nasty voice, "Vodka on the rocks."

I set the drink on her tray and said, "Would you ask the man with the loud voice if he would please lower it an octave or two?"

She smiled at me for the first time since I had refused her offer. "Of course." She squeezed a splash of lime into the drink, dropped the remains in the glass, winked at me, turned and walked back to the obnoxious customer. I don't know what she said, but I heard loud and clear what *he* said. "You tell that piss ant that I'm coming over to pinch his head off, soon as I finish my drink!"

The barmaid returned to her station and in a sickly sweet voice said, "I guess you couldn't *help* hearing that."

Ten minutes before closing time I called out, "Last chance for a drink." At that late hour there were less than a dozen people left, a few taking advantage of the last call, including the loud mouth. The jilted bar maid returned and I placed the final drinks on the tray in front of her. As she started squeezing lime in his vodka I asked her, "What can I expect from the vodka man?"

"Your guess is as good as mine, sweetheart, but I recommend that you run for your car as fast as you can when you leave the bar."

I was starting to get angry. "What did you say to him to get him so pissed off?"

"Well, nothing, sweetheart! I just told him that you said if he didn't shut his mouth you were going to come over and take his glass and cram it down his throat, that's all. Isn't that what you wanted me to say to him?"

I looked at her in amazement. "Now that I know how dangerous you are I'm glad I didn't take you up on your offer."

"You'll never know what you missed." With that she winked at me once more, delivered the drinks and stopped to talk to the obnoxious loudmouth long enough to make me nervous.

It was closing time. I had convinced myself that there was trouble afoot and that I might be facing a serious thrashing. In a shaky voice I dimmed the lights and called out, "Lights out, everyone, time to leave."

And everyone did – except loudmouth and a rough looking friend. Loudmouth was a big man, bigger then he looked when I watched him walk through the bar in search of the bathroom. The barmaid was standing at her station with a grin of vindictive anticipation on her face. Loudmouth sauntered out of the back room and walked toward the bar. He put a meaty finger down on the bar, and said, "We'll be waiting for you outside punk."

Under the bar on a shelf there was a three-foot length of galvanized steel pipe that I had noticed early on. I had determined it must be a bartender's equalizer. I reached down and picked it up. "I don't know why we have to meet outside in the dark," I said, as calmly as I could. "Let's take care of the problem in here, where it's nice and warm." Adrenaline was roaring through my body, the blood pulsating through my brain was ringing in my ears like an out of control freight train going downhill. All in an instant I had leaped up on the bar flourishing the pipe.

Out of the corner of my eye in the same moment I saw the door open – and in walked the bar manager. His timing couldn't have been better, mine couldn't have been worse. If I had waited just ten more seconds all would have been well. As it was, all he saw was a crazy bartender standing there on his bar, with the equalizer in his hand.

"Its closing time," the bar manager said firmly, looking at loudmouth and his crony. Then, "Not only do I want you out of the bar but I want you off the premises NOW!" The big boys glanced at him and then at each other, turned to walk out of the bar, only once turning their heads to look back at me. I climbed off the bar and returned the pipe to its proper place.

The bar manager looked at me in speechless disgust for a moment. Then, "You're fired," he said. "I'll send your check in the mail."

I heard the barmaid chuckle.

I had no reply. I was grateful that he showed up when he did – and as a matter of fact, I thought to myself, I didn't like tending bar anyway. The manager walked me to the door, opened it, stepped out looking around, and said, "All clear." I watched as he went behind the bar to close out the till.

I drove home to the Palms Motel, where Bonnie and I were still living. It was two in the morning when I arrived, and a customer came in behind me. I opened the door for him and stepped behind the counter. "What can I do for you?" I asked, with a tired smile stuck to my face.

In the morning I told Bonnie what had come down. Come down – that was language I had adopted while working for Big Jim. It was right I should start to use it again; it was looking like I would be shortly back in his employ. I apologized to Bonnie, for I knew how anxious we both were to leave the motel and how our plans would now be delayed. She was disappointed, but she was gracious.

"What now?" she asked, but I had no reply.

Once more, I called my mother.

"I guess we'll be staying on for awhile Mom," I told her. "I got fired last night."

"That's unfortunate. What happened?"

I gave her the short version. "I hope this doesn't make it difficult for you," I said.

"As a matter of fact it does," she told me. "I've already found your replacement." She paused – something I was not accustomed to, as it seemed my mother always had the situation perfectly under hand. "Listen, Joe, Jim and I have something to run by you. I'll send him over today and he can talk to you about it."

"Thanks," I said sincerely.

A few hours later Jim arrived. We sat down across from each other, and he lit up a cigarette. "What happened?" he asked.

I told him the whole story, the episode with the barmaid and with loudmouth, right up to the end – me standing on the bar with a club in my hand and the manager walking through the door.

"Standing on the bar was out of line," he said after a moment, taking a contemplative drag of his cigarette. He reached over and spent it in the ash tray. "But as for the rest, you handled it quite well. Now if it were *me,* I wouldn't have fired you. As a matter of fact – you didn't break the most important rule."

"What's that?"

He shrugged. "Never have sex with the help. If you do, you're asking for more trouble than a fist full of rattlesnakes. By the way, how did you like bartending?"

"It's not all it's cracked up to be," I answered with a smile.

Jim laughed. Then he looked at me with one of his looks that commanded attention. "So. Here's the problem," he said. "We hired an elderly couple to run the motel. They've been in the motel business for years and they know all the problems that come with it. We were lucky to find them."

"I'm glad for all of you," I said, and I meant it.

He paused, and looked at me. Then he waved toward the bedroom. "Listen, Joe. Have Bonnie come in here," he said. "She should hear what I'm going to say. This concerns her as well."

Bonnie was in the bedroom entertaining Joey and Rich. I opened the door and stuck my head inside, "Jim has something important to talk to us about, honey. Can you break away?"

"Give me a minute," she said, glancing up with curiosity. "I'll be right out."

She came in shortly, and sat down with Jim and me. Jim had not said a word in the meantime, and I hadn't dared. "What's up?" asked Bonnie as she sat down beside me. We looked over at Jim, and he looked at us. He scratched his head.

"Listen. I wanted to talk to you about this from the moment you arrived in Seattle. Dee – my mother had changed her name – has been worried about the consequences of telling you what I'm about to tell you. She's worried what you might think of her. I convinced her that it was inevitable, that you would find out sooner or later, and that it would be best if you found out from her. She agrees. But she asked me to tell you for her." He seemed a bit uncomfortable as he talked, which was totally uncharacteristic of him. Confidence was not a trait he lacked. I glanced at Bonnie, but she was watching Jim.

After a pause he started again. "Look, Joe, your mother has been in the business for years. And as you know, *I* have been in the gambling business since I was a teenager. I have had card rooms all over Washington and Oregon, some legal, some illegal. This is how we have made a living for our entire lives."

"Mom is in the gambling business?" I was incredulous.

He looked at me, and chuckled, amused evidently at my naiveté, and shaking his head. "No, Joe. Your mother is in the business of prostitution." It is strange to say, for I had had all the hints I needed – but I was dumbstruck. I felt like the sky was falling on me. Jim calmly continued explaining. "She started into the business in Boise, running it from a tavern she owned there. Then she opened another house in Fernley, Nevada, and another in The Dalles, Washington, where we met – that one's closed now. Her most successful house is The Mustang Bridge Ranch, just outside of Reno. They have all been doing well for years and they keep her really busy. That's why she is gone all the time."

He looked at me, and must have read the shock on my face. "You must have wondered where all the men who ring the buzzer in the middle of the night come from?" he demanded. I suppose I had, but I had shrugged the entire thing off with one or more rationalizations. I didn't respond – Jim wasn't looking for a response. He continued, "Well, your mother has a call girl service and the girls who come into the motel with these men all work for her. It's a safe place for them to do their business. She's a successful business entrepreneur, Joe, think of it that way. She pulled herself up out of the great Depression and made a life for herself, and a damn good one." He stopped, and lit up another cigarette. Then he looked at me and he said, "So, there's our story. What do you have to say?"

What could I say? I had gotten to know my mother for the first time since arriving in Seattle. Before that she had been an apparition. She had only involved herself in raising me when I had grown older and had become uncontrollable. When I was a boy she had been consistent in sending Nellie money each month, providing us with a roof over our heads and food on our table, but I had seldom seen her. She had appeared each Christmas in her Caddy with a trunk full of presents, then disappeared almost as soon as they had been unloaded.

It felt good to finally have her in my life. I wasn't about to lose her again.

I hadn't thought much about prostitution and the people involved with it. The only experience I had had with it was that one night in Wells, Nevada. I did know it was the oldest profession in the world, and I had learned from the prostitute that night that it provided women with a way out of poverty. And now I could see, looking back on my life and my mother's mysterious, aloof presence in it, that she was a fine example of her work.

I took heart, and answered, "I have come to know my mother since moving to Seattle, Jim. She's a fine and beautiful woman, whom I've grown to love. I admire her courage and only hope I can live my life as well as she has hers."

Jim nodded, evidently satisfied, and looked at Bonnie. "How about you?"

"I'm with Joe. I love her, too, and am proud of her. She can do no wrong in my eyes."

Jim sat silently for a moment and then said, "It's too bad she isn't here for this conversation. I'll do my best to tell her what you both have said. She'll like to hear it. Now, Joe, about your future. I can get you a job and I think you would be good at it, if you want it."

"I guess anything will do. Bonnie and I have to find a place to live before we leave the motel."

"In the gambling business you need connections. I have quite a few. Down the highway a mile or so is a tavern, Trudy's Tavern. It's not only a bar but it also has a card room in the back. Pete, the young man who owns the business, owes me a favor. I taught him all he knows about running a card room and there is a job there dealing cards. It's yours, if you want it. You'll make a damn good living."

"Sounds good to me, Jim," I said, "but my card playing ability begins and ends with solitaire."

Jim chuckled. "Don't worry about that, Joe. I can make you a pro in a week or less – but only if you practice every minute you can spare."

"When can I start?"

"The sooner the better," he grinned. And he reached in his coat pocket and pulled out a deck of Bee playing cards.

He explained that they were the brand of professionals, for they were tough and could be cleaned with corn starch. "There are other reasons we pros like them, too," he continued, "but we'll get to that later. At Trudy's they play lowball. The lower your hand the better. For example, the best hand possible is 5-4-3-2-1. Ace is counted as one. The next best hand is 6-4-3-2-1, than comes 6-5-3-2-1, next 7-4-3-2-1 and so on. Got it?"

"I think so." I was not sure I had, but I wanted to impress. Bonnie pushed her chair back and said, "I *don't* get it, but I guess I was thinking about my boys, so if you'll excuse me?" She paused. "Thanks for what you're doing for my family Jim. It means more to us than you can imagine." Then she rose from her chair and left to check on Joey and Rich.

Jim broke the seal on the box, withdrew the cards, turned them face up on the table and with a swipe exposed the entire deck, every card neatly spread, all were visible. Thus started my education, which was to last some weeks. He taught me all I needed to know and more.

I learned the game well.

Soon I was introduced to Pete, the owner of Trudy's. "When do you want to start?" Pete asked.

"Does tomorrow work for you?"

He smiled. "I like a little enthusiasm. Come in at five and we'll get you going."

In the 1950's and 60's card rooms in Seattle opened under a policy of tolerance. If a bar applied for a permit and if they received one there were strict rules that governed their activities. They weren't allowed to open before 6:00 PM and had to close at 2:00 AM. There was no unlimited betting allowed and they could be closed at the city's whim. A card room was a little like the Wild West contained in four square walls.

It took a few days for me to settle in and get acquainted with the other dealers and regular customers. Many of them had nicknames. There was Stilts, for example, a skinny old man who filled in as what they called a shill. A shill was usually a retired gambler who was paid by the house and sat in when there weren't enough players to make up a game. Shills didn't gamble and only played their hand if they were confident it would be a winner. Then there was Hollis, a dealer who wore a rough cowboy outfit without the guns, and Blue Boy, who was an engineer at Boeing and knew the odds of winning any given hand. He played accordingly. He won most of the time and when he lost he never lost much. There was Pinky, a part-time shill, who always had an Italian stogie in his mouth, and Pigeon, another Boeing employee who came in once a month on payday. Pigeon was an opponent's dream. He was not only a poor player, he was unlucky. He usually went home broke to his wife and four kids, and if he sat at a table without a full contingent of players there would be a scramble for players in the know to grab the empty seats. Who can say what demons he carried that possessed him to put gambling ahead of his family.

And then there was the Nail. He was a big time contractor who loved the adrenalin rush of the gamble. A true gambler. He was willing to lose four or five hundred dollars at a sitting. It didn't seem to faze him. When he sat down at a table the pros would rush to have a seat at his table.

In December of 1959 Bonnie got one of the most coveted jobs in Seattle. She would open the 1960 World's Fair as a hostess in the already world famous Space Needle. She had competed with literally thousands of applicants. She was a beautiful woman and although there were many others just as beautiful, she won the job by virtue of qualities none of the others could compete with: a charming personality, charisma, and sapphire blue eyes. That was a combination that was hard to beat.

For the first time in our married life money was not a problem. Bonnie was paid well and I was averaging between two and five hundred dollars a week, depending on whether I was dealing or playing. I was getting to be a good player, and sat at a table to play only when the stakes were high and when someone like the Nail, a high roller, was sitting in to play.

One night I was sitting in the dealer's chair. I had been dealing for several hours and signaled to Hollis that I needed a break. I cleared the table of my earnings and walked out of the smoke filled bar and card room to get some fresh air. A few minutes later a big car drove into the parking lot – and guess who came out of the car? It was the Nail. This could mean big money. I turned and walked back into the card room, hoping there would be two empty chairs at one of the tables.

The tables were all filled, except for a table with one empty seat just to the right of the dealer. I grabbed it and sat down. I looked around at the chips in front of each player noting that one player was down to his last five dollars. The play was still going on from the last hand and the fellow with five dollars left had already folded. I looked over at him, "Say, friend, it looks like the chair you've been sitting in hasn't been good to you. I'll give you twenty dollars for your chair. Twenty dollars will give you a new start at another table."

He squinted at me suspiciously. "Let me see the money."

I reached into my pocket, pulled a twenty out of my roll, folded it and flipped it across the table to him. All the professionals like Big Jim carried their money in a "roll" in their front pocket. The money was always neatly stacked, one dollar bills on the outside, then fives, followed by tens, twenties - and then hundreds if you were a high roller. It always impressed me when Jim pulled out his roll. Of course his was much bigger than mine.

The player grabbed the twenty-dollar bill and stood up to leave, but as he was rising I asked him, "Hey, would you mind keeping that seat warm for a few minutes more? I'm holding it for a friend." Just as he started to reply the Nail walked into the room looking for a table with an empty chair. "Never mind," I smiled. "Here's my friend now." The player grunted, pocketed his twenty dollars and turned and left. I raised a hand and called out to the Nail, "There's a chair at this table if you're interested."

He smiled at me as he sat down in his very expensive chair. I signaled the chip man, who walked over, and I asked him for two-hundred dollars in chips. He stacked the chips in front of me and I said, "Make a note of it, I'll settle up after the game."

"Okay," he said, glancing at the Nail on the other side of the table. "Good luck. You never know, you might need it." He laughed as he walked away. He was absolutely right, and I knew it. If the Nail got lucky – and that was not unheard of – he could, with a single strong hand, clean out all of your chips, leaving nothing but cigarette ashes in front of you. I was thankful there was a ten-dollar limit on each bet.

My chair was just right of the dealer. Last to play. The player to the dealer's left had the blind and would start the betting. The Nail sat in seat number four. The cards were dealt, and I picked up my hand. Not bad. I had caught an 8-4-3-2-1. I would have felt confident if there were fewer players at the table, but it was a bit dangerous with eight players. The best hand possible in lowball is called a bicycle, 5-4-3-2-1. I could throw the eight out to try and draw a better hand – but there are only twelve cards at most in that deck that would improve it, and the odds are poor. Whether I tried for it or not depended on what would happen in the first round of betting.

The first player after the blind looked at his cards and bet five dollars. The third player folded. I had been watching the Nail closely, but so far he had ignored his cards. They were lying on the table where the dealer had dealt them. This was how he liked to play, fast and loose. He was a true gambler, a card player's dream – or nightmare.

It was the Nail's turn to bet. He paused for a moment, and still without looking at his cards raised the bet by ten dollars. The next player shoved out fifteen dollars and called, and the player next to me folded.

It was on me. I was trying to figure the odds but I was never very good at math. Maybe I should have stayed in school. I wasn't very concerned about the first bet after the blind; he probably had a decent hand, and I figured he would draw a card, perhaps two. The player that called the raise must have something going for him, but he hadn't raised, so that made me think that he would draw at least one card. I felt the best way to play the hand was to force as many players as possible out of the game, which would improve my chances of winning with an eight high. I raised another ten dollars.

The player with the blind was next. It would cost him twenty-three dollars to play, and he folded. The dealer dragged his blind into the pot.

"That's a raise of twenty to you to play," said the dealer to the next player. The player looked at his hand again – a card player's tick, making sure he had seen right. He counted out his chips and threw in.

The dealer then looked at the Nail. "That's ten to call." The Nail raised the pot another ten dollars. And still didn't look at his hand.

The next player called. If he had raised I would have called, but because he didn't I was confident that I had the best hand – at least of those who knew what cards they were holding – so I raised another ten. The Nail raised another ten, again without looking at his cards. It was beginning to be a big pot, and people were gathering around our table to watch the action.

The next player looked at his hand and called again. I did the same. "Pot's right," said the dealer. "Cards?"

The Nail was first. At last he looked at his hand and weighed the cards for a moment. Then he did something laughable – he threw four cards on the table. "Four cards," he said. He hadn't had anything – and now once more no one knew what he *did* have. But I had helped narrow the players down to three, and my 8-4 was looking better all the time. The huge pot was definitely creeping my way.

"How many for you?" the dealer asked of the player to my right.

"Only one," he answered.

"Joe?"

"None for me. I like what I'm holding."

They received their cards and I watched the Nail. He didn't touch his four new cards, much less look at them. However, he pushed ten dollars worth of chips into the pot. The player to my right looked at his hand. I had my fingers crossed. If he threw in, the pot would be mine. He didn't make a hand and threw his cards on the table face down.

I raised ten, the Nail raised again. This went on for ten rounds before he finally looked at his cards, not showing a hint of what he had found. This was the moment I had been waiting for. I watched him eagerly to see how he replied.

The Nail once again raised the limit, and my stomach turned over. He knew he couldn't bluff me with another ten dollar raise. He had obviously made a hand. I called, hoping he had an 8-5 or worse. He laid down his hand. Against all odds he had won with a 7-5-4-3-ace. I watched him rake in my earnings from the last few weeks.

I realized in that moment that gambling wasn't all it was cracked up to be. Now I knew why Jim didn't gamble. We continued the play long enough for me to break even.

My job at Trudy's was lucrative and interesting. With Big Jim's help I knew as much about dealing as anybody in the business and was enjoying being involved in the gambling trade, and Bonnie loved her job at the Space Needle. Our only challenge at the time was that we were both working nights. Joey and Rich were still toddlers, so we boarded them with a young family who lived in the country. They seemed to be doing well under the circumstances, but we were not able to be with them as much as we would have liked. There just seemed to be no other alternative. We hoped that something would come up that would solve the problem, and something did. Just not in the way we thought it might.

SLAM! Seattle was under pressure from its citizens to close down all the card rooms in the city, and it did. I was once again out of work, but this time Big Jim had a solution to the problem.

"If you want to continue dealing you can work for me. I'll take care of finding the players. The games will start at 8:00 PM every Friday night and they'll end when they end. The game is only for high rollers, the buy-in is steep – a hundred dollars to play in a no-limit game. Stilts will take care of the chips and collect the fee to play. The tips will be good and you'll make twenty-dollars an hour."

"I assume none of this will be legal?"

"That's right."

"What's the penalty if we get caught?"

"For you, probably a five-hundred dollar fine with no jail time for your first offense. I'll take care of your bail."

I considered, but not for long. By now, I was well on my way to living Jim's kind of life. The momentum was set, and turning back would have been almost impossible. "When would we start?" I asked.

"I've rented an old house in the city. We start this Friday."

I had reservations about what Big Jim was offering me, but didn't know how to say no. I would now be venturing into a world of thick mist and darkness, one where breaking the law, and not getting caught, was a contest between the lawbreakers and the police. It was nerve-wracking, but I saw no other alternative.

I arrived at the rental house an hour early to help Jim and Sticks set up the room, one card table and nine chairs. We set up the bar on a bookshelf that banked one wall of the living room. Big Jim would sell drinks to loosen up the gamblers and make a few extra bucks on the side. We brought in a chest filled with ice. Several bottles of whiskey, vodka, scotch, and mixers, 7 up, soda water and fresh limes. We set the card table in the middle of room. There was a large window in the room and I walked over to see if it would open. "Would you mind if we moved the table over by this window?"

"Why?" asked Big Jim.

"If I sit with my back to the window, I can open it when the room gets filled with smoke."

Jim chuckled and shook his head, and looked at me as I had often seen him doing before – as if looking down on an absurdity from a great height. "You act like you've never been in a card room before, Joe. A smoke filled room is part of the game. The boys like it. Get used to it."

"Well," I said sheepishly, "if the cops come we could make a run for it out the window." This was logic more to his taste. We slid the table next to the window, leaving me with just enough room to slide between the table and the wall.

Players started arriving at seven o'clock and there were soon four players, enough for a game. By eight o'clock the table was full. Big Jim or Sticks would take a seat and play in the game if a player went broke, and one or the other would relieve me when necessary.

Such the ritual. Several weeks passed and everything was going really well. I was making, on average, close to a hundred a night in tips, plus the money I took off the table. Sometimes I made more depending on how long the game lasted. On several occasions the gambling continued all through the night and well into the next day.

"This is the last play at this house," said Big Jim one Friday night while we were setting up for the game. "We've been here long enough. It's time to move on before someone catches wind of what's going on."

It would have been the sensible thing to do – but it was already too late. Sometime around midnight the front door started dancing someone was pounding violently on it.

"Open up, it's the police!" Jim and Sticks wasted not a moment. They sprinted for the back door. The hammering at the door was getting louder and more violent; it wasn't going to hold out much longer. There was no time to follow Jim and Sticks so I did a back roll out the window behind me. As I hit the ground the door came crashing in, and three seconds later I was lost in the dark of a neighbor's back yard. Our players weren't so lucky. They all landed in the jailhouse and Jim bailed them out, at a cost of $2,000. He couldn't afford not to; a disgruntled player might finger him as the master mind behind it all.

A few days later Jim dropped by. "The way I got it figured is that the neighbors called the cops. I know just the place to have a game where we won't have that worry."

"Where would that be?"

"At the Palms Motel."

There comes a moment on the downhill slide when you see with perfect clarity just where you are going, and how impossible it has become to scramble back up. When I heard that name, somehow I knew, immediately. I had reservations, of course; but what could I do now, at this late hour? I had made the decision long ago, when the truth of my mother's profession had been made known to me, and Jim Bennett had pulled out that first deck of cards. And I believe now that my road had been determined even before that, from my very birth. I know now that there was something in all this madness I had to learn. But at that time I was just a dumb kid who had gotten in way over his head.

"I'm in," I said.

The game was arranged. We cleared out a room at the motel and set up. The players were all high rollers, gamblers who could afford to lose money, and they loved the game. Four of them had been at the rental house when it was busted by the cops. There is nothing like a serious gambler. The game started off with a bang. The first hand had a big pot, the winner hauled in over five hundred dollars. And I hauled in a big tip.

Around midnight I signaled Sticks. "Take over for me, I need a smoke." I walked out of the smoke filled room, leaving the door open, into the fresh air of the night, lit a cigarette and walked to the back of the parking lot. It was a clear sky in Seattle, even the stars were visible.

Suddenly three police cars roared into the parking lot, lights flashing, and no sirens. Six policemen ran to the open door, each with a gun in hand. Standing in the shade of the trees, I watched as the paddy wagon drove in. Handcuffed by the police, all the gamblers were loaded into the wagon. The motel room had no back door and Sticks and Jim were busted along with the rest.

SLAM. The paddy wagon door closed on that episode of my life, and the reservations I had about where my life was headed had been answered by a power much greater than my own. I called Mom and she had her attorney bail everyone out. And I decided, too late really, to fight against the current that was carrying me, and try my hand at something else.

ESCAPE TO MEXICO

Running away
to somewhere
won't
take you anywhere.

Jim and Mom said they were moving to Reno, Nevada. They wanted to be closer to the business so Mom wouldn't have to travel so much. That is all they told me. Mom didn't explain what was going on, just that she would keep in touch and if I wanted to I could follow them later. I had a hunch it had something to do with Jim getting busted; perhaps the heat was more than he bargained for.

I was unable to see my way out of the dark shadow hovering over me. I was riding *Mom's* wave, going with the flow of *her* life. I was but an actor in the movie that she was creating for herself. I thought about the day when Olive Suprell told me that we each make our own movie. All I knew for certain was that my gambling career was over and I was in need of a job again. Bonnie loved her work and was making a good living at the Space Needle, so following Mom to Reno wasn't an option.

When I was dealing cards at Trudy's, I'd become acquainted with Sid, a high roller who came in often to play cards. He owned a large used car dealership and offered me a sales position. I had hoped my selling days were over – or at least had hoped I would never have to sell anything again. But I was desperate and I was seeking, I think, some way back to the light. With no better idea in mind, I contacted him and took him up on his offer.

Selling cars was easy compared to encyclopedias or insurance. No door-to-door selling. My experience as a high pressure salesman was serving me well and I was making money. I was finally working days so Bonnie and I were able to bring Joey and Rich back home. It was wonderful for all of us to be together again.

It was a typical used car lot. In those days the lots all ran ads on television hosted by a loud, enthusiastic pitchman, bragging about easy financing and clean, reliable transportation. For financing they used what the car salesmen called a Mouse House, which was the name given to the loan companies that took advantage of people who did not have enough cash to pay for a car. The interest charged by these loan shark companies was outrageous, but if paying high interest was the only way of getting transportation people would accept it without complaint.

I had become friends with Ed, the manager of one of the Mouse Houses we used. One evening he invited me to have a few drinks at the neighborhood bar. The conversation was trivial to begin with, but after several drinks he opened up.

"I have a proposition for you, Joe, because I trust you. It will be between you and me.""I'm all ears," I said in surprise. This was unexpected.

"The home office is putting on a contest. Over the next two months, the manager of the house with the most new business wins a thousand dollars and a trip to the Bahamas. I want to win that trip."

I still wasn't following how I fit into all this, and all I could say was, "Good luck."

"So here's the deal. I can loan money to one of your customers *without doing a credit check and with no down-payment,* as long as the loan amount doesn't exceed $980. You'll be the only car salesman I will make this type of loan for. You'll have the opportunity to make a lot of money, and I'll win the trip to the Bahamas. Win-win."

At the time I had no idea that there might be ramifications. I felt it was business as usual in the kinky world I had joined. The law had become a somewhat vague and distant concept to me and I did not pay it any heed when it did not come pounding at the door, dressed in uniform. I was enthusiastic about Ed's idea, and I agreed at once.

Even though Ed said his idea was only between him and me, I couldn't sell cars without the advertising, so I explained the situation to Sid. He knew a good thing when he heard it. He changed our television advertising at once. "No down payment! No credit check! Easy payments! In need of cash, bring in your old car and we'll pay top dollar for it!"

Every flake in town was hearing about us. Soon there were more customers on the lot than cars. Every junker on the lot, no matter its condition, was suddenly priced at $980, and I was hauling customers to the Mouse House by the car load. If a car was sold by another salesman he would pay me $25 for handling the loan. The customers were ecstatic. Money was flowing into my pocket like water down a gutter.

Late one night just before closing Sid came in. Being the boss, he wrote the paychecks, and so he was aware that all the salesmen were flush with cash. "How 'bout playing a little 4-5-6?" he asked, looking round at us. "You all alive here? Anybody interested, or what?"

We were – all of us. Gambling on the lot was common. If we weren't busy, we would even pitch quarters at the side of the building. Whoever came closest to the wall won all the quarters. Anything to kill time.

4-5-6 is a dice game that involves two or more players. A bet amount is agreed upon and each player puts that amount in the pile or pot. Each player then has to roll all three dice at once. If you roll 4-5-6, you automatically win, roll a 1-2-3 and you lose, triplets beat pairs, and so-on.

Sid brought out the dice, it was decided that we would open the pot with a bet of $100 from each player. I figured that I could afford to play one hand. When the betting was complete there was $500 in the pot. We rolled a single dice to determine who went first, and I won with a six.

My first roll was a 4-5-6, a winner, and I raked the $500 off the floor. Five-hundred dollars was a lot of money in 1962. I felt lucky – that dangerous feeling that comes to a gambling man of being able to do no harm. Why not? I asked myself. And I pushed all the money back into the pot. Sid covered the $500 which eliminated the other players from the game. It was Sid's roll, he threw a 2-2-4 – not a great number. Lady Luck can be fickle but she stuck with me that day. I rolled another 4-5-6. One-thousand dollars now lay, beckoning, on the floor. I wanted to grab it and run. However even gamblers have ethics, I let the money ride. Not wanting any competition with such a big stake at hand, Sid covered the bet again.

And then he rolled again, a 1-2-3 – an automatic loss. His luck was as bad that day as mine was good. I hoped he would give it up and come back another time, but he was getting desperate. His stress was obvious and it showed in his eyes. Now it would cost him $2000 to play. He was sweating. I shifted, wanting to convince him somehow to back out – but Sid was the boss. "Don't move," he said, "I can cover this." He walked into his office and returned with the money, throwing $2000 on top of my money on the floor. He picked up the dice and handed them to me, without looking at me. "Your roll," he said.

I rubbed the dice between the palms of my hands and wondered if this would ever end. I was beginning to worry. If I won again he would be more than desperate. I didn't know what might happen. I rolled – another 4-5-6. I was so lucky that it was making me nervous. If the dice hadn't been Sid's, he probably would have accused me of cheating, because he knew about my gambling past. There was now $4000 on the floor and it belonged to me – if I had the courage to pick it up.

By now the sweat was pouring through Sid's white linen shirt, it was obvious that he had run out of cash. I looked at the money on the floor and could feel him staring at me. "This diamond ring was appraised at five grand," he said at last, his voice trembling slightly. "It will more then cover the pot." With a little effort and some spit he managed to disengage it from his finger and threw it on top of the money. I knew how much that ring meant to him. It was at least a four-carat diamond, and it was his status symbol. I had no choice. I was winning the money but he was controlling the game. The consequences of refusing the bet were considerable. I shrugged and handed him the dice. "Your roll."

He spun the dice across the floor, they hit the wall hard and tumbled onto the floor, the first dice to stop spinning was a 5, the next was a 5, the third dice slowed to a halt and landed with a 3 on top. 5-5-3, not a bad throw.

My turn. I was playing a dangerous game. Sid was nobody to mess with, and I knew it. It might be safer to lose and laugh about it than to take the chance of winning and suffer the consequences. But I couldn't make the dice land how I wanted, neither for better nor for worse. Win or lose it would be up to Lady Luck. As the dice bounced off the wall two fives rolled to the surface, and the last spun for a moment like top before landing on another five. 5-5-5, triplet beats pair. Sid got up off his knees. The look he gave me would wilt a cactus in the desert. He turned and walked out the door. He jumped in his white Cadillac, slammed the door, started the engine and threw gravel on half-a-dozen of his used cars parked in the car lot as he raced away.

One of the salesman looked at me with a huge grin on his ugly face. "*Now* what are you doing to do, Joe?" He laughed and laughed like he knew something that I ought to have known. But he wasn't about to share it. I was going to learn soon enough. I knew that was my last day in the car business, but I didn't know that losing my job was only the beginning. I was through with it, but it wasn't through with me.

I went home to Bonnie and the kids with a carload of presents. I told Bonnie the whole story and that I wasn't going back, no more selling cars. After dinner the phone rang. It was Ed and he sounded overly-excited. "I need to see you as soon as possible. Can you meet me at the Stardust Bar?"

I couldn't imagine what was so urgent, but I told him I'd be there in half an hour. I kissed Bonnie and told her I would be back in a couple of hours.

He was waiting for me when I arrived. "What's up?" I asked as I sat down.

"I got a call from the vice president of my company. They're accusing me of fraud."

"That's awful, Ed! Are they going to press charges?"

"They will if I don't cover their losses!" And he explained to me at last what he'd had his hands in. All of the loans he had made in his scheme to win a vacation in the Bahamas had been made to less than credible applicants. He had been stirring the pot without glancing into it, without wanting to see the big stew of dishonesty and fraud he'd been cooking up.

"They're threatening me with criminal charges," he whined.

"What are you going to do?" I asked.

"*Me?* The question is what are *we* going to do, Joe? They're saying *you're* involved in the fraud too. I supplied the loans, *you* supplied the flakes and the cars."

"Wait a minute," I said, feeling suddenly nervous. "*You* made it happen, I just went along for the ride."

"Well, whatever. You're involved, whether you want to be or not, and I no longer have a job."

"They fired you?"

He scratched his head. "Yeah, at least until the investigation is completed. And while that's happening I don't want to be around. Besides, I need a vacation – even if it isn't a free vacation in the Bahamas."

"What, are you thinking of skipping town?" I asked, shocked.

"*Way* out of town," he nodded. "How does Mexico sound to you?"

"Whoa, are you asking *me* to go with you?" Not for the first time, I felt everything crashing down around me.

"It would save you a lot of hassle," he said. He could see he would have to convince me. "Look, Joe," he said, gesturing nervously, "they're going to put you through the wringer, don't you get it? Mexico will give us time to figure out what we're up against."

It dawned on me that the investigators would eventually be talking to Sid, and that he would undoubtedly point the finger at me – that same finger that still had the mark on it of his lost diamond ring.

"When do you plan on leaving?" I asked, after a moment of reflection. I was beginning to resign myself to the inevitable.

"How does tomorrow sound to you?"

I went home and told Bonnie my dilemma. She was quiet about it but realized there wasn't much else I could do. The money I had won at the dice game made my flight possible. I kept $1000 for my trip to Mexico and gave the rest to Bonnie. We found a sitter for Joey and Rich. I hoped I wouldn't be gone long.

Ed and I flew to San Diego the next day, my first time on a commercial jet. At the airport we caught a taxi and asked the driver to take us to the nearest used car lot, where we bought a 1954 four-door Chevrolet for $400. We packed our bags into the trunk and headed for Ensenada, a small fishing town on the Baja Peninsula.

Ensenada was a quaint village at the time. Ed had called this a vacation, and after awhile I started to agree with him. We were having a fine time, no worries. We spent our day's ocean fishing and our evenings at a local cantina where we ate tortillas filled with shrimp, and drank iced cold beer. We even attempted to learn a bit of Spanish, but never really got beyond *cerveza, gracias* and *hasta luego*.

It wasn't long before the Mexicans noticed our car. One evening while we sat in the cantina having a beer, we watched five or six men looking it over from top to bottom.

Ed asked the bartender, who spoke a little English, "What's going on out there? Why are they so interested in our car?"

The bartender grinned at us in his obliging way. "They thinking good car for taxi, they want *buy* it from you."

A little later, several of our potential taxi drivers came into the bar and walked up to us. Their spokesman sat down on the bar stool next to me and folded his hands on the bar. Then he asked in broken English, "You sell car?"

The car salesman in me rose to the surface and before I knew it. "*¡Si!*" I exclaimed.

"How much?"

This was unexpected, but I was a good salesman, "How much will you pay?"

He was a negotiator. "No, no, *señor. You* tell *me*, how much?"

I thought about it for a second. We had paid $400 for it. "One thousand American dollars," I answered, coolly.

He turned to his partners, "*Un mil.*" He told them, with undisguised excitement.

That they were enthusiastic was obvious. I was surprised; I had been shooting high. "You have title?" he asked me.

I reached into my wallet and pulled out the document we had received from the car lot. It wasn't a title, but it was proof of ownership.

The spokesman turned back to his partners and they spewed out their Spanish so fast I couldn't understand one word. He turned back to me. "We pay one thousand, no problem. We need title."

Ed and I talked it over and decided the opportunity to make a five to six-hundred dollar profit on a car was too good to pass up. We explained to them that we would go back to the States, get the title to the car, and return to close the deal. We left early the next morning heading back to San Diego.

Once at the dealership we found that it would take longer to get the title transferred to our name than we anticipated, so we traded our car for a 1956 Ford Fairlane 500. This time the dealer gave us a title and we headed back to the awaiting men in Mexico. On the drive I noticed the car was smoking like a coal-burning train engine. "I think we bought an oil burner," I remarked.

"The Mexicans are probably great mechanics," Ed replied, grinning. "They might not care," he added hopefully. We stopped at a gas station to check the oil and fill the gas tank. We bought four quarts of oil, putting two in the car. We bought two extra quarts and checked the oil one last time before we entered Ensenada. It was an oil burner all right. We added another quart in Ensenada, just to be sure.

Our Mexican friends joined us that night at the bar and we told them the problem we had getting the title for the Chevy, and said that they could have the newer Ford for the same price.

"Too much," the spokesman said. "It not make good taxi, only two doors, taxi need four doors. We buy car but pay five hundred." Come to think of it I had never seen a two door taxi.

Five hundred was not enough to give up our only transportation. "Nine hundred." I countered.

While the spokesman and his *compadres* talked over our offer, the bartender brought us our drinks. "*Ustedes tienen problemas signores, muchas problemas.*" He had a serious look on his brown face.

We didn't need to know Spanish to understand *problemas*.

"What's the problem?" asked Ed.

"The *Federales* come here, look for you."

"The police?" The last thing we needed was the Mexican police to be looking for us while we were hiding from the American ones. Ed was so nervous that spittle was spewing from his mouth.

"*¡Si, señor!* They heard you selling cars, it *jail* for you, if they find you."

"Why?" I was incredulous.

"You break law, bring car in from *Los Estados Unidos*, and sell it! *¡No bueno!*"

"*Gracias, amigo.*" I was grateful to have learned my ignorance from someone other than the Mexican police.

"*Por nada.* It is nothing," he said with his ingratiating smile.

I looked at Ed. We finished our drinks, and headed for the door. We apologized to the future taxi drivers and left. It was midnight when we left town, spewing smoke across the countryside. We were grateful when we reached the American border at Tijuana, even if it was four in the morning.

We were now wanted in two countries – a difficult accomplishment in less than a month. I had heard rumors about Mexican jails. They said if you were unfortunate enough to end up in one it may well be the last place you would ever see. Give me a good old American jail anytime, I thought to myself.

When we arrived at the border the border guard walked up to my window. "Identification please." He didn't seem friendly and his eyes scanned the interior of the car as we handed him our drivers' licenses. "What are you two up to so early in the morning?"

"We live in Seattle and have to be back to work in a few days, so we decided to get an early start," I explained calmly. I didn't expect any trouble; when we had passed through the border earlier everything had gone well.

"What kind of work do you do?"

"I'm a car salesman," I said a bit sheepishly. I was not proud of my occupation, and it was embarrassing to admit to such a job considering the junker I was driving.

"How about you – Ed?" he asked as he looked at Ed's driver's license.

"I manage a finance company," he answered.

"What were you gentlemen doing in Mexico?"

"Deep sea fishing," I responded.

"What an interesting combination," he nodded. "A car salesman, and a manager of a finance company. We will need to search your car, sir. Please step out of the vehicle."

He waved one of his associates over and said, "We need to frisk them and tear this hunk of junk apart. There's more to them than meets the eye, they're up to something."

My stomach turned over. I knew nothing about this car. For all I knew it could have belonged to a drug runner. It had a V8 engine, and at one time it would have been fast. It had certainly been well used. All I could hope for was that if it had been owned by a drug runner, he had cleaned it up.

Soon there were three border patrolmen tearing into it. They removed the car seats and door panels, they tore the floor mats out and then jacked it up and removed the wheels. That took over an hour. We sat and watched them search the entire car, fender to fender, roof to undercarriage, inside and out. We were terrified. We didn't have a word to say to each other during the whole ordeal.

"The car is clean," they finally announced, not without a note of regret. "I don't know what you two are up to but I'm convinced it's no good." You could see the anger in his eyes. He was convinced he had nailed the biggest drug runners to have crossed the border in months. He probably was hoping on making a score himself, and getting that shiny promotion he was hankering after. Too bad for him we were just a couple of would-be international car dealers. "It will take a while to put this piece of junk back together."

"Don't worry about it," Ed said. "We're going to junk it in San Diego. Just put the seats back and the tires on and throw everything else in the back." We were anxious to get off the border, thinking it possible that the *Federales* would contact the US border patrol and warn them to be on the lookout for two Americans in a black 1956 Ford.

Fifteen minutes later we were on our way non-stop to Seattle, in a junker car that couldn't be driven over thirty-five miles an hour. Every hundred miles we would stop at a gas station and descend into the grease pit, filling three gallon jugs with dirty used oil, oil as black as tar, to pour into the engine, and would drive away polluting beautiful blue skies all the way from Mexico to the Canadian border. We finally reached the door of my house, and none too soon. The exhausted engine died the moment we hit the driveway of my small cottage in Redondo Beach. Ed went home, dispirited and anxious.

But I was glad to be home. Bonnie was excited when I got there and said she had good news for me. We put the boys to bed and Bonnie explained that Mom had called while I was away. "She has a job for you at Mustang Ranch," Bonnie said. "She needs people she can trust to help her out and wants you to be one of the security guards."

I thought about Mom's offer. I didn't have many options. There was no doubt about it – I was caught in a rerun, a movie that played over and over. Bonnie was willing to follow me again; she could see the promise in my new position. She left her job at the Space Needle. It was hard for her to leave, but she was thrilled with the possibility to become a full-time mother again.

My mother's work, and I was going to have my hand in it. I looked at my options, but I had none. With Big Jim I had been gnawing at the outer edges of the world my mother had been in for the last twenty years, but I was not about to hurl myself headlong into it, dead center. Perhaps this would be my chance to get to know her, I thought. We certainly had not spent much time together, ever.

I called Ed the next morning to find out what was happening with the investigation and tell him that I would be leaving town. When he answered the phone I said, "Well, what's up?"

"The investigation is still going on. It doesn't look good for me. They are anxious to talk to you, Joe. What are your plans?"

"There's nothing in Seattle that holds me here, so I'm off to greener pastures."

"That's probably for the best," he said. "If you leave I can blame the whole mess on you."

I laughed, though I wasn't sure he was joking. "Good luck with that, Ed," I said. "Give it a shot if you like, but I don't think it'll wash. You should have done a better job with your credit checks. I hope you come through in one piece."

Even after all these years, I try in vain to piece together the mystery of my mother's life. When and why she had turned to prostitution; how many houses she ran, and when she had started them all; what she thought about her chosen work, about the life she had made for herself. In Seattle I began to know her for the first time – but even then, I am not sure I ever really did know her. Mom held her past close to her chest. Perhaps it was because I was intimidated by her, but I cannot remember a single conversation in which we talked about her history. She was largely absent from my life and we failed ever to bond in any really meaningful way.

Sometimes you are dealt a card and the person who deals the card is your parent, and you carry that card for the rest of your days. Many of us, like the Nail, never even look at the hand we are dealt; some of us look but don't know what to make of what we've been given. But like it or not, we all have to play.

MUSTANG RANCH

History is timeless,
some desires
never pass
away.

I called Mom and told her we were on our way. We packed
our meager possessions into a small U-Haul, put Joey and Rich
in the back seat, and headed off to Reno. We were traveling
into a whole new world, leaving behind the mire of bars, card
rooms and car lots. She was waiting for us when we arrived at
her house in Reno and was obviously happy that we had come,
and that I would be working with her in her business.

This was our first time in "The Biggest Little City in the
World." That evening Bonnie and I strolled the main drag,
dazzled by all the lights, the glitter, and the crowds walking the
streets – all those strangers throwing their hard-earned money
away in the gambling houses.

Mom was anxious to get me started at the Ranch and the
next morning as we sat over a cup of coffee, catching up
somewhat superficially on our lives in the past year, she said,
"Come with me, Joe. It's time you met my family."

"Your family?" That word was strange coming from her –
stranger yet that it should stand as an invitation to her only son.
I felt at once included and excluded by that little word, and it
came to me in a mixture of pride and pain. Pride – that I should
have reached such a level of intimacy with her; pain – that this
intimacy had not been my birthright.

"Yes," she said to me. "I consider the girls who work for
me family."

I was anxious to meet them and wondered where, and how, I would fit into it. We drove several miles out of Reno and turned off the highway onto a well-maintained dirt road. Two or three miles later we came to a bridge that crossed the Truckee River.

"This is my bridge," she told me. "It cost me twenty-five thousand dollars to build it. When I started the business here I named it Mustang Bridge Ranch, and later I shortened the name to Mustang Ranch. It's got a better ring to it. What you see on the other side of the river is Mustang. It's been growing since I started it over ten years ago. It's an interesting life you're getting involved in, Joe. So far it has been good to me, and I hope it will be the same for you."

I could see the facilities on the other side of the river. It wasn't fancy, at least from the outside. It consisted of several trailer houses joined together and looked something like a train. It wasn't quite what I had envisioned, so I held my tongue until I had the chance to meet the people my mother worked with and see what the interior of Mustang held.

As we approached the building, Mom continued to tell me about the Ranch. In Nevada, in the days when I worked there, allowing or prohibiting prostitution was a decision left to the counties. Story County, a small county near Reno, had allowed it. Mustang Ranch would bring badly needed tax money into the county coffers. Some years later Mustang Ranch became the first legal bordello in the United States.

"Just down the river is my potential competition," she said, indicating a ways downstream. "You might call it a 'war' going on between Sally Conforte and me. She has moved trailers onto her property at Happy Valley but the county won't give her a permit because they've decided one house of prostitution is enough for Story County." I glanced uneasily down the river. I knew the name Conforte, and "war" was not what I had come here to find.

What my mother told me next did nothing to help my anxiety.

"Her husband Joe is in prison for tax evasion so Sally is running the show, but I'm certain that Joe is directing all her moves. Now, the only way Sally can open up Happy Valley," she continued, "is if she puts us out of business. Blowing up our bridge would make that happen. She tried it once, unsuccessfully. I don't want that to happen again. The bridge is the only reasonable access into Mustang."

As we drove across the bridge to the parking area Mom pointed out the guard house that sat at the end of the bridge. "That building is where you will be working. We have radio communication between the guardhouse and the bordello so there will be constant contact." I looked at the guardhouse, and looked at my mother, but said nothing.

The trailers were situated behind a seven-foot high cyclone fence with five strands of tightly strung barbwire on top. Mom pushed a ringer on the gate and it was buzzed open from inside. At the door we were met by Rosie, a large woman with skin as black as ebony, her huge smiling face radiating love, seemingly all for me.

"Well jus' *look* at you, Joe. I am *sooo* happy to finally meet you," she said as she stepped off the porch giving me a huge hug almost smothering me with her large breasts.

When I caught my breath I said, "You too, Rosie. I've heard so many good things about you. Thanks for taking such good care of my mother." I had indeed heard about her. Rosie was my mother's right hand, and had been with her for years. She kept the girls in line and didn't tolerate any nonsense.

A few of the ladies were up early sitting in the lounge having breakfast. They weren't dressed for business yet and looked like any normal housewife would at that time of the day. Some were dressed in slacks and blouses, some were still in their bathrobe with curlers in their hair and without makeup. They were gracious and seemed genuinely interested to meet me.

As time went on I learned that several of these women had families of their own. I often wondered how they managed their lives. I assumed that their children were raised similar to the way I had been. Rosie told me later that they were all impressed with the fact that I accepted my mother's choice of profession so easily and without judgment. It wasn't always so easy for them.

When my sojourn into this strange world began, it was a rather desperate time for the Ranch. My experiences at Mustang would be a unique amalgamation: sometimes exciting, sometimes dangerous, sometimes boring. It seemed unreal at times and during the more tedious moments I wondered how long it, or I, would last. There were moments when it seemed the entire thing was going to blow up around us – quite literally.

The bridge was the lifeline for Mustang Ranch. To protect it Big Jim hired three guards for twenty-four hour round the clock protection. He hired an ex-con named Roland Coon who had spent a great part of his life in jail. Roland reminded me of a big tough dog; he was devoted to my mother and idolized Big Jim. His gun was a .38 caliber police revolver which was standard issue for the police in those days, and he loved it, polishing it every chance he had.

I was the new kid on the block, new to the life of a guard, and new to the world of guns. Jim handed me a small .25 automatic colt pistol and a box of shells. "I hope you'll never have to use this, Joe," he said, slapping my shoulder, "but in this business we have enemies. You never know when you might be glad you have it."

"I hope that day never comes," I replied, and I meant it. I was young but I wasn't raring for a fight. I turned the pistol in my hand. I didn't tell him that I didn't think I had it in me to shoot anyone.

I told Jim that Bonnie's brother, Terry, was interested in a job and could be trusted to be loyal. They hired him as the third guard for the Ranch. He was a writer looking for some solitude, somewhere he could write his first novel, and he thought sitting in the guardhouse would be quiet and would suit his ambition perfectly. He came to Reno and moved into my mother's world carrying his typewriter under one arm and a pistol in his pocket. I had told him that carrying a gun was a requirement and he had come fully prepared. Terry was, like me, a young newcomer to this ancient trade.

The first month was fortunately quiet, a lot of time for reading. The most exciting event concerned nothing less than my immortal soul.

One night about midnight I watched a Volkswagen Van slowly crossing the bridge. The driver waved at me and continued on to the brothel. He didn't last long – fifteen minutes later he was back in his car. That was odd, I thought. When he got to the bridge he pulled to a stop at the guardhouse and stepped out of the van. I walked out of the guardhouse and said, "What can I do for you?"

"I want to introduce myself," he said with a mild tenor. "What's your name?"

"Joe," I answered.

"Well, hello Joseph, I am Jesus Christ. I have come to save these women of the night, but I was cast out of their house of ill repute. However, my time has not been wasted, for I have found you at long last. I have been looking for you!"

"You don't say," I said with a smile that would show how impressed I was. "Honor to meet you, too."

He beamed at me, his eyes filled with tenderness and eternity. "I am searching for my disciples who will follow me and help me save the world," he said.

"Sounds like you have your work cut out for you," I smiled.

"I do," he allowed, nodding. "Will *you* join me Joseph?"

My eyebrows rose. "I'm sorry Jesus, but I have a family to take care of, and that responsibility takes up most of my time."

"You must renounce all that you have to become my disciple."

"That's asking a lot, Jesus."

He gazed at me sadly a moment, and shook his head. "You are the perfect example of an excuse-maker, Joseph, more interested in the routines of life than God, whose Kingdom is coming." With that he returned to his car. As his van backed away from the guard house he stuck his head out the window and said, "If you change your mind call me and I will hear you."

"I don't have your phone number," I replied.

"You do not need it. All you must do is say, 'I need you Jesus,' and I will be there." With that he drove away.

I liked Jesus, he drove a Volkswagen Van. I watched him disappear into the night, smiled, shook my head, and went back to reading.

It would take several more years for me to recognize the truth hidden in the words of a lunatic.

* * *

The interior of Mustang was not what one would call memorable, nothing like what is depicted in the movies. The clients would first enter the lounge area, which was nothing more than two trailers joined together side to side. It was filled with over-stuffed furniture and women with smooth round breasts, beautiful and seductive, showing a lot of leg and dressed to titillate the clients. There was a long bar with a dozen stools in front of it that could serve up any drink imaginable.

In back of the lounge, there were trailers connected end to end. They were arranged like dormitories and each of the girls had her own room where she entertained her clients and slept.

A bordello would not hire a girl without a pimp, and some of the pimps had more than one girl. They were considered a necessary part of the business and controlled the lives of their girls very closely. A good girl was a gold mine for them.

Occasionally, at random times, the county administration would call and tell Mom that they were closing the place down. It didn't happen often and usually didn't last longer than a week. I imagined they were being pressured by the local citizenry, many of whom viewed Mustang as an evil. During these times, we would hang a sign on the gate at the far end of the bridge that said "On vacation. Come back next week." We still guarded the bridge and I watched as our customers drove up, at all hours, only to leave disappointed.

I was working the day-shift once during one of the closures, sitting in the guard house on a fine sunny day and reading a book. Duke, the guard dog, was lying outside on the porch. He was a giant fawn colored German Sheppard and had been trained as an attack dog. When the girls were on site he lived in the bordello. His job was to protect the girls and he did a fine job. Nobody would mess with him. When anything unusual happened Duke would growl, a low rumble, to give you a warning. And when Duke growled, everyone listened.

On that fine day Duke started his rumble, and I went out the door at once to see what he was grumbling about. There was a seldom used road that wandered through the foothills of the surrounding mountains. If you followed it from the highway you would eventually arrive at Mustang Ranch. Coming fast down the side of the hill on this back road, creating a plume of dust, was a four-wheel-drive pickup truck. Duke and I watched as the truck came to a stop next to us, dust rolling over us like a dark cloud.

"What can I do for you?" I asked coughing and spitting dust.

"I'm here to visit the girls."

"Sorry," I said, "but we're closed."

"Not closed to *me*. I go where I want." That said, he pulled out a small caliber pistol, stuck his arm out the window and pointed it at my head. I stepped back in sudden bewilderment, for I had never been threatened with a firearm before, and had not a clue what was happening. I am not sure how I would have reacted, had I had the chance – but fortunately, I did not have to decide.

For Duke, when he saw a hand holding a gun appear out of the car window, lunged immediately at the man's wrist, and tried to drag him out through the window. Blood was streaming down the side of the truck and Duke was shaking him violently by the wrist. I leapt out of the way, expecting bullets to start spewing in all directions. This guy was tough, and somehow he managed to tear his arm out of Duke's mouth and jerk it back into the truck.

I had always hoped that I would never be forced to use the pistol I was required to carry. This was the first time it had ever been pulled from its holster. I drew it out without a hesitation, feeling the danger that I was in. "Drop the gun, NOW," I said as I pointed the pistol at him.

He dropped his gun beside him on the passenger seat and stared back at me, cradling his wounded hand. "I see you got a gun too," he grumbled. "You mind if I get out of the truck?"

"Not if you leave your gun behind."

He did as he was told, opened the door and climbed out. He held his wrist high in the air while blood poured out of the ragged wound and dripped off his elbow. He was pale and shaking.

"Follow me," I said as I turned and walked to the door of the guardhouse. "I have a First Aid Kit." Duke followed my every step and I wasn't worried about turning my back to him. Duke would have attacked in a moment's need. The First Aid Kit was fairly complete; tape, gauze and iodine. The man's wrist was a mess and looked like it would need stitches. I did the best I could with what I had at hand. He roared like a lion as I poured the iodine on his wound. I covered his bleeding wrist with gauze and wrapped it tightly with surgical tape, enough to control the bleeding.

"You need to see a doctor as soon as possible," I told him. "Let's drive across the bridge and I'll open the gate. It'll save you from driving the back road." I walked around to the passenger side of his truck, collected his gun and removed the clip. I threw the bullets in the river. I probably should have thrown his gun in as well but somehow I couldn't bring myself to do it. I tossed his gun in the back of the truck. When we crossed the bridge I got out of the truck, unlocked the padlock, swung the gate open and waved him through. "Good luck," I called out as he drove away.

I walked back to the guard house, hauled a chair outside in the sun and sat down. Duke joined me and I patted him on the head, thanking him for saving me from a situation that could have gone horribly wrong. I felt weary to the bone and was sick to my stomach. I couldn't stop thinking about what had just happened and the fact that I was living in a world struck by whirlwinds of desperate violence: on the one side, people that had not much more than sexual gratification on their minds, and on the other, people that dreamt of nothing more than money; and both of whom were willing to go to shocking lengths to fulfill their cravings. I knew it was not the world I wanted to live in, nor my family to live in, but I couldn't see my way out. I acted each day like I knew what I was doing but in reality I didn't have a clue why I did what I did. Olive Suprell had told me I should make my own movie, but I didn't know how to begin and had no one to help point me in a better direction.

I walked down the bridge and pulled my gun from its holster, staring into the water below. I wanted to throw the gun, bullets, and holster into the river, but thought about my mother and couldn't do it. I knew if I threw that gun away I would be throwing my mother away with it.

I believe that my mother, at least, was deeper than appearances. There was much more to her world than the lust of the men who visited Mustang Ranch. She was involved in a business that was as old as mankind. It was how she made a living. She was devoted to the girls who worked at Mustang. She was their mentor. She took care of them when they were sick, treated them as if they were family, and provided them with an opportunity to support themselves. She did for them what she was incapable of doing for me when I was growing up, but I would not acknowledge that openly, to her or anyone else. All I know was that, for the first time in my life, I was part of her life, and I was not yet ready to give it up, even if it meant risking my skin.

So, I stayed on, with the vague hope deep in my spirit that the day would soon come when I could see a new direction, make my own movie, and live life on my own terms.

It seemed, in those days, a hopeless hope.

* * *

A doctor visited Mustang once a month to examine all the girls. He was responsible for the health of the girls and tested them to make certain they had not picked up a venereal disease that could be passed on to the customers. He had become my doctor as well, and he had tried for months to help me with something that had plagued me since the first really stressful days of trying to care for a wife and two sons – my ulcer problem. Doing tests and prescribing milkshakes – there wasn't much else that could be done in those days for ulcers. But I kept going back to him anyway. Habits are a hard thing to break.

I was sitting in his waiting room waiting my turn with a crowd of other patients when a nurse, obviously frightened out of her wits, came running out of the doctor's office. She ran straight to me – she evidently knew who I was – bent over and whispered in my ear, "Joe! We need your help - there is a patient in the doctor's office threatening the doctor – he's out of his mind and I think he's violent. Please!" She turned and ran back to the door of the doctor's office. I had no idea that the doctor's staff knew the type of work I was involved in, but now was no time to think of the implications of that.

The other patients were looking at us, wondering what was happening. I jumped up and followed the nurse as she opened the door for me; and I walked into the chaos. A large black man had indeed lost control of himself. He had thrust everything off the doctor's desk, paper, books, pencils, the telephone and the typewriter were scattered all over the floor, and the place was a mess. He was yelling at the doctor as he noticed me, and as soon as he saw me he stopped his tirade. I seized the moment: I walked authoritatively toward the desk.

"Back off!" I commanded with a calm voice. I had learned how to control a tense situation from Big Jim. This was not the first time I had put on a strong front while I was trembling inside.

The giant had stopped yelling, but he was mumbling crazily. He wrinkled his forehead, and wiped his hair back with both hands. I stood there with my hands folded across my chest, my right hand hidden under my coat. It might have been my baby face that scared him, for he had probably heard of Baby Face Nelson. Although, with my hand under my coat he might have thought that I had a hidden gun. He would have been mistaken – but I was an old gambling hand by then, and I knew my bluff. He walked by me, glaring crazily, but without saying a word, and he left the building. The doctor began to breathe again, smiled in evident relief. "Thank you," he said, taking my hand in his own shaking fingers.

By now such encounters as this were becoming normal for me. The confrontations between Sally Conforti and Mustang Ranch continued, each one worse than the one before. Jim had never let go of the anger he felt when Sally tried to blow up the bridge into the Ranch. It had taken a month to repair the bridge, at no small cost – not to mention the revenue that had been lost in the meantime. Big Jim was out to exact his revenge and decided the way to do it would be to take over Happy Valley, Sally's bordello.

Happy Valley was only a ten minute drive down the road. It was closed down and vacant at the time. Sally, unlike my mother, had never gotten the elusive permission from Story County to open, so it just set there silent and empty.

Jim and Roland drove to the gate, cut the lock and made themselves at home. It was just that easy and like something you would read in a dime store novel.

Or so it seemed. Several nights later Sally arrived with three of her thugs to take back her property.

I had just arrived at the Ranch to relieve Terry and start my graveyard shift. I had taken my place in the guardhouse, and Terry was getting ready to leave, when a voice came over the short wave radio, screaming "Mayday, mayday!" It was Roland. We raced to the radio and listened as Roland's panicked voice explained what had happened. "Sally and her gunslingers are at the Happy Valley gate, armed and threatening to shoot the place up and me with it! I need help, NOW!"

I looked at Terry. "How about some overtime?" We jumped into the Ranch's patrol car, nervous and unsure. Both of us felt we were out of our league and wondered what in the hell we were getting ourselves into.

Just then Mom's voice came through on the car radio. "Jim isn't here!" I felt my heart sink; Jim would have known just how to react in a situation like this. I was in way over my head. "Joe, what are you going to do?" Mom asked me.

I grit my teeth. "I won't know until we get there," I said. "I guess we'll find out soon enough, we'll be there in a few more minutes." I had no idea what to expect. I only knew that I wasn't looking forward to it.

"Leave your radio on," she told us. "I'll be listening, and – take care, Joe. Sally is dangerous when she's angry."

I hadn't needed my mother to tell me that.

When we drove into the parking lot I could see Sally and her boys in my headlights, all lined up at the gate leading into the compound, guns in hand. We could hear them yelling obscenities at Roland, who was locked inside. They turned to face us as our car lights exposed them. Roland was nowhere to be seen and I imagined him lying on the floor of the building, waiting for us to come and save him. Some rescue party, I thought to myself – two boys with guns they've never used.

As we got out of the car I told Terry to stand at the side of the car behind the headlights so that they wouldn't be able to see him. He nodded and drew his gun from its holster. I left the headlights on bright so Sally and her boys wouldn't be able to see me clearly through the glare. Walking towards them and showing more courage that I felt, I demanded, "What's going on here?"

"This is my property and these are my buildings!" Sally shrieked. "There's a guy in that trailer and he won't come out, or let us in, officer!" She had said the magic word. Terry walked out of the shadow behind the headlights. The adrenaline was still hot in me, but I felt myself breathing at last.

It was extraordinary; Sally actually thought I was a cop. *Sometimes fate is on your side,* I thought disjointedly as I grasped for what to say next. "Sounds like a problem for the courts, ma'am," I said, as authoritatively as I could. "I think you had better leave now and take your problems to a judge." It came naturally to me somehow. I was shocked that she didn't even argue. She gathered up her gang and slammed the door of her Cadillac as they all piled in, spraying gravel as they quickly drove away. As I watched them drive out I wondered vaguely why all Madams seemed to drive a black Cadillac.

"What the hell, Joe!" I heard Roland cry out in a shaking voice as he emerged, still timid, from his hiding. "How'd you get rid of 'em?"

"They thought we were cops," I said with a nervous laugh. "Whatever gave her *that* idea I'll never know, but it sure saved our butts."

We heard later that as Sally was speeding toward Reno she was stopped by the police. The cop who pulled her over found the car loaded with guns, including one very illegal machine gun. Sally and her hoods were taken into custody. I never heard what happened after that.

Roland left Happy Valley the next day. The bordello burned to the ground a week later. I never asked how the fire started. I didn't want to know. But I could feel the hornets were hovering.

What I have recorded here is how I remember these events. Over the years I have learned that many times in tense situations, the people involved don't share the same reality. I was talking with Terry recently and asked him how he recalled the incident that night with Sally. Here is how he recalled that moment:

"It all comes back to me now that you painted the picture, Joe. I forgot about Sally thinking you were a cop. I do remember Roland being nervous and sweating up a storm. And I remember one of Sally's boys who was facing off with Roland when I walked up to the fence staring at me with a little smirk on his face because he was amused that Roland was so nervous. I was watching him because he seemed ready to make a move. I think Roland thought we were all going to die, and the thought crossed my mind too, for a moment. Sometimes the details escape me but you brought it back beautifully. We are lucky to be here aren't we?"

And by God, we are.

* * *

Bonnie, Joey, Rich and I had plenty of time to share with each other in those days. Bonnie didn't have to work and was enjoying her days with the boys. I was earning enough money that we could eat out occasionally, or take in one of the shows that played at the casinos. We spent our most memorable night out having dinner at Harrah's Club.

After paying the tab and leaving a tip I still had ten dollars in my pocket. "Bonnie, let's take this ten dollar bill and try our luck at the crap table. You never know, we might win enough to pay for our dinner."

"It's worth a try," she said with her usual grace. We wandered over to the crap table. With only ten dollars I didn't expect to win much, but you never knew when Lady Luck might sit in your hand.

Craps has the best odds of any of the casino games, but that is only true if you know how to play the odds. Playing the odds correctly, the house had only a .3 percentage in their favor. Another lesson I had learned from Big Jim. The game works like this: if the come-out roll is 7 or 11, the bet wins. If the come-out roll is 2, 3 or 12, the bet loses. If the roll is any other value, it establishes a *point*. If, with a point established, that same point is rolled again before a 7, the bet wins. If, with a point established, a 7 is rolled before the point is rolled again the bet loses and the dice move to the next player at the table. If a 4, 5, 6, 8, 9, or 10 is thrown, most casinos allow players to *take odds* by doubling down.

I placed two dollars on the table. My first roll was a seven, and I let my winnings ride. I started rolling points, and always doubled my bet playing the odds. Soon I had several hundred dollars on the table. Bonnie kept nudging me in the ribs. "Take the money, Joe," she whispered in my ear.

But the gambling fire was in me – that strange inexplicable feeling that you can do no wrong, and that everything is going to fall in place for you. "Bonnie," I told her, "I came to this game to win a thousand dollars or leave if I lost the ten dollars we started with. Let's see what we can do." I kept rolling winning numbers and letting all my winnings ride. Doubling down, taking advantage of the odds. Soon a winning role of the dice was paying me over one-hundred dollars and I told Bonnie to start dragging in the chips. Bonnie shoveled the winnings into her purse. It seemed Lady Luck *was* with me that night – I just couldn't lose. Other gamblers were trying to squeeze into the table to get into the action and people were ten deep around the table. The gambler sitting next to me nudged me. "That woman over there is stealing your chips, partner."

"That's all right, there are plenty more where those came from," I laughed.

I watched the dice roll over the table again and again with a winning number. It finally happened, I rolled a seven. I watched the dealers rack in over two-thousand dollars left on the table. I had won, and won big time. I placed a one-hundred dollar tip on the table and thanked the dealers for showing me a great time. We walked over to the cashier and I watched as Bonnie dug handfuls of chips out of her purse. When they were all counted we had won over five-thousand dollars from our ten- dollar stake. It seemed that when I got lucky, I got very lucky.

I shook Bonnie awake the next morning. "Get dressed darlin'. We're going shopping." I bought a brand new Plymouth Barracuda off the show room floor, the first new car I had bought myself. I bought a brand new Nikon Camera, extra lenses, and all the darkroom equipment I would need to pursue my new interest, photography. I didn't know at the time just how far it was going to carry me. Bonnie took the rest and went shopping for her and the boys.

The Ranch was busier than ever in those days. The feuds between Mom and Sally continued on, and the local citizens were starting to shake their fists and howl to the heavens about Mustang Ranch and how the girls were leading their citizens into hell. And Joe Conforti was released from prison. He came back to Reno in a cold fury, determined to see Mustang Ranch closed down.

He didn't waste any time getting in touch with Jim. He wanted a meeting and Jim agreed. There are rules that must be established for a serious and potentially dangerous meeting between two men who lived outside the law. The meeting was to be held in the Nevada desert, well away from civilization. They agreed on the location, and they agreed that each could bring one body guard to the meeting. The body guards would stand by their cars out of hearing distance. It was to be a private conversation.

Jim trusted me. I had stood the test of time, and he asked if I would go with him. I agreed, of course. After all we were family by now, even though we still didn't share blood.

We drove for an hour into the desert, and Jim was strangely quiet on the way. Off in the distance we could see Conforti's car and two people, one standing on each side of the car. We sat in silence as Jim slowly drove on. We finally reached our destination and Jim slowed the car to a crawl and stopped. I could tell that he was nervous. "Is your gun loaded?" he asked without looking at me.

I assured him it was, but something else was bothering him. Conforti had parked his car in the middle of the road facing back towards the way we came in. "I don't like this," he said. I couldn't see the trouble; I still didn't have the eye for such things. He explained it to me. "If the meeting goes bad, we'll be vulnerable. I don't want them behind us when we leave." He reversed our car, backed off the road leaving room for Joe to drive ahead of us when we left, and parked it broadside to theirs.

"Get out of the car and stand behind it," he said. "Keep your eyes on the thug and leave your gun holstered. But be ready for trouble." We got out of our car and I took my place behind it as Jim had told me to do. He seemed calm and walked confidently toward them. I wondered if he was as nervous inside as I was. He stopped when he was at midpoint between the cars. Conforti walked from his car to meet him. There was no sound other then the wind blowing sand against the metal of the cars. There was no shaking of hands, no salutation. This was about business and they were hostile competitors. Their relationship was filled with enmity and it showed.

By then I had heard the rumors that Joe was part of the mafia. It was true, I realized as I looked at him: he had the demeanor of a Mafioso, and his Italian blood showed in the color of his skin and his dark eyes. They turned their backs to their body guards and walked off into the desert, out of hearing. Conforti's man kept his eyes on me, and I did the same, staring back at him, trying to feel bold, hoping he would believe it.

In hindsight, it would have seemed strange to someone watching this meeting from one of the hills that surrounded us, seeing two dusty new black Cadillac automobiles parked fifty feet apart in the middle of the Nevada desert, two men walking into the desert, two others standing beside their cars. The situation reminds me as I write this of the movie *The Godfather,* something of the sort that would have fit perfectly in that movie.

Conforti played the part of an Italian mobster to perfection. He moved with confidence and talked with his whole body. I couldn't hear what he was saying, but it was obvious he was angry. His arms and hands spoke volumes. Jim, on the other hand, seemed calm and composed.

The meeting lasted no more than thirty minutes. They walked back to their Cadillac, not smiling, not shaking hands, in total silence.

Jim opened the driver's door and told me to get in the car. "Conforti is angry. I am going to wait him out. I want him to leave first. I don't think he has the patience to wait long." So we sat there, waiting for Conforti to leave. Jim was right, a few minutes later he drove off in a cloud of dust, after it cleared we followed.

"How did it go?" I asked.

"Not as good as I had hoped," he said, looking at me for the first time in the whole episode. "We're still at war." He fell silent again, and shook his head. Then he added, "He's one tough son-of-a-bitch."

BREAKING THE BONDS

Who knows in what darkness
fearless angels
tread.

I was 40 years old before I could talk about my mother and
the experiences I had at Mustang Ranch. It was too hard for me
to feel the judgment people passed on my mother's choice of
profession, to see it in their faces, hear it in their voices. I was
not aware enough to let them pass judgment as they would, and
that in so doing I would outgrow my own and be free of it, just
as one day I had to become free of Mustang Ranch itself.

It was a dark, violent, and chaotic world, one that I never
felt I belonged in, and not one I wanted my family involved
with. It seemed there was some infernal pulse pushing me
forward, just waiting for me to step towards it. In strange, dark
worlds wondrous events do happen. It was here, of all places,
in a house of prostitution, that I found my light, and from the
most unlikely source. It was a fleeting moment, to outward
appearances utterly mundane, but it changed, unalterably, my
entire life.

I was having lunch one day with the girls, as we guards
often did. They were all interesting characters and entertaining
conversationalists, each one beautiful in her own way. I was
sitting with a young woman and we were talking about our
families. After sitting in silence for some time she looked at me
and asked, "Joe, do you believe in God?"

"Hell no," I laughed. "What kind of God would have
created a mess of a world like this - full of violence, hatred,
wars, people living in poverty, and all with only one way out -
death. You're born, if you're lucky you'll have a few good

times, for certain you'll have your fair share of hard times, and then you die. Just read the history books. Tell me – if there is a God, how do you explain it all?"

She suddenly jumped out of her chair, startling me, and with strange excitement in her voice said, "Don't you move an inch, Joe, I'll be right back." With that she headed for her room. I watched her go in curiosity. In a few minutes she returned, smiling and carrying a small book. "Read this," she said, handing it to me. "Maybe it'll change your mind."

"What is it?" I asked, looking up from the book to her, with patronizing skepticism.

"*There is a River*, by Edgar Cayce," she said; and when she saw that this name was totally unknown to me, she tried to explain. "He's a wonderful man," she began, trying to find the words. "A healer of sorts. He has cured sickness in a lot of people and is a psychic. He goes into a trance state and answers questions, questions about problems with health, and questions about God."

I thanked her and returned to the guard house, carrying her little book in my hand. I sat down in the shade of the guardhouse, looking at the book with curiosity, feeling the usual resistance to a book which you know will express ideas you think are inane. *What can it hurt?* I thought, smiling cynically to myself. If this man can really heal people maybe he'll even have a cure for my stomach ulcers.

A few hours later I had finished Edgar Cayce's little book. I sat in the shade stunned. It was as if a door I had long ago closed, opened once again and beckoned me in. *There is a River* had answered the question that had haunted me since I was six years old, the question I could never find an answer to: why do innocent people suffer?

I had heard of reincarnation but never really understood it. Cayce's explanation made sense to me, I could feel the truth of it in the pit of my stomach. An eye for an eye, a tooth for a tooth; you paid for this life's deeds in the next. Good deeds, good karma; bad deeds bad karma. Every experience a lesson, teaching one how to live a life filled with love, forgiveness, compassion, and good intention; how to bring one's soul back to God. I thought to myself, *an angel working in a bordello?* And I remembered what I had been told a million times; God works in mysterious ways.

I finally understood.

Cayce said, "You can't get to heaven without leaning on the arm of a brother you have helped." I thought about the little girl with cerebral palsy who had been the catalyst in my search for God and knew she had been a lesson, an angel disguised in a helpless body. I had carried her memory with me for years and I felt her with me now, leaning on the arm of a brother she had helped. I closed my eyes and prayed, for the first time since I could remember. I prayed that she had found some peace in her life and thanked her for the gift she had given me.

I quit my job that day. I wanted a new life, different karma, a new movie. When I crossed Mom's bridge over the Truckee River for the last time, I stopped my car in the middle of the bridge and walked to the railing. I looked at the gun in my hand and quietly dropped it into the river. I watched the silver barrel disappear as it sank, forever out of my life.

I once read that one-time-in-a-hundred a gun might save your life; the other ninety-nine it would only lead you into dangerous bravado. I recognized the truth in those words and realized that if you live by the gun, sooner or later it would fail you. I saw the rippling reflection of the gun as it lay at the bottom of the river, the dust and gravel of time beginning to obscure it from my sight. I turned, got in my car and drove away from Mustang Ranch, never to see it again.

I felt unburdened for the first time in a long time and my heart was open and full of the future – the uncertainty of it, the fear of it, the old anxiety of having no way to support my family – all of this, yes. There was also the pain from breaking from my mother, from the one world in which she and I had ever lived together, as tenuous and superficial as this bond had been. But in all this emotional confusion there was something else, as well. For the first time, there was promise in my future, and the vague and still distant certainty that I was being guided along an upward path, toward the light.

* * *

Terry stayed on at the Ranch for awhile. We kept in touch over the years and he shared a couple stories with me of what had happened after my departure. What I heard made me only the happier that I had gotten out when I had. Big Jim had found a replacement for me but the chaos and turbulence got worse. These were the stories Terry shared with me:

"My memories about that time are a little bit vague but I'll do my best. I wasn't there when Roland shot himself. I worked the morning shift that day. I heard about it later from the young Hispanic guy who Jim hired to replace you.

He told me Roland had his gun out and was playing with it, blustering like a fool. He wanted to intimidate the new guy. He was standing with his back to the wall and spinning the chamber of the gun. Then he pointed it to his head and pulled the trigger. I'm sure he thought the gun was empty, but maybe not, he was a little crazy. In any case, he never expected it to go off. He pointed it to his head and pulled the trigger several times, laughing like crazy when he saw the terrified look on the new guy's face. It was the biggest joke in the world.

The new guy told me he pulled the trigger one too many times. The gun exploded and Roland had a look of total shock on his face as he slowly slid down the wall. He was trying to talk, his lips kept moving but no words came out. The new guy was in total panic. He didn't know what to do so he grabbed the radio mike and began shouting, 'Mayday! Mayday!' "

It was a grim and sad story. I was glad I hadn't been there for it.

Terry and I both missed the last days and final demise of my mother's Mustang Bordello, but he related what he knew:

"I know you want to keep your story authentic, Joe, so I'll tell you what I heard and try to keep the story as authentic as I can. I left the Ranch a couple of days before the takeover. The county had shut the Ranch down for a week and everybody had gone on vacation. From what I heard, Conforte's boys charged in and confronted the guard on duty. The Hispanic guy just loaded Duke into his car and bailed out of there on cue. No muss no fuss. It was all very smooth.

It was a good thing it was him and not me. I probably would have done something stupid and they would have found me a few days later floating down the Truckee River. Sometimes the timing in life just seems to work out."

The hornets had left the nest.

There was no recourse in those days for Mom to get her property back. You just didn't call the police and have them straighten it out for you in a case like this. You lick your wounds and you walk away. There was a lesson here about control, one that would take me fifty years to awaken to. I can only say that it is never too late to learn, if you are conscious and willing.

The Confortis with their usual grand display opened the doors of their new business shortly after the takeover. It lasted long enough for a movie to be made about Mustang Ranch. The producers didn't hear, or maybe didn't care, about my mother being the creator of Mustang; her history has been forgotten. Joe and Sally became famous in her place.

Joe paraded his girls through Reno in his red Cadillac convertible, smoking his cigars, the ladies sitting on the back of the seats waving to the curious spectators as they cruised down the streets of the city. I heard through the grapevine that sometime later Joe was brought up on tax evasion once again, and before his trial he fled to Brazil. I imagined that Sally sent him money so he could continue living his decadent lifestyle, and I am sure that some of that money came out of Mustang.

Mom and Jim soon left Reno and moved to Lake Tahoe, Nevada, where they made an offer on a small but elegant casino. I had a hunch what they had in mind and how they could compete with the big casinos. Unlike the others, they would have elegant ladies, dressed to the hilt and available for the customer's pleasure, whatever it might be. The ladies would praise these men and encourage them to drink and gamble their money away, offering themselves as a reward for money well spent.

As for me, I had come to a crossroad and had chosen the spiritual path, the mystical path less traveled. I had finally become more than an actor in the world. I had found my way and was determined to be the creator of my own movie. Olive Suprell would be proud.

A ROAD OUT OF DARKNESS

Sometimes,
with awakened
dreams.
life begins
again.

The day the young woman at Mustang Ranch handed me her book, *There is a River,* my life changed, irrevocably. I began to see the world with a clarity I had never experienced before, and for the first time life seemed to be filled with possibility, dreams and aspirations. I knew not where it would take me, but I was willing, and for the first time I found a confidence deep in my soul that I could handle anything that came my way. All I had to do was open the door and take my first step forward. Remarkably my ulcers soon went away. I was no longer in pain.

I spent a lot of time photographing in those days, photographing anything and everything, with the equipment I had bought from the money Bonnie and I had won that night in Harrah's Club. I started to get to know the business and I began learning about cameras. As any hobbyist, I liked meeting the professionals and learning from them. I was in one of the local shops one afternoon, eying all the latest in camera equipment. There was a young man standing at the counter next to me asking to look at one of the new cameras on display and we started up a conversation over its merits. His name was Mike Martin and I could tell he really knew his stuff. We talked on for quite some time and he asked if I would like to go to his house to see his work and his studio. It was one of those great moments in life when things begin to come together; you step into blank space and a stone rises up to meet your falling foot, and you know you are headed in the right direction.

Mike was an excellent photographer, a student of Ansel Adams. His work was brilliant and he was a master in darkroom techniques. His love for photography was evident and it was the first time in my life I experienced someone living life on their own terms, involved in something good and beautiful. Mike became my mentor and generously taught me everything he knew about photography and the darkroom techniques he had learned from Ansel Adams. I truly was in a whole new world.

Photography wasn't the only thing we had in common. We were both interested in learning how to climb. In this, we were both amateurs, and we decided to begin learning together. We started by climbing the canyon walls that were abundant around Reno. We climbed together every chance we could, taking our cameras along with us. The two pursuits – climbing and photography – merged perfectly.

Mike introduced me to Doc Kaminski, who owned a studio in Reno, and Doc offered me a job. I accepted the position. I was ecstatic; to be able to make a living doing something I loved seemed beyond belief. I had never dreamed such a thing was possible. Work, for me, had always been what you *had* to do, never what you *wanted* to do.

It wasn't long before I learned that Mike was not only a photographer. He had another career he pursued on the side: he sold marijuana. Every few months he would jump on his motorcycle and ride off to Mexico to replenish his stock. I remember well the last time he rode away, because I never heard from him, or saw him again. No one seemed to know where he was and I could only guess what happened to him. It was a great loss. He was the first person in my life who had shown me how to live a truly creative life in light instead of darkness. I can see his intelligent smile as I write what I can only assume is his obituary.

I continued climbing every chance I got, and eventually joined the Sierra Club getting into some serious mountain climbing. It had become a passion. When I was in the mountains and climbing my mind was clear and I felt completely in tune with myself. Without the daily pressures of life constantly at hand, I had time to think about life and what I was hoping to gain from it. Climbing awakened me. I knew for the first time that life was more than just surviving, and I began my search, my spiritual search.

There is a River had been only the beginning. I stumbled across a book, *Autobiography of a Yogi*, by Paramahansa Yogananda, and discovered the Self Realization Fellowship. Paramahansa's words offered me what I had been searching for: "Giving love to all, feeling the love of God, seeing his presence in everyone, and having but one desire—for His constant presence in the temple of your consciousness---that is the way to live in this world."

My spiritual journey had begun and Paramahansa's words became my guiding light. I was moving into a new world in which adventure was to replace danger, and physical endurance was to replace violence, and beauty was to replace the endless search for squalid pleasures. I would be tried in this new world and here too would risk my life, but what I stood to gain would be now infinitely more precious than a buck.

PART II

A MOUNTAIN TO CLIMB

THE BREATH OF GOD

Who knows
what
God
might do to
awaken you.

I found it exhilarating being roped to a companion while on the smooth, steep face of a mountain, making decisions to avoid physical harm, or even death. The adrenalin rush cleared my mind of triviality and replaced within me a deeper sense of awareness. I loved the thrill of the challenge, of overcoming fear, of the precision required; no mistakes allowed. The euphoria is impossible to describe, there are no words.

When I was climbing I was aware that my physical body functioned much better when the three attributes I had been studying - the physical, mental and spiritual - were working together in harmony. It was another of Paramahansa's gifts and I worked at making this awareness part of my reality, carrying his words with me on every mountain I climbed.

* * *

The wind had been blowing at gale force all night, as if to warn of things to come. We didn't sleep at all and the tent was blown on its side, flattened by the gusting wind, constantly abusing us with body slaps and popping noises.

It was New Year's Eve Day, 1966, and we were on Mt. Shasta, a major mountain with an elevation of 14,179 ft., the mountain itself rising 11,500 feet from its base. I was accompanied by three Sierra Club members with whom I had been climbing for almost a year, this was to be my first winter ascent. Our goal was to spend New Year's Eve night on the summit and to descend the mountain on the first day of the New Year.

My rope-mate was Jim Bacus, the other two climbers were Bill Simpson, and Reggie Donatelli. Reggie had been my climbing mentor since I met him; we had climbed Lover's Leap in California and Echo Nine in Yosemite Park. These were my only serious climbing experiences prior to this attempt on Mt. Shasta. I had learned the importance of well chosen climbing partners and I was glad to be with accomplished climbers on Mt. Shasta whom I could rely on and learn so much from.

As I packed for the trip, I recalled everything that I had learned from my previous climbs and short apprenticeship. Mistakes had been made that I didn't want to make again, so I packed with extra care. On one occasion, in late spring, Reggie and I were climbing a small peak in Yosemite named Echo Nine and were hit by an unexpected snow storm that came from the backside of the mountain. We were only halfway to the summit when it struck and were inadequately prepared. We had packed no cold weather gear, and most importantly, no gloves.

It didn't take long to lose the feeling in our fingers. They were so numb from the cold that we couldn't feel the small nubbins and cracks in the rocks; we couldn't go on. Facing the possibility of frostbite, we drove a piton into a crack in the face of the wall, tied ourselves to it, and attempted to warm our hands in the pits of our arms. The storm continued on, wind and snow blinding us as we hung on the side of the mountain. Any hope we had that the storm might pass by dimmed with the darkness of the storm, it was not abating and we were getting colder by the minute.

Reggie, always one to think of immediate options in times of crisis, said "Joe, let's take our boots and socks off and use our socks for gloves." His idea, as had been so many others, was a winner. We struggled to remove our boots and socks. It was difficult to put our boots back on again with our frozen fingers, but working together we managed to do it without dropping them down the face of the mountain. The socks were just enough to keep our hands warm and we were once again climbing to the summit .

We finally reached the summit and sat in silence, each feeling a sense of accomplishment, and watched the storm blow in its fury. It ended just as fast as it had begun. The sun broke through the clouds and warmed the mountain for our descent. It was a lesson I would learn more than once on later climbing trips: *Never* venture forth on any climbing or back-country trip, no matter its difficulty, without proper equipment. *Always* prepare for *whatever* possibility might be encountered in the wilderness.

Someone wisely said, "Good judgment comes from experience, and experience comes from bad judgment".

My climbing partners on Mt. Shasta were, beyond everything, good company. The night before our ascent, in the comfort of the Sierra Club Cabin nestled in the trees at the base of the mountain, they told frightening stories. Stories they had heard from other climbers and folks down below; that it was an active volcano and overdue for an eruption, a sleeping giant; they talked about rumors of a vast colony of Martians living in its core who reached out from hidden doors to snatch unwary climbers. We all laughed at the tales but in the deep of night, thinking about climbing this mountain in the dead of winter, the stories seemed to take on an unnerving reality and my sleep was tinged with disquiet.

We began the climb at dawn pushing our way through the strong winds and accomplishing our set goal, that of reaching the halfway point on the mountain the first day. We pitched our tents amidst the ice and rocks on the only flat spot the mountain offered us. The wind was blowing hard and it was almost impossible to anchor the tent to the ice and rock. As soon as it was secured to the ice Backus and I scrambled in hoping our bodies would stabilize the tent. The mountain was using the wind as its instrument and our tent as a weapon to slap and beat us throughout the night, making sleep hopeless.

Jim and I emerged from our shredded tent the next morning with our ears ringing from the pandemonium of the screaming storm. The sun was blinking in and out of the clouds as we ate a small meal of dried fruit and oatmeal, warming ourselves with a cup of tea. Thankfully the storm was passing on and visibility was excellent; it was a perfect day for a winter climb.

We had separated into two teams; Reggie and Simpson in one, Jim and I in the other. Reggie and Simpson had left camp before first light, taking a different route than we would take. Jim and I had chosen a route that we were comfortable with - a couloir intersecting a ridge that led to the summit.

We set off alone. Not wanting to lose altitude, we slowly traversed the mountain meeting the couloir at a point where its slope ranged from 30 to 40 degrees, getting steeper as it rose up towards the ridge. The run-out at the base of the couloir was very wide and had narrowed considerably at the point of our interception. From here we would climb up the face of the couloir for about five-hundred feet, meeting the ridge that would take us to the summit. The run-out below us was not steep but very long, broadening out well before it reached the tree line.

The slope that we chose to climb to the ridge was not dangerous so roping up wouldn't be necessary; we would ascend without protection. It would, however, be necessary to cut steps in the wind-swept ice slope with our ice axes. We began our climb agreeing to leap-frog at fifteen-minute intervals; I opted to take first lead. Cutting steps was not so difficult and I was making good time up the face. Jim followed shortly behind and took over. As he continued onward, I cut a notch in the slope a few feet away from our snow ladder and sat down to take a few pictures and enjoy the view. A wide panorama stretched out before me; snow, bare rocks, forests and distant mountains. High above me the clouds made fantastical formations. I was witnessing the grandeur of God, and I and my camera took what advantage of it we could.

I was so absorbed in the scenery that I had lost track of time and I suddenly realized it was past time to relieve Jim of the tedious task of cutting steps into the icy slope. I stood from my perch and stepped into the steps Jim had carved out and looked up the steep ice field above to see how far Jim had gotten. I was stunned and confused. I could see nothing but white upon white. Where was Jim? I stared dumbly above me, closed my eyes, shook my head and looked again, but nothing had changed. Jim was gone!

My eyes scoured the slope. I looked down the face in panic, thinking he must have fallen and slid by me, somehow, without my noticing. There was nothing; the snow covered run-out was stark, void of all but a few large rocks. Further on I could only see the never-ending forest that surrounded Shasta. I looked up again, searching the face above me - it was open, bare, white, steep, and empty. I thought perhaps he had managed to climb to the top, but that was impossible. It was at least three-hundred feet to the top of the ridge. Even if he had quit cutting steps and sprinted he wouldn't be close to reaching it.

I was having a hard time overcoming my fear. It was just not possible that he had disappeared. There was no rational explanation, save one, that I thought upon as my blood ran cold: The stories were true. Jim Bacus had been abducted, taken into the mountain by Martians.

I looked back down the mountain, making certain that I had not missed anything, but Jim was nowhere to be seen. I was completely alone; haunting fear arose as I experienced the awful feeling of utter desolation. The stories of the Martians entered my mind once more but I rapidly dispensed with them. I was confronted with a question even more perplexing than that posed by the inexplicable disappearance of my climbing partner: *What should I do now?*

My survival instincts rebelled against the notion of moving on up the mountain, but how could I go back? What would I say to Reggie and Bill? Telling them that Jim had been taken by the Martians was starting to sound crazy, even to me. If indeed Jim had somehow continued climbing up the mountain and something had happened to him, there might be the chance that he needed me. There was only one course of action I could justify, and that was to follow him, wherever he had gone.

Cautiously I started up the steps that Jim had cut, looking left and right for any sign of disturbed ice or snow. It hadn't taken long to reach the point where the steps he had cut ended. Once again I looked up; there was no hole, no door, no crampon tracks scrambling up the face, no opening into the inner recesses of the mountain. I had a fleeting, insane thought that perhaps the Martians had covered their entrance with snow, disguising it as part of the mountain. I imagined the snow exploding as Martians, with horrible eyes and drooling lips, burst forth, snatching me down into their cave. I wondered if my mind had lost its balance and laughed nervously at my imagination.

Thus I arrived at the last step Jim had cut, and once again was faced with the question of what to do next. Do I continue alone to the summit and try to explain what happened, tell

Reggie and Bill the impossible story that Jim was missing? Tell them he hadn't fallen off the mountain and there was no sign that he had been drug into the mountain? He had mysteriously disappeared into thin air. No one would believe that tale, I couldn't believe it myself.

I wasn't confident or experienced enough in my climbing abilities to consider a solo climb to the summit. Should I turn around and retreat to the Sierra Club Cabin at the base of the mountain, and wait for Reggie and Bill to return? No, that was unacceptable; to turn back now, without having discovered the fate of my climbing mate would be unforgivable. I had no choice but to continue onward.

I stepped into the last step that Jim had cut and, with a prayer, I lifted my ax to cut the next step. Just as I started to swing the ax and as in a dream, I was lifted off the snow. For one horrified, disoriented moment I flailed uselessly, terrifying thoughts racing through my mind: *Martians. Falling. I am going to die.* But no-thing had a hold of me, and I *wasn't* falling down, I *was* falling up!

The wind had lifted me off the face of the mountain and I was flying up the slope and gaining speed, flying as fast as a rocket blasting off. I struggled to keep my body upright, reaching out helplessly with my ice ax and crampons to regain the mountain face. The wind was propelling me to the top of the ridge and as I careened up the face of the mountain I wondered how high the wind would carry me, where would it drop me. With that thought I panicked and struck out desperately with my ice ax against the mountain attempting to slow myself down, but the wind was stronger than my futile attempts. I could see the ridge coming rapidly and felt utterly helpless, then grateful when I didn't continued skyward - the wind hurtled me, light as a feather, over its ledge.

Ahead I could see jagged rocks jutting out from the ice like gargantuan teeth. Throughout all the wind and constant jarring I was able to keep hold of my ice ax and I continued driving the point into the frozen ice below me. I was unable to drive it completely into the ice, but had managed to slow down the speed of my body as it slid over the ridge. I struck a field of rocks, bouncing off of them, dazed but unharmed. I was heading towards another barrier of rock spires and grabbed out for one, but was unable to hold on. The wind was relentless as I careened through the rocks. I made one last attempt, successfully, to wrap my arms around one of the spires. I was bouncing around like a sheet in the wind, clinging to my last anchor, and was slowly losing my grip. I looked over my shoulder and all I could see was blowing snow, a total void. I had no idea what awaited me on the other side of the ridge, which looked to be only ten or fifteen feet away. It took everything I had in me to keep a hold on the rock. I could only pray that I could outlast the gale, but I felt my grip slipping as the wind slowly pried me loose from my lone salvation. Like it or not, I was going to find out what awaited me on the other side of the ridge.

Amidst the chaos and tumult of howling winds, blinding and stinging snow, and overwhelming confusion, I was coherent enough to realize that I had to go over the ridge feet first and face the inevitable head on. It would be my only chance of surviving. As I let go of the rock I flipped myself over on my butt and let the wind carry me into nothingness.

Airborne again, I felt the wind loosen its grip and drop me, like a stone, over the ledge into the unknown. I was no longer flying, but falling with the blown ice and snow. I looked between my legs and saw below me a huge white ledge of snow and on the edge of it was my rope-mate, Jim, sitting alone amidst the white.

I landed hard beside him and the snow gave way under me like a huge feather mattress. I sank up to my armpits and for the first moment in what seemed a long, long time, I was no longer moving. Everything was peaceful, infinitely quiet. I sat stunned and was unable to speak amidst the sudden silence, my mind grappling with confusion, latent panic, and blessed gratitude.

So we sat, Jim and I, motionless in unending quiet when suddenly I heard Jim's voice break through the wall of timelessness around me. "What took you so long, Joe?" Jim was a man of few words.

If we had landed anywhere but in that small snow deposit we would have fallen to our death, one of those 'once in a lifetime' events that sets one to think.

I have been told, and I believe, that nothing happens by chance.

A RETURN TO OUR ROOTS

How deep down do
they dig,
how far will they travel
to find you
and bring you home.

Mountains had lured me back to my beginning, I wanted to return to *my* mountains, the Sawtooth Mountains, where I was born and raised. Bonnie and I packed up and returned to our roots in Idaho. Glen Michels said he would be happy to have me back and I returned to a job I thought never to do again, plumbing. I wasn't excited about it, but was grateful to have a job; it would put food on the table until something better came along.

When we were settled in, the first thing I did was to start looking for a climbing partner. I went to the local sporting goods store and asked the owner, who was clerking that day, if he knew of any climbers around. He told me that climbing wasn't happening in Idaho, but he had heard about one guy who was climbing in the surrounding mountains by the name of John Zapp.

I found his name in the phone book and gave him a call. It turned out to be another one of those 'meant to be moments'; he was also looking for a climbing partner. He had more experience than I did, but it seemed that my enthusiasm made up for any lack I might have had. He asked me to meet him at the rock quarry on Table Rock, just outside of Boise, the following weekend.

He was there waiting for me and when we introduced ourselves I had a gut feeling that we would be climbing many mountains together. He asked pointed questions about my climbing experience and then he put me through the ringer. We climbed every bolder in sight. He was impressed with my ability and I knew I could learn a lot from him, so we made plans to meet again.

John was my age. He was tall, with dark hair, and his face was tanned from spending so much time outside. He was a handsome man, elegant in manner and a total gentleman. He learned how to climb in Switzerland, where he had lived for several years. He was born in Idaho and had been raised with skis on his feet and ski poles in his hands. When I met him he was coaching the ski team at the College of Idaho. Skiing was in his blood. He not only taught his pupils to ski but also insisted they be superb athletes. He followed his own advice; he was either running a hundred miles a week or riding his bike twice as far. He drove his car only when absolutely necessary. He was abnormally strong and had superb balance. He was a true all-around athlete.

He put me through a grueling physical education, and it was just what I needed to awaken the potential my body held. At first snow we would go to the mountains and run through thigh deep powder, until we could not take another step. I had been of an average strength before these extreme workouts, but now I found myself gaining a power of body I never thought I could possess. Soon we were climbing every weekend and making a list of all the mountains we wanted to climb. Mt. Regan would be the first.

My life had been altered completely. I had closed the doors on my past burying secret memories in the dark closet of my mind, but change was on the way. Past memories would soon be buried in another grave, with the death of my mother.

DEATH OF A MADAM

Life
is but a
feather
falling from
the nest.

My life had changed so much, and so rapidly, that the day my mother called me to tell me she was not well, I felt that I hadn't spoken with her in years. Her news was not good. She had been diagnosed with lung cancer and the doctors told her it was incurable. She was determined to fight it and needed my help.

She had heard of a clinic in Mexico that claimed to have a cure and asked if I would ride with her and Jim to Mexico. I left for Lake Tahoe early the next morning, trying mentally to prepare myself for what was to come. Despite my determination to depart from my mother's life, the strings of love and history were strong and I didn't hesitate to turn back to confront it once more.

We arrived at the clinic two days later. I was amazed at the number of people sitting there, waiting to be called into the doctor's office. While Mom was being examined I started visiting with the other patients. Word of the clinic had spread and people had come from all over the world in hope of curing their cancer. Some were there for the first time, others had already started their treatment, and some had been cured and were returning for a final exam. For the first time since I learned of her illness I had hope that perhaps she really could beat it – until I saw her face as she came back into the waiting room.

Her cancer was too far advanced, they could do nothing to help her. The next three weeks were devastating. Mentally she remained strong during that time, but physically she was deteriorating rapidly. Her body was not getting sufficient oxygen. All I could do was sit with her as she faded, hoping I was giving her some small relief just by being there with her.

The silence in her room was broken one day while I sat at her bedside. She gasped suddenly, trying to get a breath of air, "Joe," she whispered with an exhausted voice, "Bring me one of those silver orbs, they will cure me." I was not in her reality and could see nothing. I was totally dumbfounded and tried to explain to her that the orbs were invisible to me.

Tearfully and utterly helpless, I said, "I'm sorry Mom but I'm unable to see them."

"There, over by the window, catch one please, please." her voice fading as she spoke. She tried to sit up and extended her arm, pointing a finger at the invisible orbs. With a shudder she fell back on the bed and faded into unconsciousness.

A week or so before she died she asked Jim and I to come into her room. She told me that she was proud of me and thanked me for the conversations we had these past few weeks. Conversations about what it meant to live with spiritual awareness and that she had no doubt that she would be back again. She wanted me to know that she had finally found peace. Her comments touched me deeply, they were the kindest words she had ever said to me.

She took a piece of paper from her bedside table and said, "This is my will. I'm leaving all my money to you Jim, but only on the condition that when you die you will leave half of your money to Joe." Jim said he would. She handed me her will and I laid it on the bedside table. I left the room to give her a few moments alone with Jim and when I came back the will was gone. I never asked Jim about it. I never expected anything from him anyway. I was not of his blood.

Mom's last words to me were, "I'm the lucky one, Joe. I'm leaving this insane world." She was only forty-three years old when she died, and she died impenitent.

Jim had lost his life companion. Mom had been the strong force in their life, and with her death he was deprived of direction. The last time I saw him, or spoke with him, was at my mother's funeral. He and I had become almost strangers to each other.

My time in Mustang Ranch had been the nearest I had ever come to sharing a life with my mother, and those last days in the hospital were the nearest I had ever come to bonding with her. It was not much, in the end – a few frail strands that joined us together. She departed from this world as mysterious to me as she had always been. But I felt at least that, for a brief and fragile moment, she and I had joined hands, and understood one another.

Now I had my life ahead of me. I turned to it with full faith in the future. There was nothing more I could do for the Madam of Mustang Ranch, but live *my* life, the life she had given me, as fully as I was able – to turn my face to the world she had called insane, and to learn from it whatever it had to teach me, so that when my time at last would come, I could face my physical end with tranquility at the past, and faith in the life to come.

THE LOST AND WANDERING

If the door is
open
angels will
enter.
If the door is closed
you must
listen for
the knock.

The lake at the base of Mt. Regan, Sawtooth Lake, is a place of many memories and one of the most beautiful places on earth. I have skied to Sawtooth Lake more than 50 times, the first time in 1966 and the last in 1987 - twenty years, and each trip etched forever into memory. So many winter adventures here, so many blue-sky mountain days, so many near disasters.

Climbing Mt. Regan became my life's passion for four winters - four attempts made, three attempts failed. It began in 1966 when my climbing partner, John Zapp, and I set our stars on being the first climbers to make a winter ascent of Mt. Regan.

In those days there were only two means of transportation available when traveling mountainous terrain during winter months – snowshoes or alpine skis with seal skins attached by leather straps. When you were climbing the hair on the skins would dig into the snow to keep you from sliding backwards, and was laid in such a way that it would allow skis to slide forward fairly well. Seal skins were used by the military in WWII and worked quite well for climbing, but they were heavy. The ski boots were heavy and the cable bindings and

Marker toe plates were awkward - skiing uphill was hard going.

We had researched all the newest skis and hardware and had learned that the Norwegian army used lighter skis, with light-weight pin bindings. They had created ski wax that would adhere to the snow when climbing and had no resistance on the downhill run, but their waxes, pin bindings, and touring skis were not yet available in the United States. Even REI didn't have them in their store or catalog. They were common in Europe for skiing in rugged terrain and, as we discovered later when we bought ours from Norway in 1970, they made winter access into the mountains not only more reasonable, but traveling on them was efficient and pleasant.

Given our choices at the time, John and I decided that alpine skis and seal skins would be the best alternative for us. Though they would be tedious and slow on the climb into the mountains, and more difficult than snowshoes, the trip back out would more than make up the difference, exhilarating and fast in the steep terrain we would encounter.

It was Christmas vacation. We had seven days to get to Stanley, where our journey would begin, ski to the base of the mountain, climb it, ski out, and get home in time to return to our jobs by day eight.

Stanley is a small town in central Idaho with a population, in 1966, of approximately 50 people. The setting is beyond beautiful. It is nestled in the Sawtooth Valley at the base of the Sawtooth Mountain Range, with the Salmon River meandering through the valley. The first time I saw the Sawtooth Mountains and the little town of Stanley was in 1957. I was eighteen years old and will never forget the moment. It was then that I began dreaming of living there one day - a dream that eventually came true.

There was a narrow road following Iron Creek that ran through the tree line at the bottom of the Sawtooths. It was an easy four-mile ski following Iron Creek Road to its end, where we would begin our ascent to Mt. Regan. The distance from the end of Iron Creek Road to the base of the Regan was about ten miles, a total distance of about fourteen miles, with an elevation gain of approximately 3,000 feet.

We packed our gear Thursday evening and left for Stanley after work on Friday, driving through Sun Valley on Highway 93. In those days it was the only way into the Sawtooth Valley in winter, a slow winding road that climbed over Galena Summit. At its summit you could see the entire Sawtooth Mountain Range – a breathtaking site. We took a room that night in the old Sawtooth Hotel, a historical landmark built sometime in the 1800's.

There were three bars in town: the Rod and Gun Club, the Casino Club, and the Stanley Club. That seemed like a lot of clubs for a population of fifty and we decided there must be some heavy drinkers in town. The Stanley Club had the most cars parked out front and we could hear the roar from the Club a block away. Guessing there just might be some fine local entertainment going on inside we sauntered down the street and opened the door. Local entertainment there was – happily provided by a couple of Forest Service employees, Tom Kovalicky and Bill James. Tom was the Forest Ranger for the Sawtooth Forest and Bill worked under him - in the summer months they were both smoke jumpers.

When we walked through the front door Tom and Bill were standing on the bar, three sheets to the wind, teaching their rapt audience the proper way to land after parachuting out of an airplane, explaining that when your feet touched the ground you must immediately do an Alan roll.

"This might be something we need to know just in case we fall off that mountain." commented John, so we found a place at the bar and became as enthralled with the words of wisdom provided by these two drunken smoke jumpers as were the rest of the listeners.

Totally enraptured with the story they were listening to, the onlookers started applauding and chanting, "Demonstration, demonstration!"

Tom and Bill started waving their hands and yelling, "Alright!

The people sitting in the front row started rearranging the tables and chairs, clearing a space in front of the bar for their lesson. When the space seemed large enough, Tom and Bill yelled "HIYA!" and in unison they dove off the bar, as if they were diving into a swimming pool. It was something to see. Even though they had both consumed their fair share of liquor, they landed on their shoulders, in unison, as smooth as rabbit hair, and rolled to their feet. The crowd cheered and applauded with gusto, John and I right along with them.

They took their bows and turned back to the bar laughing. They bellied up beside us and looked us up and down as if we were some strange beings that had been dropped from the sky, our knickers had drawn them to us like a magnet. "You two are the first strangers we've seen in town since I can't remember when." said Kovalicky. "Not many people visit Stanley in the wintertime."

"What the hell are you doing here?" asked Bill.

"We came to climb Mt. Regan." John answered.

"Mt. Regan?" they both said at once. Kovalicky's eyes grew to the size of a large snow ball.

"Hell man, you know no one's ever climbed that mountain in winter before? That mountain is in middle of the Sawtooth Range! Do you realize how far that is?"

"Yeah, and dangerous. You know there's a storm coming in?" asked Bill.

"It can't be much more dangerous than that dive you guys did off the bar. I thought you were both going to break your necks." I laughed.

"Just how do you plan to get to that damned mountain?" Bill wore a serious frown.

John answered, "We thought we would ski in."

"*Ski* in?" said Kovalicky. "Are you guys nuts? It's almost 15 miles to Sawtooth Lake and you still ain't there - you still have to cross the lake and Sawtooth Lake ain't no puddle."

Bill looked at Kovalicky and said, "Can't we stop them? There must be something we can do. These guys will get into trouble and guess who will be the ones to have to rescue them."

Kovalicky thought a for moment. "Well, I can't think of anything. After all it's a free country. I guess it's alright as long as they know what they're getting themselves into."

"Do you?" Bill, had both elbows on the bar and was looking back toward us. "I mean, have you done this before?"

John commenced to give them a short resume of his climbing experience. "I climbed and skied in the Alps while I lived there, I'm a ski coach for the College of Idaho, and I have climbed all over the Sawtooths in summer, including a solo climb of Mt. Regan a few years back."

I saw Kovalicky look at me out of the corner of his eye. "What about you?"

"I have climbed in Yosemite, the Sierras in the winter, and I climbed Mt. Shasta last January." I didn't tell him that I was blown off the mountain.

Kovalicky nodded to Bill. They walked a short distance away, just out of earshot, and spoke to each other, arms flailing. When they came back Kovalicky declared, "We've decided to lend a hand. What if we pull you to the end of the Iron Creek Road on our snow machines? That would save you four miles of grunt work."

In those days I wasn't as strong as Zapp. The man was an animal. He rode his bicycle every day, and when he wasn't doing that he was running the foothills of Boise, regardless of conditions; nothing would stop him, not mud, or snow, or rain.

"Would you do that? That would be fantastic." I said, trying not to sound *too* eager. I didn't want to admit that I was worried more about the trip *in* than the climb *up*.

"What time tomorrow do you plan on starting out?" Kovalicky asked.

"Early." answered Zapp.

We made our arrangements and headed back to the hotel. It was a long, sleepless night.

We met Kovalicky and Bill for breakfast in the Sawtooth Hotel dining room at seven o'clock sharp the next morning. They had calmed down a bit but were still concerned about the risk they knew we were taking.

"So, you're *determined* to do this?" Kovalicky was still concerned.

"Don't worry," Zapp replied, "we'll be fine. If we see things aren't going well we'll turn back. We're not insane, neither of us want to get killed in an avalanche or fall off the mountain."

I nodded in agreement.

We finished a hearty breakfast, knowing it would be the last decent meal we would have for the next five or six days, and went outside. In the parking lot awaiting us was a truck pulling a trailer with six snowmobiles on it. Shortly thereafter we were joined by several more Forest Service employees who didn't want to miss out on the fun. There was no question about it, entertainment was in short supply during the winter in Stanley.

We climbed into the pickup and off we went to the Iron Creek Road, where it intersected with Highway 21. We watched as the men unloaded their snowmobiles off the trailer and loaded them up with our cumbersome frame backpacks, heavy with all the gear we were taking: climbing ropes, ice screws, ice axes, pitons, hammers, crampons, sleeping bags, water bottles, climbing boots, collapsible shovels for digging snow caves so we would not have to carry a tent, a Seva stove for cooking and enough freeze-dried food for six days.

Kovalicky and Bill had each brought along a rope about 50 feet long. Giving both John and I one end of the rope, they tied the other to their machines and off we went, flying like birds tied to a tether. The four miles from the highway to the trail head was a breeze, the next ten miles would not be so easy.

"Tell us when you plan on coming out, perhaps we'll come back to meet you and give you a ride back to Stanley." offered Kovalicky.

John said, "That would be great. With the ride you just gave us we should get to the mountain by dark and weather permitting we should be able to climb the mountain in one day. If we can get back down the mountain by dark we could be out day after tomorrow. If we're forced to spend the night on the mountain we won't be out until Tuesday."

"That sounds about right if all goes well. If we don't get to the mountain tonight, add another day to the trip and we won't be out until Wednesday," I added. I was already getting apprehensive; a light snow had started falling while John was talking. Kovalicky, Bill and the others wished us good luck and watched as we skied away.

We were making good time. The trail was fairly flat and our skis weren't sinking too deeply into the snow, but that didn't last long. Soon it was snowing hard and with each inch of snow that fell we were using more energy breaking trail, the person who breaks trail always expends more energy than those behind and we were trading places more often as the snow got deeper.

Before long we started up a steep ridge and were forced at times to sidestep on steep narrow areas. By noon the storm had turned into a blizzard. Snow was falling about an inch an hour and visibility was poor. We had been lured into what seemed to be an easier route, only to find ourselves deep in a canyon, too steep to climb out of, and we were forced to backtrack. By the time we started up the ridge to Alpine Lake it was getting late and we were getting tired. Sawtooth Lake was still two miles away and two-thousand feet higher. We pressed on but darkness was coming rapidly, between the blizzard and the twilight, visibility was bad, to say the least. We were on a narrow ridge with steep slopes dropping out of sight on both sides. We were traveling blind. The only things visible were large snowflakes falling and swirling around our faces, so thick we could barely see our skis. I knew if we weren't careful we could easily ski off the edge of the ridge.

We were forced to stop for the night on a flat spot just above Alpine Lake. It was wind-blown and there wasn't enough snow for a snow cave, but there was enough for a snow trench that would keep us somewhat sheltered from the wind. We starting digging trenches just wide enough for our ground pads and sleeping bags, and hit bedrock only two feet down. It was going to be long, long night and I knew we wouldn't be getting much rest.

After what seemed to be hours, I had finally fallen asleep. I woke abruptly, dreaming that someone was throwing ice water in my face. I sat up and looked around but I couldn't see a thing, the world was black, but I could feel freezing water percolating through my down sleeping bag and into my clothes. It took me a few minutes to realize what was happening and was momentarily stunned. We were in the middle of a rain storm at 7,000 feet in December. This scenario fell far out of our planning, and worst of all, we hadn't brought rain gear. My memory flickered on one of the more interesting facts I had read about the Sawtooth Mountains, that they are noted as being one of the coldest places in the continental United States. Unhappily, I recalled Bill's words of admonition, "It is *dangerous* out there."

"John, John!" I called with a tinge of panic, "It's raining!"

"I know." he called back. "I thought if it wasn't bothering you, I must be hallucinating, but I guess not. I think we should pack up and move on. We'd be better off if we were up higher, maybe we can climb above the rain and get back to a nice pleasant blizzard."

"That's a good idea." I replied, "All hell is going to break loose when these steep slopes get saturated." We could already hear the thunder of avalanches breaking loose all around us. We were safe from avalanches on the ridge, but we were getting soaked and were 15 miles from town. It *was* a dangerous place to be, much more so than we had anticipated. It was about nine at night and pitch black when we got our gear gathered up, stuffed in our packs, and got our skis on. Our sleeping bags were too wet to put in the packs so we rolled them up, squeezing the water out of them as best we could, and strapped them on the outside of our packs and started up the mountain.

At the time it seemed the only sensible thing to do. We figured if we got high enough to get out of the rain we could find a suitable place to dig a snow cave, just enough shelter to prevent us from freezing to death. We didn't get very far. The wet snow on the surface was mixing with the dry cold snow beneath. Our seal skins were icing up layer, upon layer, and building up so fast that we were accumulating stilts of frozen snow on the bottom of our skis. It was impossible to move forward; we had no choice but to remove our seal skins. Without their traction we were forced to side step as we climbed, and there was a lot of climbing ahead, at least one-thousand vertical feet of it.

After struggling for some time against these hopeless conditions, we were finally forced to stop moving up. The situation was grim. We couldn't just sit and wait for the rain to stop, we had to keep moving lest we freeze to death. Avalanches continued to break loose all around us, but avoiding avalanches was only one problem. The more urgent concern was that if we decided to turn back, we could trigger an avalanche and be carried to the bottom of the slope, buried beneath tons of snow. Visibility was non-existent. It would be impossible to determine how steep the slopes were that we would be skiing down. We could easily lose our sense of direction and ski off a ledge or a cliff. Regardless of what we would face if we turned back, there seemed no alternative but to descend. We couldn't continue on and we couldn't stop where we were.

We began our descent, listening to the roaring coming from the surrounding mountains as they released their burden of wet snow. The ridge we were on was so steep and narrow that we started carrying our skis, floundering through the snow. It was impossible and before long we decided it would be better to ski than to exhaust ourselves post-holing through the deep snow.

As the ridge widened we were able to traverse the slope on our skis, but were concerned that we might cut an avalanche so we stayed well apart from each other. It was during a traverse that the rain stopped, the sky started clearing, and the stars came out, although our initial relief was short lived. Before long we became conscious of the extraordinary change in temperature, it was dropping so rapidly that we could feel our fingers start to freeze in our wet gloves. We kept on moving trying to keep our body heat up. Finally we could see the outline of trees ahead that would lead us to flatter terrain, but the going would not be easy. We came to the first of several deposition areas where the run-off from avalanches above had filled the bottom of the canyon. We had to remove our skis and climb over mounds of ice and broken trees, the snow had set up like concrete. Our clothes had started to freeze, emitting crackling sounds each time we moved.

The snow on the mountain slopes above us was setting up with the cold temperatures so the danger of being hit by an avalanche had decreased, but we had to keep moving. To stop at this point would mean certain death. Each step was brutal, we were breaking through the ice crust that had formed on top of the snow and trail-breaking on the flat proved no easier than on the slopes.

I suggested to John that we discard everything that wasn't absolutely essential and return later to recover the cache. We dropped our packs and discarded our down sleeping bags, now frozen and hard as steel. I knew my bag was heavy but was shocked to find I had been carrying a 50 pound block of ice. We also discarded our climbing equipment. Having abandoned the better part of our equipment and hoping, with the reduced weight, for faster travel, we set out again. But still the ice crust wasn't strong enough to hold our weight, we continued to break through the ice and our skis became all but invisible. It seemed a never ending and constant battle. Our legs were cramping with fatigue and there was a heavy ice crust that was constantly cutting into our ankles. There was no alternative and we pushed on.

At this point I was feeling not a little despair, although it wasn't something that I wanted to communicate to John. I was sure that he was probably feeling some despair himself. He stepped to the side of the trail allowing me to take over. Trail-breaking and freezing temperatures were wearing us down, and we were both exhausted.

I estimated that we still had six or seven miles to go before we reached the highway and for the first time I wondered if we could possibly survive. Even if we reached the highway we would then have to walk or ski to Stanley, another five miles. The temperature continued dropping rapidly and it felt like it was already well below zero. I could feel the hair in my nostrils freeze with every breath I took. Our bodies were expending tremendous amounts of energy just trying to stay warm, and our wet frozen clothes were no longer adequate to retain our heat. Our lives were definitely in peril, but we continued on, pushing one ski forward and then the other, moving like zombies. We were traveling less than one mile an hour, it would take at least six hours to reach the highway.

I tried to focus on anything that would keep me going, keep me from thinking about how cold and tired I was. So I thought about all the stories I had read and heard about the people who had found themselves in a similar situation, fearing the inevitable, but refusing to give up. These adventures and epic struggles that had become part of our collected inheritance. I thought about the people whose story no one had ever heard of, some making it to safety, others who didn't, and were lost both to life and to memory.

My thoughts had given me some small energy and I knew if we were going to be among the survivors we would have to focus and give everything we had to the task at hand - shove one ski forward at a time, transfer weight to the forward ski and pull the trailing ski on, through the thick crust, ignoring it as it rasped against our aching legs, and doing it all over again, one ski at a time, one step at a time. Just keep moving. Sort of a meditation - a meditation on survival.

The repetition went on endlessly, indifferent to the complaints of the mind and body. In this trans-like state I continued moving forward. Suddenly I was startled out of my reverie. The stillness of the mountains was broken by a voice, not mine and not Johns, but a woman's voice, clear and inspiring. "*He watches over the lost and wandering.*" That's all I heard, and just as suddenly as her voice came, the quiet returned again. It was a mythical moment, leaving me at once humbled and astonished.

Some years later I read a book titled *Men Who Have Walked with God.* Many of the men written about in this book had, at some point in their spiritual journey, heard a female voice speak to them. Her voice had guided them and had given them courage to go on when they thought they could go no longer. Her name was Sophia. Perhaps it was her voice I had heard on my trip, guiding me on my way, giving me the courage, determination, and strength I needed to continue on. Throughout history there have been mountaineers and explorers who have written of similar experiences.

Shackleton wrote about "the sense that someone else was present. A presence encouraging me to make strenuous efforts to survive. On expeditions, when I had been at death's door, I couldn't identify the stranger, but was aware of a benevolent presence, insisting I shouldn't give up."

I have always wondered if those who push themselves to and beyond their limits, and understanding the chances they take by so doing, have a spiritual inclination and faith in a higher source. My spirits were instantly lifted, my body not as cold, and my skis moved with less effort. The voice had filled me with such energy and joy that I wanted to *sing*.

John must have wondered what had happened to me. I know he could feel my energy, but he didn't comment on it. I didn't tell John about the voice, I was afraid he would think I had gone out of my mind.

It seemed like only a few minutes had passed when we finally reached the trail-head at Iron Creek. It was almost midnight and the sky was crystal clear and filled with stars, giving off enough light that we could see quite well. What I saw under their glow was help for "the lost and wandering." What John saw were fresh snowmobile tracks.

Tom and Bill had come looking for us and we probably hadn't missed them by much. We *had* missed a quick ride out, but at least we wouldn't have to break trail any longer. When I stepped onto the snowmobile tracks there was yet another miracle. They had come looking for us *before* the freeze and their snow machines had packed the snow hard as granite while it was still wet. The dropping temperature had given us a two-foot-deep downhill frozen toboggan run, mostly downhill all the way to the highway. All we had to do was stand on our skis, close our eyes, and let the tracks lead us to the highway.

And that was just what we did. We were flying down the road, gliding effortlessly, like we had grown wings as we flew on towards the highway. Fifteen minutes later we were standing in the middle of Highway 21 with only five miles to go. We were safe, we would make it. We dropped our packs at the inter-section and started skiing down the highway. We had only gone a few feet when we saw headlights in the distance, headed our way from Stanley. Kovalicky and Bill had decided to come back one last time.

Never have I doubted the voice I heard that night. I have called it to mind many times since, when I felt that perhaps I was "lost and wandering." Always it has remained with me, and many, many times it has spurred me onward. I have often referred back to a passage from *Men Who Have Walked with God*:

"For mystics, indeed, for all those whose minds are set upon God or Ultimate Spirit as the one goal, it matters not much what is the helping figure the mind fixes upon *in route*. The way may prove easier because the pilgrim reverently asks for guidance of the Virgin Mary, or of a collective Ancestor, or of Sophia. Wisdom, visualized as a guardian other self."

THE LOST AND WANDERING - PART TWO

*Persistence
can be a
virtue,
or a
  demon.*

After surviving the first attempt at Mt. Regan John and I began planning our next winter ascent of Mt Regan.

"Joe, while we were skiing out Iron Creek Road, I started thinking about what we could do differently on our next try at Regan." I didn't tell him at that moment thinking about another attempt at Regan had been the one thing furthest from my mind at the time. He continued, "Next fall, say in October, we could take everything we don't need for the ski in and cache it near the mountain. When we return in December for the climb we would be free of the weight, and could get to Mt. Regan easily in one day. All we would be carrying is our trail food, some tea bags, our Seva Stove, some extra clothes - and this time we will take rain gear. We wouldn't be carrying more than twenty pounds each. What do you think about that?"

"That sounds good to me." The prospects of a quick and easy ski in was enticing; I still thought that the easiest part of the trip was the climb. "Let's do it!"

When October came around John and I gathered up our climbing gear, everything we thought we might possibly need; ropes, ice ax, pitons, ice screws, hammers, crampons, shovels. This time in the event we would have to sleep on the mountain, we decided to take a tent along with our sleeping bags, freeze-dried food, climbing boots and extra clothes. For the next two weeks we watched the weather closely waiting for perfect weather as we had only one day to hike to the base of the mountain, stash our cache and return home. The weather looked good for the second week in October, so we planned our preliminary expedition for then.

Our day arrived and on Thursday we packed our gear in John's Volkswagen van and were ready to leave Friday after work. Highway 21 was still open for the summer season so we didn't have to drive through Sun Valley and over Galena Summit. We drove up the Iron Creek road and parked the van at the trail head, and pitched our tent in the dark, winter was already setting in - there were 6 or 8 inches of snow on the ground.

Next morning, after a quick breakfast of oatmeal and a pot of tea, we headed up the trail as dawn was breaking. We were making good time, carrying about forty pounds each, and the snow wasn't slowing us down much. It seemed that the trip in December would be a piece of cake. We arrived at Sawtooth Lake in early afternoon and hiked around the east end of the lake looking for the perfect place to cache our gear.

We hadn't found the perfect spot yet. It had to be easy to find and a place where it wouldn't be buried under tons of snow. We stopped under a huge old tree for lunch and while I was breaking out the salami, bread and cheese, I noticed Zapp looking hard up the tree. "This is it," he said after a few minutes of reflection. "We climb as high in this tree as possible and tie our gear to the branches. It's a no - brainier. It will be easy to find the tree - we could even find it in the dark if we had to." I enthusiastically agreed, and after lunch I climbed up the tree 30 or 40 feet and tied the stuff-bags that contained our cache to the tree. The canvas stuff-bags were made of tightly woven oiled canvas and would keep even our down sleeping bags dry. As I climbed back down the tree I thought, when we return in December there will be 10 to 15 feet of snow on the ground and it will be an easier climb.

Secure in the knowledge that our gear was safe, we hiked away. Our trip down the mountain was peaceful and unhurried - the alpine glow on the mountains was beautiful, as if auguring well for our coming winter expedition.

The next two months passed quickly. Christmas vacation arrived and it was time to head to the mountains. We were ready, excited and certain that this, our second attempt to climb Mt. Regan in winter, would be successful. We called Kovalicky and asked if he was interested in giving us another ride up Iron Creek.

"You guys sure like to suffer," he laughed.

"Pain is the spice of life," I laughed back. Then came the bad news - he and Bill were off to Montana for the holidays.

"Would you like me to find someone else to pull you in?"

"That's all right, we're traveling light this time." I explained our cache and told him we should have no trouble. We felt we were already beholden to Tom and Bill and didn't think it quite right to get the whole town of Stanley involved in our follies.

We arrived in Stanley late Friday and grabbed a room at the now familiar Sawtooth Hotel. We decided not to go carousing this year and after arranging an early ride to the Iron Creek Road turnoff, we went to bed hoping for a good night's sleep.

The next morning when we sat for breakfast, we were given a note from Kovalicky - "Bill and I snowmobiled up Iron Creek before we left for Montana and packed the snow for you. Good luck up there. It has been a heavy snow year, don't get yourselves caught up in an avalanche." Our ride took us to Iron Creek and we unloaded our gear from the pickup and thanked our driver.

The tracks Tom and Bill left for us were a day or two old but they helped nonetheless – it only took a couple of hours to arrive at the trail head and it had been a pleasant ski. Once we entered the forest it became a totally different thing. We were suddenly pushing 12 to 14 inches of snow ahead of us with every step and the higher we climbed, the deeper it got. With our light packs it did not seem too bad and we congratulated ourselves thinking about our cache waiting for us at the base of Mt. Regan. By our calculations we would be at Sawtooth Lake before dark. There would be plenty of time to collect our gear, pitch our tent, have dinner and get a good night's sleep. We stopped for lunch on a flat spot below Alpine Lake, right on schedule. Soon after lunch, as we reached the ridge just above the lake, a light snow started falling. The wind came along the ridge with force and we were being pushed around a bit, but with our light loads the going wasn't bad.

Wordlessly we skied over our old campsite from the winter before. It was just getting dark when we topped the ridge to Sawtooth Lake, and in the beauty of the waning light we removed our seal skins and skied off towards the lake. In short time we arrived at the lake and started around the east side to retrieve our gear. Ominously, the landscape was much different now than it was last October. Nothing seemed the same and it seemed there were trees and even some rock cliffs missing – I was disconcerted and felt like we were in a different place altogether. Everything was white, smooth and rounded - nothing rose out of the snow except Mt. Regan. Anxiously, we skied around a ridge expecting to see our tree.

But our tree was gone - it was nowhere to be seen.

We looked around us, both of us silently wondering if this was the right place. But all the markers were in place - we recognized our position but our tree was gone.

"It's hard to believe it is buried under fifty feet of snow." I finally commented. "It would be easier to believe it just up and ran away."

"A tree can hide but it can't run." John was trying to make a joke, I didn't catch the humor. The only other explanation was that it was blown over by the wind. There was no possibility that it had been knocked over by an avalanche; the terrain here wasn't steep enough.

"Well at least we aren't wet to the bone like last winter." I guess John was trying to cheer me up.

"Yes, and aren't carrying a 50 pound block of ice on our backs," I was trying to join in the humor. "I suggest we have a spot of tea, old chap, before we carve some turns out of here."

Tea was all that we had left and we were both cold, tired and dehydrated, and in need of food. We had been anticipating a sort of feast at this point from our stored provisions. I broke out the Seva, primed it, lit the stove, poured the last of our water in our small pot and slowly added snow as the water warmed. I had learned earlier that melting snow to drink or cook with was not as simple as it seemed - it was easy to burn snow if you added too much to a pot and it required patience or else you would be in for a bad cup of tea.

The water was finally getting hot and we brought out our tea bags and cups. When the water started boiling, I reached for the handle on the tea pot, I was getting dull witted and clumsy, my gloved fingers weren't behaving well and I knocked the pot over. For a stunned moment we both looked at the hot water melting a hole in the snow-pack.

I gave Zapp a sheepish look, "Sorry about that, shall I try again?"

He didn't look at me when he said, "I think we better get off the steep part of the mountain before it's so dark we have to crawl down." I apologized again and packed up the stove. We strapped our seal skins back on our skis, put our packs on, turned and dishearteningly started out. I felt so guilty about spilling the tea that I went ahead, determined to break trail all the way to the top of the ridge. It was snowing harder and the wind had picked up.

John was close on my heals. "Let's try Castle Peak next winter." he said with little enthusiasm.

"OK. It could be that this mountain doesn't like us, we haven't even touched it." I replied, gesturing at the austere mountain face gazing down at us from above. I felt uneasy and wondered if we were in for another epic as the wind and snowfall increased.

By the time we reached the ridge it was so dark that the difference between snow and objects was difficult to distinguish, and the wind was howling around us driving snow into our faces. It was hard to keep our eyes open against the wind and snow and the steepest part of the descent still lay ahead.

"If any avalanche activity is happening we won't be able to hear it above this wind," I shouted.

"There could be some slab avalanche happening if this wind keeps up," John yelled back.

That was the last of our conversation on the ridge. We post-holed down - it was too steep and dark to attempt skiing, even without heavy packs. We made it off the ridge in one piece and the wind was less of a problem in the forest below where the trees, swaying above us, absorbed most of its impact. The track we cut on the way up was nowhere to be found so we kept going down, keeping Iron Creek on our right and hoping not to stumble into it. The prospect of repeating our icy descent of the prior year was enough to send chills through our bones.

With our light packs the trip out was easier than last winter and we weren't breaking trail through ice crusted snow. We didn't feel the panic of the previous winter and were still confident that all was well even though we had been on our skis for over twelve hours with little to eat and we had run out of water, we were dehydrated, forced to warm snow in our mouths before swallowing it. Iron Creek was close but it was impossible to get to the water because of the deep snow and lack of visibility. Fortunately we found a large dead tree that had fallen across the creek. We knocked enough snow off the tree to lay down on it and reach the water to fill our water bottles. It was just what we needed to give us the energy to make it to the trail-head.

We stumbled onto Iron Creek Road around 10 PM and Highway 21 a little over an hour later. We weren't so lucky as to get a ride into Stanley this time and had to endure the five mile hike through a wind-driven snowstorm and we staggered into town around midnight. The only lights on were at the Rod and Gun Club, and they were a welcome sight. We entered the bar covered with snow - there wasn't a soul in the place. The bartender heard us come in and anticipating a late customer came through the door behind the bar.

"What in the hell happened to you!" he exclaimed. "Dora, Dora, come out here!"

While we were waiting for Dora we started to tell our story. The bartender only had one ear and the missing ear looked as if someone had bitten it off. I thought to myself that the Sawtooth Mountains must be a tough place in more ways than one.

Dora came from the back in her night clothes. By that time the snow we were wearing was melting, creating puddles on the floor. When she saw us she threw her hands up, "Glen!" she cried, "Bring these young fellows into the kitchen so we can thaw them out!" I could tell by the sound of her voice that she thought Glen was a bit slow figuring out what to do.

Dora rushed ahead while we followed Glen into the kitchen. It was located in a room behind the bar and she was already stoking the wood cook stove. "Bring some chairs, Glen," she demanded. We must have looked as bad as we felt. Dora was obviously concerned, and Glen quickly complied as we sat down in front of the already hot stove.

"Coffee will be ready in no time," she said as she put the pot on the burner over the fire box. "Where did you boys come from?" she questioned. "Were you in a car wreck?"

"No, nothing like that, we just skied out of the mountains." I wondered what she would think of that. "My God," she exclaimed. "Are you those boys that were here last winter and nearly froze to death up there?"

"I guess that would be us."

"Tom Kovalicky and Bill James have been telling the story of how they saved your lives last Christmas, and here you are back again. Are you crazy? What's wrong with you, are you trying to kill yourselves?"

" I *am* beginning to think that we aren't too smart," I replied.

"I guess that must be the way of it," said Glen.

While Dora poured our coffee, one-eared Glen left. He soon returned with a bottle of whiskey and poured a generous splash in our cups. "This ought to help thaw you out." He laughed as he poured some in his cup.

I didn't know which was thawing me out the fastest, the hot stove or the burning whiskey going down my throat. Dora, left the room, and returned with two heavy wool blankets.

"You get out of those wet clothes," she ordered. She laid the blankets on the kitchen counter and pushed a drying rack closer to the stove. "I'll be back when you're decent." With that she exited the room so we could get undressed. "Glen, tell me

173

when they're decent," she called as she closed the door behind her.

We undressed, hung our wet clothes on the rack, and pulled the blankets around us.

"Glen, are they decent yet?"

"It's all right, Ma. You can come out now."

Dora came out mumbling about how we should know better than to traipse around in those mountains in the dead of winter. Glen hadn't said much for awhile. Without asking he filled our cups with coffee, and topped it off with another generous shot of whiskey. I thought maybe Glen wasn't so slow after all.

"Do you boys know how cold it can get around here in the winter? Why I've seen 60 below or better. Stanley is the coldest country this side of the North Pole, you're damn lucky you're not stiff as boards. If you froze to death in those mountains nobody would find you until July and maybe not *then* if a bear found you first." Glen took a drink from his cup.

Dora wasn't finished with us yet. She threw a large frying pan on the stove, filled it with eggs and bacon. "You boys need some food to finish off that chill."

We hadn't had food since our salami-and-cheese lunch and were famished. The whiskey was going right straight to our heads.

"I hope you're smart enough to stay out of those mountains from here on out," she said as she started scrambling the eggs. "You're already the talk of the town. If you try another stupid stunt like this and freeze to death, I'm going to carve a sign in your memory, and it will read: 'These two fellas came here three times, the third time they stayed forever."

John and I smiled and contentedly sipped our coffee. As I thought about my trips to Stanley - the breathtaking beauty of the mountains here, the land that felt like God Himself had molded it, the friendliness of the people I had already met, I realized that that was exactly what I had in mind: I wanted to stay here forever, winter, fall, spring and summer.

* * *

John and I returned to retrieve our gear in May and to solve the mystery of our missing tree. We found the top of the tree sticking out of the snow and had to dig fifteen feet down to find our gear. Evidently, we had under-estimated the snowfall of the Sawtooth Mountains. Our tree, and our gear with it, had been buried the previous December under at least fifty feet of snow. With the deluge of snow that covered the mountains, and the powerful winds that blew fresh drifts around like sand-dunes, our tree, and thus our expedition, had never stood a chance.

FAILURE ON CASTLE PEAK

Failure
exists only
where it
is tolerated.

It was early in the month of March, 1968, and true to Zapp's request after our last failure on Regan, we were on our way to climb Castle Peak in the White Cloud Mountains. Castle Peak is the highest and biggest in the White Cloud Mountain Range of Idaho – a mountain big enough to make its own weather. The start of the attempt began as usual with our trip to Stanley.

We arrived in Stanley late in the evening, got our familiar room at the Sawtooth Hotel and went to the Rod and Gun club to say hello to our old friends Dora and Glenn, "Not again!" Dora looked shocked. "You boys are a caution - I give up."

Glen asked, "Where are you headed this time?"

"We thought to attempt a climb of Castle Peak in the White Cloud Mountains this winter, we decided we would give Mt. Regan a rest, she has probably had enough of us for awhile." I answered.

There was a man sitting at the bar that couldn't help but overhear our conversation. He looked at us and asked, "Where are you starting from?"

"The East Fork of the Salmon River - we think that way into the mountain would be the easiest in winter." answered John.

"How about that, I have a cattle ranch on the East Fork - the name's Joe Perry." he stuck out his big callused hand to give us both a shake. "I have been hired by a company who is hoping to mine that area for Molybdenum. They have a mining camp at Baker Lake and they hired me to shovel the snow off the buildings they had helicoptered in there. There is no road in that country yet."

"Are they mining Castle Peak?" I asked.

"That seems to be their intention."

John looked at me, "If we are going to climb that mountain we better hurry - it may be gone soon. That would be a shame."

"A sorry event." I replied. "We may be the first and the last to climb it in the winter or the summer." Mining for molybdenum was devastating - entire mountains had been erased from the landscape and when a project was completed they looked like it had been bombed with a nuclear weapon.

"That could be true if the dammed conservationists don't stop them. They have managed to stop the road construction, and until the company has a road up there about all they can accomplish has been done." explained Perry. "I have an idea that might save you some time and effort, help you to get your mountain climbed."

"What do you have in mind?" I ignored the bit about the dammed conservationists.

" Well, as I said they hired me to shovel the snow off the buildings. I tried to get to the camp a month back but the snow was so deep that my horse couldn't handle it - I was turned around before I was half way there. There is so much snow up there it is impossible for me to get there on horseback, and I don't know how to ski!" he laughed. "The camp sits next to Baker Lake at the base of Castle Peak, and there will be a lot more snow there - I just don't see how I am going to get there this winter and if the snow isn't shoveled off the buildings they could collapse."

"That would be a shame. It sure would put a wrench in their plans." I said, but all the while thinking something like that would be a blessing. I was beginning to see where the conversation was leading, but couldn't figure how it was going to help us climb the mountain.

He continued, "The camp has a generator, a freezer full of meat, a propane cook stove, propane heater and all the fixings and food you would need. You two would have a nice cozy camp - it even has bedding so you won't have to carry much in. I will give you the key to the place and tell you how to get there if you agree to shovel the roof while you're there."

"How many miles to the camp"? Asked John.

"About 12 miles in, but the first two or three are free of snow so they will go fast."

Here we go again, the possibility of traveling light and fast, we decided to take advantage of the opportunity *again.*

"We'll do it - can you show us on our map how to get there?" John asked.

The next morning and well before first light, Dora was kind enough to fix us a big breakfast of bacon, potatoes and eggs. We left Stanley and drove to the trail head on the East Fork of the Salmon River. Dawn was breaking as we tied our skis across the top of our packs and started walking - we walked about two miles before we encountered enough snow to ski and debated putting our skis on, but the snow had no base. It was granulated and felt like sugar, so we continued walking. A mile or so later we came around a corner and found a freshly killed deer, with mountain lion tracks all around it. We picked up speed and continued on, looking over our shoulders with each step.

The snow depth increased rapidly - it was time to break out the skis and skins. We were making good time and reckoned we were almost halfway to the camp. Breaking trail was not bad and I felt certain that we would be at the cabins before dark. We were traveling light again and had only trail snacks and our Seva stove for tea.

I started feeling weak earlier that morning and I wasn't getting better, Stomach cramps had been troubling me for an hour or so when suddenly I began sweating, became nauseous, and soon after began vomiting violently. Wracked with chills, I was getting weaker by the minute and was beginning to wonder just how sick I might get. John was ahead trail-breaking and I was rapidly falling far behind. When John decided it was my turn to lead he stepped to the side of the trail and for the first time realized I had fallen far behind. He skied back to see what was wrong.

"Are you all right?" He asked.

"No, I said, I don't feel well at all - I have been vomiting, and have the chills. I'm so weak that I can't keep up."

"Sounds like food poisoning," he looked quite concerned. "You don't suppose that Dora was trying to teach us a lesson do you?"

"How do you feel?" I asked.

"Fine" he replied.

"I don't think Dora would do such a thing," I said. "If she did she would have included you in her plan. But that doesn't preclude the possibility of it just being bad food - the bacon this morning didn't taste so good. I hope you don't start feeling bad."

John gave me a worried look. "Do you think you can go on or should we turn back?"

"Let's go on, but only if you are willing to break trail the rest of the way."

"I'm feeling strong - that's not a problem. Besides, sleeping in a warm cabin tonight would probably help you feel better."

"Go on ahead, I'll just follow your tracks and catch up later. Keep the cabin warm!"

John left and I slowly followed. When it started getting dark I began to worry – I was weak and tired. I was still vomiting and the chills were getting the best of me. I realized I was too weak to go on and needed to rest awhile so I stopped under a large fir tree and took my pack off. I knew lying in the snow would be a death wish, so I took my pocket knife from my pack and cut as many branches as I could reach off the tree laying them on the snow for a bed. Perry had told us that there were plenty of blankets in the cabin so, stupidly, again, we had left our sleeping bags in the car. All I had was my down parka so I tied the hood tight and lay down on my bed of branches.

An hour later John came back.

"How are you feeling?"

"The vomiting has slowed down but I am very weak and I still have the chills. How far is it to the cabin?"

"I didn't find it. I gave up when it got to dark to see and decided to come back and check on you."

John gathered up his own bed of branches and then melted some snow for tea. He handed me some gorp and tea, but I just couldn't keep it down. Realizing we were not making it to the cabins that night, we put our hands in our pockets, got as comfortable as we could on our branch beds, and spent the rest of the night kicking our boots together to keep our feet from freezing. It was one of the longest, sleepless nights I can remember.

At first light John started melting snow for tea and our water bottles. "What do you think?" he asked. "Should we go back or continue on?"

"Do you think you can find the cabin?"

"I don't know why not, with light it shouldn't be a problem."

"Let's go on then, same as yesterday, but if it starts snowing hard you had better come back for me. It's doubtful if

I will be able to find the cabins without your trail to follow." I was feeling a little better and the vomiting had stopped, but I was still not able to eat any gorp.

John's trail was straight and he followed the trail he had made the day before. Several miles further John's trail began wandering and he had pushed snow over the tracks he made the day before, saving me from the confusion of which one to follow. I followed his tracks to the base of Castle Peak and at that point his trail started gaining altitude. I struggled slowly after him, until I came to the top of a buttress where, to my joy, I saw the frozen lake. This must be Baker Lake! Daylight was fading as rapidly as my hopes had risen, they fell again just as fast - there was no cabin in sight.

John soon arrived and said, "It's not here. I skied around the open side of the lake looking for it, making sure it wasn't hidden lower down over the edge - it just isn't here." We pulled our map out again and realized we had climbed to Castle Lake. Baker Lake was lower down and to the north of us, so down we started. All I could handle was skiing long traverses, stopping at the end of a traverse, doing a kick turn to change direction and doing the same again and again. All the time it was getting darker and darker. When I caught up with John he had stopped and was packing down the snow with his skis, preparing a bed for another bivouac. "Even if we know the direction to go it will be impossible to find the cabins in the dark with so much snow - the cabins are probably buried. I think we should spend another night out and search in daylight."

I agreed. I had reached my end and couldn't go much further anyway so we cut more branches for our beds and lay down in our parkas preparing for another sleepless night. Fortunately it wasn't snowing - the nights were cold but not desperately so. John started the Seva and shortly we had our tea. It was a difficult night but we managed to stay warm enough, hands in pockets and slapping our boots together to ward off frost bite in our feet.

It seemed forever for dawn to come. When finally it did, we melted more water for tea, ate some gorp, and started off, John breaking trail.

"If I don't find the cabins in the next two hours I think we should start back - that should leave us enough daylight to get to our car."

I agreed and suggested that we should cache our climbing gear again and return later to retrieve it.

"Good idea." and with that John skied off and I followed. Twenty minutes later John's tracks led into a clearing, he had skied straight into a cabin, the snow was as high as the roof, and we would have been hard pressed to find in poor light.

For the next two days I laid in bed in that toasty little cabin recuperating. The first day my stomach could only handle honey and tea, but on the second day I started eating solid food from the cabin's well supplied food bin. John fulfilled Perry's request and had shoveled masses of snow from the cabin roofs.

Failed again. There just wasn't time to climb Castle Peak this trip, so very early on the morning of the third day we ate a hearty breakfast of fried pork chops taken from the freezer and thawed the day before, and left as soon as we could see our ski tracks in the snow. It hadn't snowed so we expected the skiing to be fast on the hard packed snow, and it was. We covered the first ten miles in less than an hour. The hiking was slower, and the deer kill that we found on the trip in was totally gone - the only remaining sign was blood-stained snow and cougar tracks.

We reached our car about nine in the morning and I felt a tinge of disappointment as we drove away, we weren't having much success with our climbing attempts. It was still morning when we arrived at Clayton, Idaho, a small silver mining town above the Salmon River. It sits in a canyon so narrow and deep that in winter the sun comes up about three in the afternoon and sets at around three thirty. The people who inhabited Clayton in those years were miners who worked underground all day - they probably didn't notice the lack of sunshine. Clayton consisted of a post office, an old hotel that had seen better days, and a few other buildings that didn't amount to a hill of beans. Most of the miners lived in houses scattered up a side canyon that got just a touch more sunshine.

The Clayton Post Office was open and we stopped and asked the post mistress where we could get a cup of coffee and something to eat.

"Cross the street, go down the stairs," she said, trying to suppress a smile. We looked and probably smelled pretty bad. We were wearing knickers - our long wool socks were exposed just below the knees and our hair was longer than normal. We just didn't look like miners - we probably didn't look like anything the post mistress had seen before. But, I had the feeling she would have enjoyed closing the post office and following along as we crossed the street to find our coffee.

We walked across the street and down the stairs, noticing on the way that there were a lot of cars parked on side of the highway - more cars than you would expect in such a small town so early in the morning. We came to the door at the bottom of the stairs, opened it, and were stunned by the volume of noise generated in such a large space. As we stepped inside we were confronted with at least a hundred people - men and women, but mostly men. They were all rugged miners, and their ladies looked like they could handle just about any problem that came along. If you lived in Clayton, Idaho in those days you needed to be strong - and searching the crowd, I could find no exception.

Hesitating, I looked at John. We had both heard stories of small town Idaho and a close-knit mindset that didn't tolerate strangers, particularly peculiar looking ones - but we shrugged at each other and ventured onward. It was early in the morning. What could possibly happen?

The hush that fell on the room started one by one as each person turned their head to the door and laid their eyes on us. Several jaws dropped and no one lifted the bottle of beer or the glass they held tightly against their chests. From the moment we opened the door and entered the room the noise diminished until you could hear a mouse wiggle his whiskers. As the door closed behind us the crowd started to clear a path - everybody was stepping back and in an instant there was a path cleared all 100 feet to a bar, the lone bartender was looking down the aisle at us. He gazed with such intensity that we had the sensation we were the only new customers he had seen since the roaring 20's. People sitting at tables stood to get a better look.

We started the long march to the bar that lay ahead with all eyes boring down upon us - mostly they were eyes of curiosity. They roamed from our ski boots up the long socks hugged tightly to our legs, and on to the bottom of the wool knickers - short pants that had a leather strap that tightened around the leg below the knee. Above the leather knickers we looked normal - until the eyes arrived at the hair that hung down to our shirt collars.

Their eyes seemed to narrow as the brains behind them searched for a clue as to the nature of these two strange creatures. At one point in the long walk I felt like we might be long-awaited dignitaries who had finally arrived after much expectation and waiting. As we moved toward the bar the miners and their ladies opened a generous aisle which they closed again as we went by, filling the space behind us, all moving along as if to join the procession. Nearing our destination, the miners who had been standing at the bar backed away. I guessed they were all grown far-sighted in the dark underground and couldn't see us if they were too close.

We had come there for breakfast and a cup of coffee, but the closer I got to the bar the more I realized that bacon and eggs were not on the menu, and neither John nor I were about to ask to see one. The bartender laid his big calloused hands on the bar like he might bolt over it, and after a short pause he said, "What'll you have?" Drinking alcohol in those days wasn't something that either of us did much of, but under the circumstances a big glass of whiskey seemed appropriate - I was not about to ask for a glass of milk.

"A whiskey for me thanks," I replied, trying to sound natural. John asked for a Budweiser. The bar didn't have stools and so we didn't have to worry about getting too comfortable. In no time the bartender was back with our drinks and John laid $5.00 on the bar. We both picked up our drinks and turned, trying to smile to the audience who were all on their feet, staring at us. They gave us plenty of room - they were standing back about 20 feet, and there seemed to be a no-man's land separating us. The bartender had given us room too. He had moved to the far end of the bar but was also looking our way, his gaze full of suspicion and ill-wishing. Our tentative smiles received no response.

About that time a commotion began off to one side and another aisle began to form. This time it started by a door in the side wall and spread through the crowd. We couldn't see what was creating the opening in the crowd, but again the crowd filled the opening behind whomever or whatever was coming in.

When the separation reached the front row and the last of the miners parted, a man appeared. Not at all of impressive size, only about five foot six. He looked at us with cold eyes and slowly headed our way. As he came nearer - he swaggered, walking toward us in no hurry whatsoever - my mind struggled to grasp the situation - who was this man? He couldn't be the toughest guy around, for there were some monstrous men in the crowd. Could he be the meanest? He certainly didn't have to be the bravest. Could this be their leader? He wasn't moving fast and was taking his time, appraising us as he came on. He was obviously trying to sort out what he was seeing, against all the possibilities of what we *might* be.

I was nearest to him and as he approached me, his eyes never left mine. His body closed in on me and he stuck his face in mine - I could smell his sour and reeking breath when he said, "What in the hell are you? He paused as if waiting for an answerer. I didn't have one so he provided some alternatives. Hippie?... Queer? He paused again for a moment and with a demanding look and in a low voice, he said, "Or Mountaineer?"

Hippie, queer, or mountaineer, left me no welcome choice - I didn't know which might be the right answer. In *his* world mountaineer could mean those damned environmentalist!

I took a step back trying to avoid his bad breath, I lifted my glass and drank the last of the whiskey screwing up my courage and stalling for time. "Mountaineer?" I said in a quiet voice, making my gamble.

He turned to the crowd, "It's all right," he yelled as he addressed the audience, "they're Mountaineers!" Everyone seemed to start talking at once and they all moved in closer, asking a million questions. One asked "What mountain are you climbing?" Another asked, "This time of year? You must be crazy!" A pair of the local women seemed to be casually moving closer. They had twinkling eyes but under the circumstances the last thing I needed was a budding romance. And so it continued.

One last drink and we said our goodbyes. I couldn't help winking at the two young ladies as I threw back the last of my whiskey. Several of the miners, including the bartender, asked us to come back again - an invitation we accepted warmly, but had no intention of following through with. As we left the bar, John and I both wondered aloud what might have happened if my answer had been different. We were glad we didn't know.

The lesson that I had learned once before, and had not heeded this time, really set in and I vowed, once again, *never* enter the wilderness without all the necessary gear that might be called upon for survival – in *any* situation.

John and I finally reached the summit of Castle Peak in May of 1969. John moved to New Zealand in 1970, he never did reach the summit of Mt. Regan in winter and I saw him for the last time in 1990. He was on his way to Turkey. I think of him often and hope he has gotten everything out of life that he has wished for.

He was an inspiration for me and without his guidance as my climbing mentor, life would have been much different and considerably poorer.

I have no doubt he has found other mountains to climb.

SUCCESS ON MT. REGAN

Emotion is the only difference
between
success
and
failure.

The next year I found two new climbing partners, Norm Garrison, and Kim Johnson. We made an attempt on December 24th of 1970 to conquer Mt. Regan - my third and, yet another, failed attempt. As before, the trip began well, but night descended too soon and we ran out of light about 100 feet from the summit and were forced, once more, to descend into the dark.

* * *

Our successful winter ascent finally occurred on the last day of winter of 1970. My fellow climbers included Norm Garrison, Ron Sargent, and Bill Weaver. We arrived at Sawtooth Lake in beautiful weather and spent the first night camped at the base of Mt. Regan. We started climbing early the next morning, successfully climbing the east face of the mountain and were on the summit before noon. We descended the mountain in beautiful weather, and skied back to Stanley, all in the same day. Three failed attempts and finally, we had made it.

It was getting late when we arrived in Stanley, but not too late to stop in the Rod and Gun tavern for a quiet celebration. There were four locals drinking at the bar, grinning at us as we ordered our beer. We paid for our drinks and settled down at a table to enjoy our accomplishment - the first winter ascent of Mt. Regan.

As we were recalling the details of our trip and just starting to relax into our cold bottles of beer, one of the local cowboys backed away from the bar, slowly turned round and sauntered over to our table. Sargent had a huge red beard that grew out of his face like a broom and the cowboy walked directly towards him. Putting one hand on each side of Sarg's face, he grabbed his massive beard and lifted him off his chair, turned to his friends and yelled "Hippie!" It made me think that he had been waiting for years and he had finally caught one.

Bill Weaver was as fast on his feet as he was on his skis and he calmly told the cowboy that he was mistaken - that Ron was no hippie, he was a hippie cowboy. All was hushed for a split second then all at once the cowboys began hooting and laughing. The big cowboy dropped Sargent back in his chair, I guess hippie cowboys were out of season. The other cowboys set back on their stools and grabbed for their drinks laughing. I breathed a sigh of relief and realized once again what a different world this was – the people as unique as the mountains they lived in, and I once again decided I really, really liked it.

Finally reaching the summit after all the failed attempts was anticlimactic. The speed in which it occurred was because we had finally acquired pin bindings, ski wax and ski boots from Norway. We cut the edges off wooden alpine skis to decrease weight and attached the pin bindings. The light weight ski equipment made all the difference. And the beautiful day full of warm sun didn't hinder us in any way.

ROBINSON BAR RANCH

Paradise
has
many faces
waiting
to be
 discovered.

While Norm, Ron, Bill and I camped at the base of Mt. Regan, awaiting first light to begin our ascent of the mountain, we talked about how beautiful the mountains were in the winter and I mentioned the fact that I just couldn't understand why more people weren't out climbing and skiing. I knew in the mountains of Europe it was quite common. Being somewhat of an entrepreneur, a trait I had inherited from my mother, I shared with my climbing partners a dream I had carried in mind for quite some time. I wanted to start a new business: back-country ski trips that would start from the doors of a beautiful lodge, such as those I had read about in Europe. I wanted to share the beauty of the winter mountains with friends, family and anyone else who had a longing for adventure – wanting to provide them with the opportunity of experiencing what I had, in hopes their lives would be as enriched as my own had been.

I must have done a pretty good job of explaining my vision, for when we finished our conversation, all three offered to join me in the dream. We decided right then that our first step would be to find the perfect location in the Sawtooth Valley for our base of operations and in April of 1970 we started looking.

There were two ranches between Sun Valley and Challis that would be perfect for our base; the Idaho Rocky Mountain

Ranch and Robinson Bar Ranch. On a beautiful spring morning in April, Norm and I left Boise early and headed towards the mountains, filled with great expectations.

We stopped at the Idaho Rocky Mountain Ranch first. It was perfectly situated in the Sawtooth Valley, near Stanley and only fifty miles away from Sun Valley, where we hoped we would attract many of our clients. The visit with Mr. Bogart, the eccentric owner of this beautiful property was disappointing to say the least. His life on the ranch was one of quiet repose and he had turned it into a private museum of sorts. He was not willing to open it to the public, and nothing we could say would change his mind.

Discouraged but undaunted we continued on to Robinson Bar Ranch. We drove through Stanley and followed the Salmon River, crossed the bridge that spans the Yankee Fork of the Salmon River, and finally arrived at the turnoff that would lead us into Robinson Bar. The road into the ranch was still snow covered but we had our skis and looked forward to some exercise after driving for so many miles. The quaint bridge that crossed the Salmon River into the ranch was built in the eighteen hundreds and at one time the road was the only access from Challis to Stanley and Sun Valley. It was the original stage coach route between these small western towns, and Robinson Bar was the overnight stopping place. The Ranch was full of history and was undoubtedly one of the most beautiful ranches in the American west.

We skied across the bridge and followed the road, which meandered along the river for three miles where it began its slow climb up and out of the river canyon into a small valley where the ranch was located. The scene was beautiful beyond description - a majestic two-story log lodge solidly stood next to Warm Springs Creek with the White Cloud Mountains rising beyond as a back drop. When we finally stopped gazing at the beautiful log building, and the cabins lining the creek behind, we noticed the steam rising out of the natural hot water pools. It was breathtaking and it seemed almost impossible to imagine that this ranch could become the home of my dream.

We met the caretaker, a nice young man, who seemed delighted to see us. He hadn't had many visitors that winter and was happy to give us as much information about the ranch as we wanted. Everything about the ranch was perfect: good snow in the winter, plenty of firewood in surrounding forests, every kind of skiing you could imagine, and hot springs to rest a weary body. He told us the owners and their families would all be arriving the second weekend in May and we could meet them then. He explained that most of the owners were well-connected executives from Idaho corporations and wealthy families from Sun Valley.

The next weeks seemed interminable, but May finally arrived, and all four of us left Boise in high hopes, arriving at the ranch in the afternoon. There were lots of people working outside on one of the cabins, clearing rubble that had accumulated over the years. They were so preoccupied with their project they didn't pay much attention to us. After watching them for awhile, we realized these folks were the owners and if we pitched in clearing the rubble we might win some favor when we told them we wanted their ranch. We set to work almost without introducing ourselves, and in short order all of the rocks and rubble had been separated into three or four piles.

While we were working I noticed people glancing at us and quizzing each other trying to figure out who we were and why we were working so darn hard. When the work was finished, Patsy Young, a niece of Idaho's Senator Frank Church, who was the manager of the ranch invited us to dinner. We protested, saying that we had arrived unexpectedly and didn't want to put them out, but she said there was nothing to worry about, the food was served family style and there was more than enough. We cleaned up at a long metal wash basin, with several faucets from which flowed natural hot water at a pleasant one hundred-and-five degrees. The smells from the pine forest and meadows – everything surrounding my sight - brought back memories of my childhood on the ranch at Deer Creek, on the other side of the Sawtooth Mountains, and I knew in my heart I had found my new home.

After cleaning up as best we could, we were shown into the dining room and offered cocktails and hors d'oeuvres – we felt welcome and tried to stay calm and relaxed, realizing our moment was soon coming. The dinner, which was fabulous and served with excellent wine, was filled with stories. I shared some of my wild survival tales with them, and we finished with the story of our successful first winter ascent of Mt. Regan. Even though it was obvious they all led lives quite different from ours, they seemed to enjoy our company. By and by the inevitable question was finally asked - "What brings you to Robinson Bar?"

I looked across the table making eye contact with each of them, including their beautiful wives for a brief moment, trying to calm my beating heart and I answered, "We want to start the first back-country skiing enterprise in the United States this winter and we would like to use your ranch for lodging our skiing and climbing clients. We are not well financed, so we thought in place of paying you for leasing the ranch we'll winterize all of the cabins and the lodge."

Nothing but what seemed unending silence - and then at last a question. "What is *back-country skiing*, Joe?"

They heard me out and said that they would make a decision and get back to us. We said our final farewells and left the ranch.

I lived the following days in a tension of expectation. Every time the phone rang I would jump for it. Then, one afternoon the phone rang and the secretary of one of the owners was on the line. "Is this Joe Leonard?" My stomach was flip-flopping like crazy as I said, "Yes it is."

"I am calling to see if you could meet with a few of the ranch owners in regards to your proposal. Would 6:00 tonight at John Fery's office work for you?" John was the president of Boise Cascade, an Idaho Corporation. I agreed at once.

At first it seemed the meeting was going well. All the owners were very open and friendly, asking many reasonable questions. I was hoping all the while that I was answering to their satisfaction. The last question they asked was if I realized that we wouldn't make much money, adding that we would make, most probably, none at all.

"That is a possibility," I allowed, "but none-the-less, making money isn't why we're passionate about the venture. Back-country skiing is popular in Europe, and it will be popular here one day. We will at the least be the fore-runners. That is a fact. All of us involved will share in that reality."

The owners looked at each other. I could see them deliberating silently, and I felt suddenly the great weight of the moment. I was stunned when all of them without exception agreed to our proposal.

We all shook hands and in June of 1970, Bonnie, Joey, Richard and I moved to the ranch.

Some things are just too good to be true. The years I spent at Robinson Bar were full of constant wonder, and the most exciting of my life. Over the years since, I have had the great pleasure to spend time with the people who we guided, worked with, and visited the Ranch, and they, inevitably, felt the same as I. It was magical in so many ways. During the winter months the only way into the ranch was by skiing or sleigh, pulled by our extraordinary team of Clydesdale horses, and as one traveled down the winding road leading to the ranch you had a sense you were entering another world, in another time. The lodge had thirteen guest rooms and an enormous kitchen and dining area. The living room carried a sense of the old west, setting one's imagination afire.

Our guests came from around the world, and many a night they sat in the warmth of the big stone fireplace listening to tales, old and new. The ranch became so popular it was soon opened year-round and we began guiding back-pack trips, horse-pack trips and mountain climbing expeditions. In the summer of 1972 we opened a kayaking school and provided the first guided kayaking trips on the Main Salmon River and Middle Fork of the Salmon River.

Soon after, we held the first White Water Rodeo in the U.S. on the Salmon River just below the ranch. When I look back on those years I am always filled with deep emotion - that I could have been so blessed to have lived some of this fleeting life in such a remote and beautiful paradise. I was truly living my dream.

"Whatever you can do or dream you can begin it. Boldness has genius, power and magic in it. Begin it now." *Goethe*

* * *

Before we even began the summer projects, Ron Sargent was offered a position training and coaching the 1972 U.S. Woman's Olympic ski team for the Sapporo Olympics, which of course he could not refuse to accept, and Bill Weaver left Idaho for greener pastures. Norm Garrison and I went on alone to accomplish our goal starting the first back-country skiing enterprise in the United States.

THE FIRST AND LAST ROUNDUP

*Eventually even
cowboys grow old.*

We spent the first summer at the Ranch winterizing the lodge and cabins, cutting enough firewood to get us through until summer, and stocking everything we would need for the winter months. The lists were endless and the days were long, but we had been really fortunate and found strong, capable, fine people who became the ranch crew. Many of them chose to stay on through winter as they had all fallen under the spell of the ranch and were loath to leave.

Fall was passing rapidly and winter was soon to follow. One afternoon, after a morning of hard work, the crew and I were just sitting down for lunch, looking forward to a good hot meal and a moment of relaxation. From the kitchen we heard a booming voice say to the cook, "I wanna see the foreman," and we all waited for the door leading to the crew's dining room to open. I was sitting at the head of the table, facing the door, surrounded by my crew and we all turned our eyes towards the door as a cowboy entered the room - he was a huge man and stood before us in intimidating glory. I felt alone and a bit exposed as he picked me out and looked directly in my eyes, a match stick rolling from one side to the other side of his mouth. He must have been six-foot-six and his Stetson hat was taller than the door jam. If he weighed an ounce he weighed nearly three hundred pounds and being fat wasn't a problem, he was solid muscle.

"Who's the foreman here?" he growled, not taking his eyes off me. Before now I hadn't thought of myself as 'the foreman' but in that moment none of my crew stepped up to take the job.

Surprisingly my voice didn't waver a bit - it must have been the three lucky glasses of wine I had before sitting down to the meal - and I replied, "I guess that would be me."

"I been grazing 150 head of cattle in the burned meadow at the head waters of Warm Springs Creek. I went up in them mountains last week to bring 'em out for the winter - I only found 130 cows and calves. I'm missing 20 head. So, I'm going back for the rest of my cattle next week and BY GOD they better be there." With that he turned and started out the door.

"Hold on," I said rising from my chair and following him out of the door, "We plan on putting a ski camp up there for the winter, if we run into them who do we call?"

"Chote," he replied. "Call the Gay Club in Challis and ask for me. If I ain't there leave a message." With that he spun on his cowboy boots and left. I should explain that in 1970 the new definition of the word "gay" hadn't arrived in Challis, Idaho.

It was a cold day in October when Chote entered the kitchen at Robinson Bar Ranch, and snow was imminent. We were in a hurry to get our ski hut set up in the mountains behind the Ranch before snow set in and Chote wanted his cows back in his corral in Challis. I thought with any luck we might run into his cows while we were setting up our ski hut and help him out.

A couple of days later Norm and I rounded up six head of horses. We saddled a couple and packed the others with the wall tent we were using for our hut, along with all the necessary tools and supplies we might need, and headed into the White Clouds to set up our first ski hut. At the head of Warm Springs Creek we found a perfect spot out of the wind with good downhill skiing nearby.

We spent a couple of days cutting firewood, framing the tent, and building bunks and kitchen counters out of lodge-pole pine. We were pleased with how it had turned out and spent our last night enjoying the new bunks and the warm tent heated by a stove made of tin. We left early the next morning to head back to the Ranch. As we were riding out and were passing through the burned meadow we smelled them - the cows that Chote was looking for were just ahead at the edge of the meadow, peacefully grazing the fall grass, unaware of the wrath of their owner. I counted 20 head - 10 cows and 10 calves - just the number I wanted to find. Chote had more or less accused us of cattle rustling hippies, at least that is what we thought.

When we arrived back at the Ranch in late afternoon I called Chote at the Gay Club. "Is Chote there?" I asked the bartender. The noise was so loud in the back-ground I could hardly hear the bartender as he called - "Chote! CHOTE! PHONE!" And then at the other end of the line I could hear that booming voice, "This is Chote - whadya want?"

"Chote, this is Joe at Robinson Bar, we rode up to the burned meadow today and saw your cows."

"Whatsa?"

"Your cows, Chote, all 20 head in the burned meadow, at the bottom end." I thought to myself that Chote was obviously well on his way to never-land.

"Zat right?" he asked after a moment.

"Yeah, they're there all right."

"OK then I'll see ya t'morrow.

About ten o'clock the next morning Chote showed up in his big truck pulling a huge cattle trailer - I could see his horse inside through the openings on the side. I walked up to his door and he rolled down the window. His hand came through the window, clutching a bottle of Early Times whiskey. "Finder's fee," he said tersely. "Where'd you say those cows was?" He opened the door and got out. My grandfather Bill would have admired Chote, he was a real honest to god cowboy.

"They're at this end of the burned meadow grazing on plenty of grass - they seemed happy. I think they'll stay right where we found them."

He opened the back of the cattle trailer and brought his horse out. The horse was a big gilding, probably 17 hands high. He saddled the horse, put on his bridle, stuck his foot in the stirrup and rode away without a word the more. I cradled the bottle of whiskey lovingly in my arm and headed for the lodge.

We quit work around five, went behind the crew's quarters and filled our tin wash basin with the natural hot water flowing out of a pipe, washed up and went into dinner. We always had a couple of drinks before dinner and several after if there was any left. We usually had wine but that night, thanks to Chote, we drank whiskey. We drank *all* the whiskey.

It was well after dark when we heard Chote ride up and Norm and I went out to greet him. We wanted to see if he found all his cows and help him load them into his trailer, but when we got to his truck he had already unsaddled his horse and was starting to load him up.

"Chote, where are the cows?" I asked.

He spun around violently and said, "There wasn't any cows there."

I found myself in a real dilemma - I couldn't say, I'm sorry, here's your finder's fee back. All I could say was, "I swear they were there yesterday, there was plenty of grass and I didn't think they would go far..."

He stepped into the trailer and tied his horse to the rail. He came out and closed the doors, and as he started for the truck he leveled a stiff finger at me and said, "I'll be back and there had damned well *better* be 20 head when I see ya again." It wasn't hard to hear the threat in his words.

As he drove away, I thought, I don't think we're doing well on Chote's friendly side. I was hoping that if we helped him get his cattle out of the White Clouds the people in Challis would quit thinking of us as the Robinson Bar hippies, which had been our reputation there for as long as we had been around. But more than that, I wasn't looking forward to dealing with Chote himself, angry or drunk or both.

Next morning during breakfast I talked to Garrison and we decided to ride out to find the cows and drive them back to the ranch. It was starting to snow when we rode out of the corral which was a blessing because it would be easy to spot their tracks. Now, truth be known, neither Norm nor I had any experience with herding cattle. We figured most of the trail had Warm Springs Creek on one side and steep terrain on the other, which would make moving the cattle a lot easier. We arrived at the meadow around noon and there they were, contentedly chewing away, as stationary as ever. We sat in the saddle and carefully counted them - all 20 head, 10 cows and 10 calves present and ready.

Rounding the cows up was easier than I expected. I reckoned it was the heavy snow fall and that they were as anxious to get out of the mountains as Chote was to get them out. The cattle followed the trail all the way to Robinson Bar as easy as you please and we left them back of the ranch near the corrals. I called the Gay Bar once again, "Is Chote there?"

"Hang on," said the bartender. "Chote, CHOTE! PHONE!"

A few minutes later Chote answered, "Whadya want." He was definitely three sheets to the wind and it was only late afternoon – but, I excused him, after all it was Friday.

"We brought your cows out of the mountains and they're here at the Ranch."

"Whadya say?"

"Your cows Chote! They're here at the Ranch. Can you pick them up in the morning?"

"Yea, in the mornan, OK, in the mornin." And with that he hung up.

The next morning arrived, but Chote didn't. Then the next day - still no Chote. Norm said he would ride out and check on the cows. When he returned he said they were getting restless - the grazing was sparse and he thought they might start looking for greener pastures, so we decided to try to drive them into the corral. We knew we would need help so we brought everybody who worked at the Ranch and made a human fence - the cows would have no place to run but right down the human fence and into the open gate of the corral. Norm and I rode our horses out and gathered the cows in a bunch and slowly drove them in, and again, easy as you please, in they went through the gate. Everybody was happy and I ran to the phone.

"Is Chote there?" I hadn't supposed that Chote had had so many calls ever before in the same week.

"CHOTE, CHOTE!" yelled the bartender, in a ceremony that was becoming all too familiar. Chote picked up the phone with some trouble – I listened as the phone banged and slid around on the bar and hoped he wasn't on a drinking binge. When finally he managed to lift the phone, he said - "Whosis?"

"It's Joe, Chote, the foreman," I hoped the word foreman might ring a bell, "from Robinson Bar Ranch. We've got your cows in our corral! You have to come and get them tomorrow for certain - we don't have any spare feed."

"Corral - in the corral?" he asked.

"Yeah, we put them in our corral! Can you get here in the morning?"

"You betcha, in the mornin." He hung up.

The next morning we finished an early breakfast and went about our chores. It was about noon and we were getting a little anxious when we went in for lunch and sat down.

We heard Chote's truck drive up and the whole crew went out to greet him. I walked up to his open window with a big grin on my face - but Chote wasn't smiling.

"Where's the cows?" he asked.

"There, in the corral," I said pointing in that direction. He stuck his head out the window and looked in the direction of my pointed finger and the first smile I had ever seen on that huge face broke out like the sun. Looking at me he said, "Have a beer!" And with that, just like magic, a beer appeared in his hand. Gratefully I took it, popped the cap and said, with a gesture to his cows, "Here's to you and yours."

He backed his trailer against the loading chute. The chute was built in the late 1800's - it was at least 70 years old, but we had used it earlier to load some of the Ranch horses to take to winter pasture, and it had been strong enough for that. When all was ready Chote climbed into the cow trailer. When he came out he had a coiled bullwhip in his hands and opened the gate. All forty eyes of the ranch crew were on him and wide open - those of the cows were even wider. I thought to myself, those cows have seen Chote and his bullwhip before.

It was something us hippie cowboys and cowgirls had yet to experience. He laid the whip out full length in front of him and said something like GEHA!! Every cow, suddenly in a panic, started running to the only opening in the corral, the opening that led to the loading chute. Chote kept calling out GEHA! He wasn't yelling but his voice was deep and strong, and the cows were definitely paying heed - they were all lined up, waiting their turn to get in the trailer.

That obviously wasn't satisfactory and Chote started laying that bullwhip on the backs of the cows in the chute. He laid a hard hit on a cow somewhere in the middle of the bunch, and that definitely got her attention. She started climbing on the back of the cow in front of her - anxious, just like me, to do whatever she needed to please Chote. Unfortunately, she lost her balance while trying to climb up and fell, landing upside down between the cow she was trying to ride and the chute fence. The fence exploded and cows were running in every direction but into the trailer. It took only a few seconds for the dust to settle - there wasn't a cow in sight. Chote lifted his hat, scratched his head and saddled his horse. In silence, Norm and I did the same.

We were about to get some lessons in a real cattle round up.

We spent the rest of the day rounding up the cows and calves finding only 19 - we were short one calf. We repaired the chute, and Chote, who had become a bit gentler, herded the cattle into the trailer along with his horse. In relief, we all waved our hats as Chote drove away. The last thing he said to me as he drove off was, "If you find that calf call me at the Gay Club." We nodded that we would.

Norm, said, "I don't know about *you,* but that was *my* last roundup."

"I couldn't agree more." I replied.

About a week later on a Friday evening the phone rang, and it was Chote. The noise in the background was raucous and I wondered if maybe Chote lived at the Gay Club. "Is this the foreman?" he demanded.

I said, "Yeah Chote, this is Joe."

"I decided that if you find that calf you can have him."

In relief, I thanked him and the next morning Norm and I were on our horses once again tracking the lost calf - it would go a long way in feeding our crew of twenty hands. We spent a long day hunting through the pines and never found sign of the animal.

INDIAN VALLEY

Traveling
back into
  timelessness.

Before the snow flew we had to find a means of transporting our guests into the ranch during the winter months when the road would be impassable because of the snow. We decided to keep the transportation rustic. Our guests could ski the three miles into the ranch, but we expected a lot of beginners and most people wouldn't even have skis. After hours of brainstorming, we decided the best solution would be a team of horses and a large sleigh that could carry guests and supplies into the ranch.

We put the word out to some local ranchers hoping to locate a team of horses, and sleigh runners that we would build a sleigh on. One old timer told us about a rancher in Indian Valley who was involved in a forced bank foreclosure and had to auction off all his farm equipment and livestock. He said the rancher had been around long enough that he would certainly have used a team of horses and a sled to feed his cattle in winter.

The lodge had three fireplaces, two wood stoves used for heating, and Nellie Bell, a double-oven-wood-fired cook stove. Nellie Bell had been brought to the ranch back before the turn of the century, and was something of a working museum piece. We would need a *lot* of firewood, and a vehicle to haul it from the forest. With all this in mind we started looking around for a truck that could transport our horses and haul the firewood. We finally found the perfect vehicle - a nineteen-forty-eight Chevy dump truck for five hundred dollars, and we named our new-found treasure Mister Natural.

Norm and I, driving Mister Natural, headed to Indian Valley for the auction. This was the first time I had visited the valley where my grandparents had spent their youth – the famed valley of milk and honey that had brought my mother's family out West long before I was born. When we arrived in the valley I could see the beauty of the land that had attracted Nellie's parents out of Oklahoma.

It was an early Saturday morning when we arrived at the ranch, well before the auction began. The auction was to be held in the front yard of the ranch house, a beautiful old hand-built log building. I wondered if this ranch had entertained my family in the old days. I could almost see Bill and Nellie dancing to country music in the dust of the front yard. Perhaps it had even been built originally by my ancestors; perhaps my grandmother had grown up in this fine old log building.

Walking through all the equipment we discovered two sets of runners. One was old and well used, struck through with dry rot. At the very end of the rows and rows of the equipment - equipment, I thought to myself, that had been so precious and necessary for the pioneers who had struggled, at risk of life, to bring plenty out of this land - was another set. They looked brand new, still covered with the original yellow paint protecting the wood. I elbowed Norm. This was our lucky day.

The auction started early, run by an old-timer with a lot of talent, who clearly had years of practice. His voice rang out like music as he guided the bidding. As such things happen, the first item up for bid were the runners with dry rot. Only one person bid on them. The auctioneer started the bidding at twenty-five dollars, and they went for that amount. We didn't bid because we had our hearts set on the unused runners. We felt secure that nobody else would want sleigh runners; all the farmers and ranchers at that time used tractors to pull wagons to feed their cattle during the winter. No one was stupid enough to want runners anymore. We were sure we would take our prize home for no more than fifty dollars.

The auctioneer started the bidding at the far end of the line of equipment for sale and wouldn't get to the second set of runners until late in the afternoon. We didn't mind. We bid on a box full of farrier tools, all in good condition, and got the set for ten dollars. We were happy with our buy; we didn't know how to shoe a horse, but would have to learn.

At last the auctioneer arrived at our sleigh runners. He started the bidding at fifty dollars. It was a bargain, Norm raised his hand. "I got fifty," sang the auctioneer. "Do I hear seventy five?" Norm and I held our breath.

A man, who was obviously a well-to-do rancher, dressed in fine western clothes, a black Stetson hat, expensive cowboy boots, and a bolo tie, raised his hand and nodded his head. We knew instantly that we were not going to get a set of runners on the cheap. We wondered why *he* would want sleigh runners, and what he would possibly hope to do with them. He could obviously afford a tractor to pull a wagon through the deep snow. I think it dawned on both Norm and I at the same time, even if these ranchers used tractors, a sleigh would be more efficient than a wagon in the dead of winter.

We had no choice. We had to go all the way. The chances of us finding another set were poor, sled runners were rare and winter would soon be upon us. The bidding to our horror seemed never to end, and began to spiral truly out of control. The auctioneer kept singing his song, always in twenty-five dollar increments, and suddenly we found ourselves on the threshold of four-hundred dollars. We were nervous, even frightened. How far was this damned rancher willing to go? He was a lot wealthier than we were and we were going to run out of money very soon.

Our opponent bid four-hundred and seventy five. Norm looked at me and raised a shaking hand and bid five-hundred. The auctioneer was having a grand time. He was in his element, singing his song and smiling over the heads in the crowd. This was the first bidding war he had seen all day, and he wanted it to continue as long as possible. The well-dressed cowboy must have set his limit at five-hundred, you could see his mind turning. He hated to give up and unfortunately that was the part of him that had the upper hand. He hesitantly raised his hand and raised the bid to five-hundred and twenty-five.

I looked over at Norm, raised my eyebrows and confidently called out, "Five hundred and fifty dollars!" The confidence in my voice was not justified. It was our last bid, we couldn't go higher, we were finished, and I was bluffing hard. The auctioneer pointed his finger at the rancher and said, "That is five-hundred-fifty to you sir." Norm and I held our breath. The rancher hesitated, looking down at the ground, contemplating. When he raised his head Norm and I were still holding our breath. Our opponent looked up at the auctioneer and shook his head. He was obviously unhappy, but we were dancing with joy.

We found a beautiful team of Clydesdale horses in Hailey, Idaho, named Chuck and Shorty. We built a wagon on top of the runners with benches to sit on, side boards to keep our clients from falling off, and a roof to keep the snow out, with a bench in front raised high enough for the driver to see over the team. Ray Seal, the rancher whom we bought Chuck and Shorty from taught us how to harness the team to the sleigh and how to handle the reins and drive the horses, and we learned how to shoe a horse.

FIRST SNOW

The first shall
be last
and the last shall
be first.

When we started guiding skiers into the mountains in 1970, we provided all of the necessary back-country skiing equipment, as it was difficult, even impossible, to purchase in the United States. We bought forty pair of wood touring skis, pin bindings, touring boots, and bamboo ski poles, all in assorted sizes, and a variety of wax for different snow conditions, from Norge Equipment Co. in Norway. The total cost for all this equipment was under $500, including shipping. We waited patiently for our shipment to arrive and when it finally came it was like Christmas. We were stunned at their quality, efficiency, and how light the skis and boots were. We were determined to provide everything we could possibly think of to ensure that our guests would enjoy their stay at the ranch and their trips into the wilderness.

The first winter at the Ranch was superb – it came and went so fast it seemed but a dream, and even in our great optimism, we had done better than we had expected. Guests came from afar to ski into the huts, climb, or just to stay at the lodge and soak in the restive natural hot-water pools. All left vowing to return again. That winter we guided Dean Conger of National Geographic Magazine skiing into the White Cloud Mountains and climbing in the Sawtooth Mountains - he too planned to return again the following summer. The owners of the Ranch came often – they loved it so much they asked Bonnie and me if we would run it year around, and we happily agreed. If every winter would be like that!

But of course, it would not be. Hard times were coming fast, disguised by the coming of a beautiful spring and the unexpected rediscovery of an old friend.

THE RETURN OF CHOTE

Cowboys
can be
angels too.

Spring arrived in its mountainous glory – I have yet to read a description rich enough to describe the wonders of it and the ranch was a jewel set in its midst.

It was a beautiful spring morning and our first summer guests were arriving the following week. Bonnie and I loaded into the pickup and headed for Challis to purchase supplies for the ranch. I would rather have gone to Sun Valley where I was liked and respected, but Challis was closer. The cowboys of Challis had no respect for hippies and they had tagged everyone who worked at the ranch as a hippy, long, long ago. It was about 10 o'clock in the morning when we drove into town.

I had what was is known as a mountain man's bladder - a bladder that never fills to its capacity because in the mountains you don't need to hold on until you find a bathroom to relieve yourself – but that morning it was full to the brim and demanding attention. I was wiggling around in the driver's seat in great discomfort. I needed a tree badly and there was not a tree in sight on the main street of that cowboy town, but just down the street was the Gay Club, and the Budweiser sign was lit-up like a welcome home sign.

I had heard several stories about longhairs stopping in Challis for a beer at the local pub, and instead of a beer they left with the worst haircut of their lives. The bars in Challis were not places that a Robinson Bar hippie would go for a good time. However, it was still morning, my bladder was about to burst, and I had some shopping to do.

I pulled up in front of the Gay Club, told Bonnie I would be right back, and stepped into the bar. As the door closed behind me and as my eyes adjusted to the light I could see, reminiscent of my climbing trip into Castle Peak, that the bar seats were all full. Each one had a cowboy hat over it, and under each cowboy hat was a drunken cowboy.

I hesitated for a second, wondering if my little sojourn was really necessary. I started for the bathroom, but first had to pass behind the cowboys at the bar. I was hoping they wouldn't notice me but elbows were punching ribs as I passed each seat. In the mirror hanging over the back-bar all I could see were sets of eyes, all watching a stupid hippie wearing a cowboy hat. I could see the signs in their eyes, I was here just to make their day.

I opened the door to the bathroom with one hand and unzipped my pants with the other, relieving myself with a sigh. I had been in tricky situations before and survived, yet I wasn't looking forward to walking through that cowboy laden bar again. I looked around hoping to find a window to climb out of, but there was only one way out - the door leading back through the bar. I took a deep breath and opened the door. I wasn't running - that would have been embarrassing, but I was definitely a hippie cowboy who was in a real hurry.

The cowboys were already off their stools and coming for me - they were determined to prevent their entertainment from escaping. Realizing the inevitable, I stopped, crouched, doubled up my fist, wiped my nose on my sleeve, scraped the floor like a Brahma bull with one foot and tried my best to scare the hell out of them. It didn't even slow them down, not even a little bit - they kept coming. I wondered if they had a pair of scissors, or was my scalping to be done with one of the knives they each carried on his hip. Three or four came within my hippie cowboy punch range when a voice out of my past bellowed out -

"LEAVE THAT BOY ALONE - he's a friend of mine!" Without hesitation every cowboy spun on his cowboy boots, their spurs carving half moon circles in the wood floor, and headed back to his assigned bar stool.

"Hey foreman! Come over here and I'll buy you a drink!" It was my old friend Chote - all three-hundred pounds of him and smiling like he'd just seen his lost cows. I've never loved a cowboy more than I did at that moment.

"Did you ever find that calf?" he asked me.

"No, Chote, I never saw hide or hair of that critter."

"Probably cougar shit by now." Chote said.

"Probably so..." I responded, nodding at his wisdom. "Hey, bartender, bring us another drink!"

The conversation continued long enough for us to finish our second drink and had covered all the common ground we had to share. I didn't think it would be a good idea to bore Chote for long so I made my excuses and left.

Bonnie was still waiting for me in the truck. Smelling my breath, she said, "Joe, where in the heck have you been?" By the time I finished the story she had calmed down.

I looked in the rear view mirror admiring my full head of curly hair and thanked God that it was still on top of my head, right where it belonged.

CHUCK AND SHORTY

Horses
live forever
in
the mind.

I had changed my life completely, had become a different person in a different world. I had left behind me a realm of self-destruction and awful greed, and had in its place found a beauty in life I had never suspected could exist. Such a total alteration in my life was inspiring, and gave me a sense of possibility and a feeling of great power in the face of my experience. These were both positive emotions, and I owe many of my achievements to them; but they were at the time untempered. I think I believed that I could do anything, that anything was possible. But there are lessons in this life that we must learn, whether we want to or not; and at least that much is out of our hands.

The winter of '72, '73 was bad. It snowed a skiff in November and temperatures dropped to minus twenty degrees Fahrenheit and then to forty below. We were able to drive into the ranch all through November, which was unusual. In December it got colder, but had finally snowed enough that we could no longer drive into the Ranch; the only way in for the rest of the winter would be by horse-drawn sleighs, or skis.

My son, Joey, had been out gathering wood for the lodge, as one of his responsibilities was to see that the wood boxes were filled each day. He ran into the lodge to tell me that he could smell propane and I went out to see what was going on. I too could smell propane in the air and panicked when I saw a mist of the stuff hovering above our thousand-gallon propane tank. I ran over to it and closed the valve but it didn't help, gas was still escaping - the valve was broken. I raced back into the lodge and started throwing water on the fires we had burning in fireplaces and stoves, yelling, "Bonnie call the gas company and tell them we have a bad leak in the valve of our propane tank – hurry!"

The whole crew was helping and soon we had all the fires extinguished. Bonnie had reached the gas company and they were on their way. I harnessed Gem to the cutter sleigh, a gift from one of our wealthy guests, and raced out to meet them at the highway. They loaded into the sleigh and we returned to the Ranch as fast as we could. Fred, the owner of the company, was able to remove the defective valve, suffering from frostbite on his fingers in the process. Fred was one of the few people in Challis that didn't think we were hippies. He had watched how hard we worked installing gas stoves in the cabins, burying gas lines with pick and shovel, and he had noticed many improvements. He was born and raised in Challis and his respect went a long way in improving our image there.

Everything was back to normal, but normal didn't seem to last long. We had lost a lot of propane, and we ran out altogether a few weeks later. We couldn't run the Ranch without propane, it was used to heat the cabins that our guests stayed in. We always refilled the tank when the roads were clear of snow, but this year we would have to find some way of getting a thousand gallons of propane into the snowbound Ranch. I called the propane company and asked Fred if he thought we could haul in a replacement tank with our team of Clydesdales, Chuck and Shorty. He said it would be no problem if we had a sled to put the tank on. We built a sled out of logs that we could harness to the horses, called Fred to tell him we were ready and made arrangements to meet him at the highway. He came with a crane on his trailer and lifted the

1000 gallon tank off his trailer and lowered it onto our log sled.

After securing the tank to the sled, Fred and I climbed onto the bench behind the horses, crossed the bridge over the Salmon River, and started up the grade to the Ranch. It all went well until we reached the steepest section of the road. Half way up the grade I could tell that Chuck and Shorty were struggling; the sled was digging in and was plowing huge amounts of snow in front of it. It was hard on the horses and they finally slowed to a stop, breathing hard. I let them rest just long enough to catch their breath, but no longer. It was cold and I didn't want them to stiffen up. I slapped them halfheartedly on the rump with the reins and they lunged, trying to break the tension between the snow and the log sled runners, throwing all of their enormous muscular weight against the obstruction – but the sled didn't budge. I was distraught. I tried a while longer to get the horses to budge their load, but there was just no way. I reckoned that it was all over and the sled, with its load, would sit on the road for the rest of the winter. Fred, who had sat in silence for the duration of my struggles, could tell by the look on my face that I thought it was hopeless.

"Do you mind if I give it a try?" he finally asked.

Reluctantly I handed him the reins. He took them confidently, let out a little slack, slapped the reins hard on the horse's rumps and in a strong voice called out, "Yaah." He had a touch and sent them a message through the reins. The message had released their power and the sleigh, with the huge propane tank, almost jumped off the snow. Fred had been very quiet about it, but obviously knew how to work the horses. Twenty minutes later we found ourselves back at the ranch. Chuck and Shorty weren't even breathing hard when we arrived. Fred attached the new tank to the propane lines and it seemed once more that all had returned to normal. Unfortunately, as I was soon to learn, normal *never* lasts long.

* * *

On a very cold December day I was up before dawn building fires in the lodge, trying to warm the old log building. The temperature outside was hovering, as it sometimes did, at fifty below zero. I went out the back door for more firewood and felt that something was wrong. I stopped in the cold and realized I was smelling smoke. It was not unusual for a log building to catch on fire in very cold temperatures. It was definitely something we worried about. I scanned over all the buildings for any sight of flame. I looked at the lodge, cabins, the crew's quarters, the original barn – but saw nothing.

The barn had been built in the late eighteen hundreds, and we had resurrected it and put it back to use. It housed our matching pair of Clydesdale horses, Chuck and Shorty, and an Appaloosa stallion that we were breeding, hoping to increase the population of our twenty-seven dude horses, many of which were getting old. We wintered twenty-four head of dude horses in Challis, where it was warmer, but Chuck, Shorty, and the Appaloosa along with Marty's horse Gem were in our barn.

Marty, our wrangler, loved horses more than anyone on the planet. She had taken a portion of the barn and turned it into a cozy little home, room enough for a wood stove, a table and a bed. She liked being close to Gem. She also had a couple of pet chickens that lived in the barn with the horses during the winter. That morning she had gotten up early and was in the kitchen with the cook having a cup of coffee. She had lit her little wood stove before coming to the lodge so her small room would be warm upon her return.

The ranch hand who was to feed the horses that morning had made the fatal mistake of not arriving on time. It was fifty degrees below zero and he decided to have another cup of coffee to help ward off the cold before heading to the barn. It was cold and the horses were hungry. They were always fed at the same time each and every morning – except this one.

This morning no one came with their hay and they grew restless. Chuck and Shorty shared a stall on the opposite side of the wall from Marty's room. I could only surmise that one of them lost patience and kicked the wall between his stall and her bedroom. They were huge horses and capable of kicking a log wall hard enough for it to cave in. The wood stove, unfortunately, sat behind the wall and was rent apart, spilling its contents out onto the wood floor.

I didn't see any smoke or flame as I scanned the buildings and assumed I had only smelled the fires in the lodge. I continued gathering firewood, but the smell of smoke grew stronger around me. I stood up and looked again and was horrified when I saw that the roof of the barn was covered in a mist of smoke. In one shattering moment I watched as flames shot out through Marty's window. I dropped the firewood where I stood, screamed as loud as I could, "*FIRE! FIRE!*" and ran to the barn to get the horses out.

The door to the barn was on the far side of the building. I ran to open it and it was jammed, it wouldn't open. I rammed it with my shoulder, kicked it hard with my feet, but it wouldn't budge. The horses were screaming, a horrible shrill sound, and I was screaming along with them. In desperation I ran back from the door a few feet, turned, and ran as fast I could, jumped in the air, and flew horizontally into the door, slamming it with both my feet. The door didn't open but I had managed to break one of the boards, smoke bellowed through the hole. I stuck my hand through the hole trying to find what was keeping the door from opening. It was barred by one of the corral doors from the stall closest to the door, Gem's stall. I was able to push the obstruction out of the way and pushed the door open.

Gem charged through the door knocking me over. He was followed by an explosion of smoke and flame. The chickens tumbled out of the door, blackened from the smoke and fire and squawking in panic. Gem's back was smoking, a few more seconds in the barn and his hair would have burst into flame. The inside of the barn was an inferno. The roof was totally engulfed in flame and suddenly collapsed, blowing sparks high in the air and forcing flames out the door. It was too late to do anything. Our horses were lost.

Gem was the only horse that survived. It all happened so fast. The fire had spread through the dried logs of the old barn so quickly that the other horses didn't have a chance. They had been silenced, their death had been horrifying. It had been the greatest tragedy of my life. A horrible loss that perhaps, in some small way, was preparing me for much greater tragedies yet to come, but it still brings tears to my eyes even now, forty-three years later. They died on December 7, 1972. I drink a toast to them every year on that day.

Some say, "That which doesn't kill us makes us stronger." There is truth in that statement. Every tragedy comes with a lesson. Mine was the realization that loss is an inevitable part of life.

Life continued on at Robinson Bar, but some of the magic had vanished from our lives, vanishing with the smoke of the barn, vanishing like the sparks falling from the sky that had turned to ash. Catastrophe has a way of removing the luster of things and replacing it with doubt. I was no longer infallible.

KAYAKING THE ONE-HUNDRED YEAR FLOOD, 1974

The circle of life,
dew to rain
puddles to
streams to
rivers to
oceans to
vapor
to rain.

In late May of 1974 spring came early and hot to the Idaho Mountains. It had been a heavy snow year, one of the heaviest seen in many years. All the creeks and rivers in the Sawtooth and White Cloud Mountains were flooding - experts were calling it the hundred-year flood.

The Salmon River borders the northern-most side of Robinson Bar Ranch, and Warm Springs Creek wanders through the middle of the ranch, running by the lodge and under the bridge which, in those days, provided our only access into the Ranch.

Warm Springs Creek was the drainage for Ants Basin and was one of the major drainage points of the White Cloud Mountains, and in May of 1974 it had grown to the size of a river. Uprooted trees and other debris were floating down-stream and were piling up against the bridge, threatening our access to the Ranch. The piled debris quickly inhibited the flow of the creek creating a lake upstream of the bridge and it soon became obvious that the fast rising water was going to overflow the road, perhaps washing it out completely. The turbulent waters in the middle of Warm Springs had created a whirlpool that was large enough to swallow a cow. We tried to remove the debris by every means possible - we used our four-wheel drive truck, come-a-longs, and even used our team of horses to remove the trees, some of which were long enough to span the creek.

We fought the battle for several days and one morning after finishing an early breakfast we set out to start the battle anew. The water was overflowing the road and as we neared the creek we were stopped by a rumbling sound. The ground was shaking, the road started moving, and we watched the bridge and much of the road disappear in a huge wave of water and trees. Under our very eyes the mass of trees and debris creating the small lake were washed downstream into the Salmon River - if it had occurred five minutes later, there is no telling how many of us would have gone with it.

We had ten guests staying at the ranch at the time and they suddenly found themselves isolated by the destruction of the bridge. The only way out was to hike 25 miles through the mountains, call for a helicopter, or swim to the other side of Warm Springs creek, which was really not an option because the water was moving fast, cold, and furiously down-stream. Our guests, anxious about the isolation and disquieted with the natural forces at hand, wanted to leave the Ranch and return to their more tranquil lives at home. None of the options for transport out of the Ranch seemed possible, so after brainstorming for some while Norm and I decided to try building a footbridge across the creek.

We walked upstream until we found two trees long enough to span the creek and big enough in diameter to support the weight of several people. After falling literally thousands of dead trees for firewood for winter heat, we were good with the chain saw and were able to cut them down.

We dropped the logs across the creek, side by side, and about four feet apart. We nailed planks across the gap between the trees, cutting off the limbs as we went, and then for safety, we built a rope railing to hang on to. The bridge was a success. We were able to get our guests safely out of the Ranch and sent them on their way. We would have to wait for the high water to recede before we could replace the road - but for the moment, we had re-established contact with the world.

* * *

The Salmon River peaked in June that summer, and during May and June we were kayaking the biggest water any of us had ever seen. In early June a local commercial outfitter had clients who booked a raft trip on the river. Sadly, their raft flipped over in some violent white water in the Salmon River Canyon just below the Ranch, and two people were drowned - it wouldn't be the last time lives were lost in the river that summer.

The Salmon River below Shoup, Idaho, was in flood and running wild. That section of the Salmon runs over a hundred miles through the Idaho Primitive Area and anyone who runs that section, even in a normal year, needs to know what they are doing. Three of my kayaking friends and I decided that we didn't want to miss the greatest ride we may ever have the opportunity of experiencing. It could be the trip of a lifetime, and definitely one to tell our grandchildren about. We decided to do it.

Bonnie drove us to the put-in at Shoup where we unloaded our kayaks and stuffed them with only bare necessities; in our dry bags we packed food, clothing, hiking boots, and sleeping bags. We also brought ground pads and a tarp in case the weather turned bad. A heavy kayak is slow and hard to maneuver, so we were keeping ours as light as possible. The river was moving so fast we estimated that we could run the whole 100 miles of river in two days and I asked Bonnie to return for us in the afternoon of the following day at the take-out, just upstream from Riggins, Idaho. I kissed her goodbye and waved as she drove back to the Ranch.

A RETURN TO THE DEMONS IN HELL

Sinking, spinning,
 time slowing down,
 spinning -
 memories
 of life
 flashing
 back....

The whirlpool finally collapsed and spit me out with a belch, as I dropped back in the violent water I landed facing downstream, I had won a battle with death. But I was back again stabbing and jabbing at the maelstrom of water. I felt my paddle blade go deep as it was grabbed by some strange underwater torrent - I was turned over once again. And again I forced my knees hard against the cowling to keep from being pulled out of my boat.

Under the water I opened my eyes and looked up, the water was full of bubbles. It was sometimes luminous, swirling to green, turning to black, to blue, full of violent motion, surging and sinking. Sometimes it was very dark, sometimes I could see light from the sun as it filtered through the water. As I fought to push my paddle to the surface I could see that if there was a little light my paddle would move up, but when it was dark it was forced down by a surge of heavy water. All at once it became obvious - when I saw light coming toward me from above I was in a trough, when a boil or a wave came over me my paddle was pushed down. I realized the time to push the paddle to the surface and roll up was the moment I saw light moving over me.

As I watched the water above me grow lighter, I pushed hard on my paddle feeling it break the surface, and in an instant I swung the paddle in an arc above and snapped my hips. My body burst through the surface and I was upright again, bracing and slashing at the violent waters. It seemed this horror story would never end - the water was not moving in any one direction, there was nothing but turbulence.

The log jam was not far away, waiting for me. I had to avoid it, I had to make my move at just the right moment, and timing would be everything. It was more difficult than the first time, but this time I knew what I had to do, and I knew I couldn't screw it up. I had to turn the bow of my kayak into the eddy and reach the upstream current before I was sucked into the log jam. I was exhausted - turning into the turmoil of the eddy was dangerous, but I had to do it. The bottom end of the eddy was a shorter distance to the upstream current then in the middle of the eddy. So, with a silent prayer, I paddled with everything I had left in me down the eddy line towards the log jam. Waiting to the last minute, before it would have been too late to avoid the jam, I reached to the very front of my kayak with my paddle and used a draw-stroke to pull the front of my boat away from the eddy line. With a few more strokes I managed to cross the brutal water and gratefully entered the current that was headed back upstream.

Relaxing for a moment trying to gather my thoughts, I knew I had to try something different if I was going to survive this nightmare. To my left was chaos, to my right was the shore - the way I longed to go. For a moment I pondered the possibility of abandoning my kayak and trying to scramble up the eroding cliff of mud and loose rock, but I could see nothing to hang on to, and if I failed, the current would carry me to the wall of water. I would end up back in the eddy, but this time without my boat - drowning would be inevitable.

A thought came to me from another dimension, could it have been help for the lost and wandering? Some years before, I read in the book *Dune* that "fear is the mind killer". I have no idea why that thought came to me just then, but recognizing it as truth, I was immediately calmed. *Instead of thinking about drowning, I began thinking about living.*

I began to look for a weakness in the wall of water that separated me from my freedom. The wall got lower further downstream, but paddling across the eddy to reach the wall would be impossible. It would be impossible to paddle in a straight line, and it would be impossible to hit the wall with any speed. I would end up back on the eddy line, or worse, if I tipped over I could end up pinned against the log jam. Paddling in the very center of the eddy where turbulence was at its worst was out of the question - it would be like trying to mount a horse that was already bucking.

I knew there was only one way out, and that was through the four-foot wall of powerful, fast moving river at the top of the eddy. I could reach the wall, the problem would be punching through it. It might as well have been made of concrete, but concrete or not, through it was my only deliverance. My body and mind were fully exhausted at this point and I realized that this attempt would be my last.

I started paddling hard and as I approached the wall I changed the direction of my kayak slightly. I wanted to hit the wall at an angle and not square on. If I hit it at too much of an angle the river would simply push me backwards into the eddy, not enough angle and it would slap me back into the nightmare as had happened before. That move had always worked for me in the past, but in my first attempt to breech the wall, not only did it fail, it failed miserably.

If I was going to survive I had to break the rules - not an easy thing to do if you are in a state of panic. Breaking the rules always brings up fear and fear in this case was of the unknown, for I was in a situation that was other-worldly.

With all of my strength I drove the boat into the river wall. The kayak instantly started to turn downstream and at the same time I drove my body upstream into the river wall – instantly flipping me upside down. I knew this would happen - it was part of my desperate plan. As my body went underwater, I drove my paddle as far out into the current as I could reach, and held on pulling the blade of the paddle toward me, hoping the paddle would pull me away from the eddy line. With indescribable relief I felt myself in the downstream flow of the river and rolled up. I moved rapidly knowing I was still upstream of the wave that had thrown me into this horrifying mess.

By the grace of God I was given a second chance. I was again climbing the face of the monstrous wave that flipped me into the chaos, nothing had changed, and it was still nasty at the top. I wasn't about to take it on again. This time I quickly turned the kayak sideways on the face of the wave, and began the climb. When I felt my boat start to slide down the face I turned the bow down the face and began surfing. I was surfing forward and away from the eddy, right into the maelstrom that I had so stupidly avoided last time I was here.

I was entering a dream world. My kayak was tossed about like a toy boat in a hurricane on the ocean. Straight ahead of me were two holes that had a water bridge between them. I managed to stay on the water bridge and looked down into the deep holes on either side of me - the thought of being trapped in either one of them was more than I could bear. I thought of my kayaking partners and prayed they all had managed to avoid them.

Now I was in manageable whitewater, waves only five to eight feet high. Compared to the boiling eddy I had just escaped, it was like a stroll in the park. No more was I slashing and slapping the water. I was surprised at how relaxed I was, and at how easily I was maneuvering my boat. Everything seemed to be happening in slow motion. Instead of fighting the turmoil of the river, I felt I was dancing to the music of it - no longer afraid, and without fear as my companion, I began to think of the river as a challenge and not a death-defying act.

I had passed through the torrent of the wild whitewater and the river quieted some. There was not a soul in sight, my kayaking partners weren't there. I was alone. The river had a mind of its own, there was no controlling its forward motion – my mates could be anywhere. Stopping to wait for me would have been out of the question, so I continued on, doing my solo dance with the river.

A few miles downstream there they were - *they were alive and out of their boats* - standing on the bank of the river waiting for me, or my body, to come into sight. They had found a huge eddy backing up into a side canyon, paddled up the bottom end and parked their kayaks. I did just the same.

"You were missing for so long we thought for certain you had met your maker, we were out here looking for your body." Bob hollered, as they came over to me.

"Where the hell have you been, what happened?" asked Vane.

"The last time I saw you, you were back-surfing on the wave. We didn't want to crowd you - there wasn't room for all of us, so we headed on down the river." John was laughing hysterically.

"My time in that eddy showed me how insignificantly mortal I am," I said. I told them of my harrowing experience and how I finally managed to escape the nightmare. While I was telling the story I had the sensation that I was living in a higher state of consciousness. Yet, it may be that gratification of being alive made me more grateful of life itself. It was never the less an emotional moment.

"We realize it's a bit early for camping but since we are on dry land we figured that we might as well make camp, this river is hard enough to kayak in the light of day, we sure don't want to be stuck on it after dark," John said in a tired voice.

The next morning, in trepidation, we continued on our journey the minute it was light enough to see. We noticed the river level had dropped several inches during the night. It must have been a clear night in the mountains and we hoped the river wouldn't pick up more steam later in the day. My attitude hadn't changed much - I still felt the calm I had experienced after my battle with the eddy the day before. All went quite well most of the morning - the biggest event was floating by some holes that were, thankfully, easily avoided. Looking down in them as we floated by was like looking into the Grand Canyon. It seemed we were in the strange terrain of some water world, hovering above precipices and bizarre watery canyons that could easily swallow a man and his kayak into their depths, never to be seen again.

Later in the morning we came around a corner and saw just ahead another ugly gigantic wave - if possible bigger than the one that had pushed me into my death-struggle the day before. And what was worse, there was no way around it. The entire Salmon River was crashing up against a cliff and creating a diagonal wave at its peak that wanted, once again, to send everything that came its way hurtling into an eddy on its left. We all turned around and started frantically paddling up stream looking for a way out of the river - but to no avail. It didn't take long to realize that like it or not we were committed, and wasting our energy trying to escape would do nothing for our chances below.

"Keep as much distance between each other as possible, and get as close to the cliff as possible!"

During the night I thought about the breaking wave that threw me in the eddy and wondered if I had been closer to the wall would the wave have let me pass? This wave was giving me an opportunity to test it.

I turned around and paddled for the wave. I started climbing. I was so close to the wall that my paddle blade was almost scraping it and when I reached the breaking wave at the top I laid my kayak on its side, keeping the bottom of the boat facing in the direction that the diagonal wave would send me. This time I drove my paddle deep into the heart of the wave, trying to catch the current hiding there. I stuck my body in her belly as well, trying with all my might, determined to break through the power of the collapsing wave. The next thing I knew, I was airborne, twenty feet in the air on the backside of the wave. I was right-side up and flying like a bird. The wave had sucked me under and vomited me back out, right where I wanted to be. When I landed, I was right-side up, facing down-stream and maneuvering through the river with ease.

I turned my kayak around and paddled upstream to watch the others come through, praying that they would come out as easily as I had done. Vane emerged first - but too bad, he missed the flight. Moments later John was sliding down the wave. Both he and Vane were in one piece, but both had missed the thrill of flying in a kayak. Perhaps I had been over-zealous when I stuck not just my paddle, but my whole body into the wave.

"Where is Bob?" I shouted.

John yelled, "Here he comes!" Bob's boat came through the top of the wave tumbling end over end, but he wasn't in it. "Catch the boat, I'll find him!" I yelled and started paddling up stream.

Suddenly Bob popped out of the bottom of the huge wave looking desperately in all directions for his kayak. I noticed gratefully that he still had his paddle. I raced upstream and came along side of him. "Grab the handle behind me!" I yelled. I had pulled a lot of swimmers out of the river over the past couple of years while teaching kayaking and had installed a handle just behind the cockpit of my kayak. It proved to be a big help in pulling swimmers out of the river, and having the handle near the center of the kayak decreased the drag caused by the weight of a submerged kayaker.

Bob grabbed the handle and I could feel the difference immediately as my kayak became unmanageable and sluggish. "Are you unhurt?" I asked.

"I am so far," he answered.

"If I tell you to let go, let go immediately and try to swim in the direction that I take." If we were to fall into a giant hole, the kayak would get stuck in the backwash but a submerged swimmer would float deeper and might find a current at the bottom of the hole that would flush him out.

"OK." He said it firmly enough that I knew that I wouldn't have to ask twice.

I looked downstream to see what was happening. John and Vane had corralled the kayak and were trying to dump the water out of it, but they weren't having much luck. A kayak full of water is heavy and trying to empty it in big waves is next to impossible. I had done it before and thought if the river stayed as calm as it was now we could do it again. "Put your boats side by side, leave the kayak upside down and slowly pull one end of the kayak up on your spray skirt," I called to them. Vane caught hold of one end of the kayak and started trying to lift his end up, but he didn't have any leverage and came close to tipping himself over. "John!" I called. "Lean over on Vane's kayak and help stabilize him." He leaned on Vane's boat and between the two of them they drained one end of the kayak.

By that time Bob and I had caught up with them. "Drag the kayak over the top of your boat John so we can drain the other end." I said hoping it would work. "*And in a hurry!*" I added. The sound of whitewater downstream was getting disconcertingly louder. All of us pitched in and finally Bob's kayak was dry enough to float. We put his kayak between Vane's and John's kayaks and Bob was able to climb across my boat, over John's, and into his own. He fastened his spray skirt over the cockpit rim and we were once more on our way.

"That must have been Chittam Rapids - if it is, it's the last of the big ones that we'll have to run," mused John. We all wanted to cheer but were afraid we might wake the river demons.

We had been on the river for two days, but only about 12 hours in our kayaks. We figured that to be in the neighborhood of about one-hundred miles in 12 hours. We were entering the lower end of the canyon and the river was starting to spread out. We were ecstatic. We had had enough big water kayaking to last us for some time, if not a life time. If I remembered correctly, there were still a few rapids ahead in the lower end of the river, but it would be a fun ride, without the terrors we had just experienced for the last couple of days. Bonnie was scheduled to meet us at the end of a dirt road that started in Riggins and followed the river upstream for about five miles.

We had made it, and we were grateful to be alive. We paddled over to the boat ramp - or at least where the boat ramp used to be - and got out of our kayaks. I fell on my knees and, for the second time on this journey, kissed the earth. We were also thankful that we didn't have to run the rapids between here and Riggins - it was certain that they would be monsters.

Three o'clock came and went and no shuttle had arrived, then four o'clock came and went, still no shuttle. We were starting to get restless and anxious, none of us wanted to get back in the river. "Something must be wrong, perhaps the van broke down." Bonnie was always dependable and had never let me down before, but it was getting late and we wanted off the river and out of there.

"The way I see it we have four choices, we can get back in our boats and watch for the shuttle from the river; we can pick up our boats and carry them down the road; or, we can leave our boats here and walk down the road until we find our shuttle. It doesn't look like Bonnie is coming, but if you want to we can just wait here until she shows up. Do any of you have a suggestion?"

Everybody was quiet for a minute, pondering our choices. John finally broke the silence. "Well, our kayaks are still in great shape. It seems to me that to get caught walking down a road in our wet suits leaving our perfectly good kayaks lying on the ground would be embarrassing to say the least. It might be alright if we didn't have that river right there for transportation."

I looked around waiting for *someone* to admit that they would rather be embarrassed then to tackle that river again, but not a word grazed a lip. I silently picked up my kayak and headed back to the river. We hadn't gone far downstream when a man with a small boy walking down the road began waving and yelling at us. We paddled over near the bank so we could hear him better as we drifted by. "I don't know where you came from but if you knew what was around that bend in the river you would break your asses getting out of those little boats!"

We didn't tell him that we came all the way from Shoup, Idaho. He probably wouldn't have believed us anyway.

"Have you seen a van with 'Leonard Expeditions' written on the side around here?"

"The road is washed out a couple of miles downstream. There won't be any cars on this road for some time." All this time we were drifting on, downstream, gradually comprehending our situation. It wasn't a pleasant moment, but again there was no choice left. We were back on the river.

Just like the man said, around the corner was a big rapid, with a familiar looking wave in the middle that was breaking white at its crown. "Well at least I don't see a big eddy," I said, praying that I was right.

It would have been anti-climactic the way the trip was ending before we put back in the river and this last rapid put the frosting on the cake. I avoided the big wave and headed for the rapids to the side of it. They were familiar, and I felt like I had been there before. We all came through, laughing, exhilarated, and continued on. That was the last big rapid we would run. We could see Bonnie and the van waiting for us just ahead on the far side of the washout.

The journey had been a supernatural experience, a force beyond understanding. On that river, during those two days, I can only say that there is nothing finer than being with brave companions, my intrepid mates on that trip were the best of companions. I believe that considering the hazards we had faced our escaped from death was nothing less than miraculous.

In that violent eddy I had learned important lessons, lessons that have been with me ever since. I learned that fear is the thief of all things precious in life. The Course in Miracles says, "Fear has no justification in any form." I had learned that only by abandoning my fear would I find divine help through spiritual energy, finding the courage and strength to face my trial - and I did so, burning with wont of life. There have been times over the past years that I have forgotten my lesson, but its truth has always comes back and has carried me through, again and again. I discovered the spark of Divinity that lies dormant in all of us, and put it to use.

THE END OF AN ERA

Life is
fleeting
like time
 like a
river
flowing.

In 1973, Nancy Reynolds, one of the owners of Robinson Bar Ranch, was working for Ronald Regan, then the Governor of California. She convinced him to provide unlimited time at Robinson Bar to all of the California POWs who were returning from Vietnam. Four airmen, who had been shot down over North Vietnam, took the offer and stayed at the ranch for several weeks while recuperating. John McCain was among them, and he arrived at the ranch with his wife and son.

John and I became friends and Sheila and I visited him in Washington DC. He shared with us his world, a world much different from our own, but exciting in its way. We saw him again some years later, and when I stood before him with my hand extended he had but one word to say – Biblical.

It was an honor to have these dedicated servicemen, who had risked their lives for their country, come to Robinson Bar Ranch, and we did our best to share all the peace and tranquility the Ranch could offer them, in hopes it would help them heal, and go forward after the horrors they had suffered.

The time had come for Norm to leave Robinson Bar and he returned to Boise to run his family's business. It seemed the end of an era, but another end was on the way, an end that had always lurked in the dark recesses of my mind.

Winter was over, it was a sunny, warm, blue-sky day in spring. Bonnie had been visiting friends and enjoying some time off in Boise. When she drove into the ranch, I had hardly the least suspicion that it might be for the last time. I could see from her expression, however, that she had something to tell me, and it was something important. She did not waste much time in getting to the point. "Joe," she said, looking frankly into my eyes, "I have to go back to the city. I want more out of life than this, I am too young to spend the rest of my life in this isolation."

We had been married for seventeen years, half of our lives. We had two teenage boys who had spent half of their lives on the ranch. For me it was the life I had always dreamed of – every day was meaningful, full of adventure, and I was my own boss. Everything I had wanted to accomplish was just outside the door of our log cabin. I loved Bonnie and was torn in half. But the school of life had changed us, made both of us aware of our need to discover our true selves. We both had gained the confidence that we could control our own destiny.

My life was fueled by passion, the loss of which would cripple me. Everything I had ever dreamed of in life was here at Robinson Bar and I could not leave it without forever looking back, wondering what I had lost. I honestly believed that nobody on the planet was as fortunate as we had been to live so wonderful a life, and I still say that to this day.

Before the ranch our lives had been filled with dark times. Bonnie had followed me through the cards, the cars, the motels and bordellos. She had never complained, even when life was filled with hopelessness and despair. She always firmly believed that one day we would find a way out and life would be better for her and our family. I thought we had found that better life, but in the end, it was only I who had found it.

I considered deeply what she was saying to me; I weighed the options. But there was in the end no decision to be made. There was nothing for me in the city, only dullness and routine, an eight-to-five job. Also, making money no longer held me in its grip, I considered it a waste of life; a deadening of the spirit.

I didn't know it at the time, but looking back, I realize now that it felt to me like another form of desertion - as I had experienced from my father, from my mother, as I had learned to expect from the world. I didn't deserve love and unconsciously had expected Bonnie would leave me sooner or later. It wasn't her fault, it was my weakness. I responded with the only words I could find, which were truth for me. "I can't go." I was not capable of living my life to suit her or anyone else.

Bonnie left the Ranch and I stayed on. Perhaps it was for the best. When we parted she was still young and beautiful, still vibrant. I see her always in my mind as she was; for me, she has never grown old.

Even despite my confidence and my certainty I was riddled with guilt. It is a guilt which lasted into my seventies, but while writing this book I finally realized that, contrary to what I believed at the time, Bonnie had never asked me to return to Boise with her. *She* was going to Boise; it's possible that she never expected me to follow. In this realization, I finally let my guilt go. I know now that if I had said that I would follow her, she would have taken me. She didn't desert me, I didn't desert her, we followed our separate paths, the choice was ours to make.

Destiny will not be denied.

* * *

In the summer of ,1975 the owners called me and asked that I come to Boise for an owners' meeting. I went feeling anxious and depressed. I had heard through the grapevine that someone was interested in buying the Ranch, and indeed, it was sold that year. The new owners asked me to stay on, but I recognized that it was time to go and I moved to Stanley, Idaho.

Carol King, the singer, owns the Ranch now and she has made it her own, changing it from rustic to sophisticated. Her changes are beautiful, but I will always remember it as it was when we skied down the road into the ranch for the first time, in its original, wild beauty. She has listed the ranch for sale. Her asking price is high, twenty-one million dollars, and I heard when she was asked why so much, she replied that Robinson Bar Ranch is one of the spiritual spots on the earth. I couldn't agree more, and if I could afford to buy it I would, in a New York minute.

My time at Robinson Bar was an experience that I hoped would never end, but nothing lasts forever. At least not in this world. In the end nothing is perfect – but Robinson Bar Ranch is as close as it gets.

THERE AND BACK AGAIN

Dreams require
a
dreamer.

Robinson Bar Ranch had been another chapter in my life, but the book was not closing. Indeed I had learned from Robinson Bar a single priceless lesson: that it was always possible to start again, and to make life ever more beautiful than it had been before.

Leaving the ranch was not easy, but it didn't mean the end of my life as a mountain guide. My dream of sharing the mountains and rivers with all who wanted to join me continued and I was determined to start a hut system in the Sawtooth Mountains. It would be the first commercial hut system to be set in America and would follow the example of the European style hut systems. My goal was to start with three huts, four miles apart, running along the face of the Sawtooth Mountain Range above Stanley. The huts would be placed just out of the wilderness boundaries, with each hut providing access to the immense downhill powder bowls that skirted the mountains in the wilderness area.

I met Sheila for the first time in 1972 and some years later she moved to Stanley. She loved to ski and I taught her to kayak - she was good and she loved it, she loved the mountains, loved living there, and best of all she loved me. We were both coming out of precedent marriages, and her parents were worried we were moving too fast. They made us promise to separate for two months, to be certain of the endurance of our feelings for each other. I made it through about half this time and then could bear no more. I broke down completely, lost my head, and drove up to the bar where she was working, burst in and whisked her away.

We married and spent our honeymoon hiking the mountain trails, picking locations for our first huts.

Bill Hon was one of owners of Robinson Bar before it was sold and over the years he and his wife, Bev, had become great friends of mine. He owned a piece of property on the banks of the Salmon River in Stanley that would be a perfect location for a lodge. Sheila and I would sit on the property imagining just how perfect it could be - we would be able to launch our kayaks into the Salmon right from our back door, and could house and feed our winter guests, before and after skiing them into the ski huts.

One morning I called Bill to tell him I was heading for Boise and asked if we could meet for lunch. We met in the old Idaho Hotel in downtown Boise. As we sat enjoying our food, I asked him, "Bill, that piece of land you own on the Salmon, is it for sale?"

He folded his hands on the table and considered. "Are you asking for yourself?"

"Yes," I replied, and proceeded to tell him what I was hoping to accomplish.

Staring across the table at me he said, "Sounds like you, Joe. Have you got any money?"

I smiled and shrugged. "My circumstances are pretty close to what they were when I came to you asking for Robinson Bar."

"Well," he said after a moment, "that worked out better than we could have imagined. What do you have in mind this time?"

And I told him. "If you will give me the deed to the property, I'll go to my banker in Boise and use the deed for collateral against a building loan. When the lodge is finished,

I'll convert the building loan to a mortgage, and pay you for your land." It seemed a long shot, but I didn't have anything to lose and hoped Bill would see it in the same way.

"No problem, Joe," he said with surprising rapidity. "It sounds like a fine idea to me. I think it will work."

I had been involved with a bank in Boise for several years. I had never deposited much money in it, but I was well known to the banker, for I had met him at parties the owners of Robinson Bar had thrown, all of whom he had done business with. I called him and set up a meeting, arriving in my typical fashion - cowboy boots, Levi's, a leather vest and cowboy hat that had seen better days.

When I walked into his office, cowboy hat in hand, I was warmly greeted.

"Joe, what can I do for you?" he said, rising and extending a hand.

I shook hands and we exchanged a few pleasantries as I sat in the chair across from his desk. Then I looked him in the eye and said, "I am here for a loan, Eric. I own a piece of land in Stanley on the banks of the Salmon River. I want to build a ski lodge on it and need a building loan to get started."

He sighed deeply and shook his head. "I'm sorry Joe," he said, "damned if I'm not, but we don't loan money that far away from Boise."

My body slumped a little in the chair as I tried to hide my disappointment. It never entered my mind that a bank wouldn't be willing to make an investment in one of the most beautiful places in the west. Even worse, this was my only connection with a bank anywhere.

He paused, watching my reaction, and then he said, "But, there is something I can do. I can loan you $15,000 for 90 days on your signature."

My mind started spinning as I wondered where in the hell I could get $15,000 in ninety days. I had just spent the whole summer with a team of horses in the forest, falling trees and dragging enough logs out of the forest for a two-story lodge, because I couldn't afford to purchase the lumber. $15,000 would go a long way towards the building, I thought, and may even be enough to finish it. But the banker had said 90 days, and winter was coming. Could I possibly complete a two-story lodge with all the snow and cold that would come with it? Should I take the money in faith that I could not only complete the building in ninety days, but also find $15,000 dollars to pay him back? I ran the scenarios through my head trying to answer a million questions at once.

Earlier that year I ran across a quotation of Goethe in a climbing book by W. H. Murray. This quotation never left my mind, and has never since: "When one is committed providence moves too. All sorts of things occur to help one that would never otherwise have occurred."

Well, I thought, I was committed, and if I really believed in Goethe's words, I really must start living them. I thought it over for one more second and said, "Thank you Eric that would be a great help." I drove back to Stanley, grabbed Sheila, took her to our new property on the Salmon River and asked, "How far from the river should we build?"

After a moment of stunned silence she said, "So close that we can lay in our bed and watch the river run by under the window."

We broke ground for the foundation in October. It was getting cold and we had to pour the concrete foundation before the serious freezing started.

I hired Fred Brubaker, Steve Gordon, Bev and Tom Angel, and Brad Bever, one of my ski guides. All of them, except for Brad, had worked for me at Robinson Bar and I knew they were hard workers. We dug the foundation in a week with pick and shovel and a week later were ready to pour cement. The closest cement mixer to be found was in Ketchum, Idaho. When I called the cement company to make arrangements for delivery, they asked if water was available on site. Because of the possibility of wet cement freezing in their truck while driving over Galena Summit with temperatures dropping rapidly, they would bring dry cement and mix it on site. That was fine with me.

The night before delivery the temperature dropped to ten below zero, and it was going to get colder. I called the cement company first thing in the morning. "Are you going to deliver today?"

"I don't think so," he laughed. "You can't pour cement in below zero temperatures. It will freeze before it dries and when it does dry it wouldn't support your dog if he walked on it."

I had anticipated this and bought four giant propane space heaters, one for each corner of the building, and enough plastic sheeting to make a tent over the forms. The temperatures had dropped and would not be getting any higher. Winter had come to stay.

"I understand," I replied, "but I can keep the concrete from freezing so that's not a problem. I have to build this winter, I don't have a choice. I have to pour the foundation now."

"There is another problem," he said. "Pouring at ten below zero is dangerous. At that temperature it could freeze in the mixer, and we can't take the risk."

"If I provide you with natural hot water at one-hundred-and-twenty degrees will you pour?"

He paused, and then, "It sounds like it might work, we've never poured cement at ten below zero before. Hell, it'll be a first. I'm willing to give it a try if you are."

Ninety days later we had all the walls up. The spirit of endeavor had led me straight along the path, and others were following after me – so I hoped to God it would not fail me now. For although we had ourselves the rudiments of a fine lodge, the building was not finished.

The roof was on, but there were no doors or windows. It was like a great gutted animal sitting out there by the river, not at all the finished building I had hoped for. With photographs of the lodge in hand, I returned to Boise and went back to my banker.

"Joe, good to see you!" Eric said. His voice was filled with the usual mild friendly enthusiasm I imagined he used for all those who fell in his good graces, and as I sat once again across his desk I thought to myself that he had probably checked on what accounts were due today.

"Good to see you as well, Eric," I said. Then I paused, looked him in the eye, and finally said, "Unfortunately, Eric, I haven't been able to come up with the money to pay back your loan."

"WHAT?" he practically screamed, as his face and neck turned as red as a beet swelling over his shirt collar.

I tried not to feel intimidated as I continued on. "*However*," I said as I reached into my cowboy shirt pocket and extracted the 4x6 photographs of the lodge, "If you will loan me $15,000 more, I will give you a first mortgage on the lodge I have built."

He snatched the photographs out of my hand and looked at them for a moment. He slowly shook his head, and looked up at me with an illegible expression on his face. "Joe, do you know what *bankers* call what you are doing?" he demanded.

"I am not certain I want to know," I replied nervously.

"Why, they call that, *Creative Financing!*" He was shouting and laughing hysterically all at once, and I feared he might have lost his mind.

Goethe, once again, entered my mind: "A whole stream of events issues forth from the decision, raised in ones favor all manner of unforeseen incidents and meetings and material assistance which no man could have dreamed would have come his way. Whatever you can do or dream you can, begin it. Boldness has genius, power and magic in it. Begin it now."

And so had it gone. We paid Bill Hon the money we owed him when our two-story rustic log lodge, twenty feet away from the river, was completed. We started kayaking lessons out our back door and we skied from the front door through the town of Stanley, across the meadow behind, and on into the mountains to our first ski hut. We opened a small shop where we sold back-country clothing and equipment, which we called There and Back Again, and opened our lodge for Leonard Expeditions. Sheila was pregnant with our first child, and the future was rich, to our eyes. As I put my hand on the rough logs walls of the lodge, and looked out across the river, where the sun was glimmering over the face of the water and shining off of the white of fresh-fallen snow, once more I felt the hand of providence guiding us on.

But I know now that we are not sent to this earthly garden to delight in its fruits, like children in a perfect innocence, but rather to undergo a deep spiritual education, at times through toil and tragedy. Providence is a force that works always and ever for our benefit – but, when need be, it works on us at the expense of our present happiness.

I was shortly to learn this lesson with a devastating force.

JESSE JOE

Some angels
stay only
long enough
to teach
one
lesson.

Jesse Joe was a beautiful baby, his eyes were as blue as his Grandmothers. His hair was golden, the color of fall meadow grass, abundant with curls, elusive like ripples on a stream. His skin, like his mothers, was smooth and soft, the color of ivory. Sheila and I were enraptured and I was sure that one day Jesse would be a great skier. He was born in the spring, a good time to be born when you live in the mountains where winter temperatures would sometimes reach minus sixty degrees below zero.

The first summer of Jess's life was warm and pleasant, a joyous time for all of us. He was a healthy and happy child, easy to care for in the busy days of running our lodge. Our guests came from all over the country and were active people, their days were filled with fishing, backpacking, biking, and kayaking. They were delighted to be in the mountains and loved the relaxed environment of our lodge, their enthusiasm was contagious and it was impossible to resist being swept up in their energy. Like the rest of us, it seemed that Jesse looked forward to each new day.

Fall arrived early that year. The first frost kissed the sego lilies in early August and by mid-September the mountain peaks were showing a dusting of snow. In early morning the edges of the streams and rivers were heavy with ice waiting for the afternoon sun to set it free. Fall was a special time for us, not only because of the vibrant colors and sparkling clear air it brought, but also because we closed the lodge in fall, freeing ourselves of the responsibility of caring for our guests, and giving us time to enjoy our beautiful home alone.

In October we started preparing for the upcoming ski season and planned to spend the next couple of months in the mountains setting up our huts. It was a dream time and didn't feel like work at all. Jesse came with us while we worked. Sheila carried him in a pack in front of her, and on her back she carried another, filled with clothes, sleeping bags, and food.

Sheila is the kind of person everyone loves from the moment they meet her. She is naturally lovely with blond hair bleached by the warm mountain sun and has a smile that will melt a pillar of stone if exposed to it for long. She isn't tall, only about five foot six, and because she is small of bone she doesn't look to be particularly strong. But her appearance is deceiving, her strength comes from within, and she could carry a heavy pack with no trouble at all. She had to be strong - every fall we packed thousands of pounds of gear into our camps, and back out again each spring.

My pack averaged about eighty pounds and on occasion would go over one hundred; Sheila's pack, including Jesse in front, would average about sixty pounds, sometimes more. We carried wood stoves, wall-tents, yurts, rope for bunks and foam mattresses, and all the cooking equipment and necessaries to feed and care for ten to twelve people. We even carried a wood-fired hot tub into our Goat Meadow camp, consisting of a five-foot long galvanized horse trough and a copper boiler. The people who came to ski with us were well cared for.

Jesse naturally took to the mountains. He loved being carried in his pack and quietly watched the world go by as we hiked through the forests, totally absorbed by the natural surroundings. He would lie contentedly on the ground for hours watching the pine trees sway in the breeze, and he especially loved sleeping outside. He had his own sleeping bag, an old bivouac sack that I used on summer climbing trips, and when wrapped up in it he would sleep soundly.

It was a magical time. In Goat Creek meadow we watched the beaver for hours, working in their ponds, preparing for winter. They grew accustomed to our presence and if we stayed a respectful distance from their homes they would pay no attention to us at all. In the evenings I would light my pipe and the three of us would sit at the edge of the meadow listening to the coyotes yapping and wailing – we imagined they were curious to know if we planned on staying through winter. We watched the golden autumn meadows turn to brown, and in the mornings, before the sun melted the frost off the meadow, we would search for tracks of the animals that had passed through in the night. We would often see deer tracks, bear tracks, and signs of elk passing by on their way to better wintering grounds. The time passed all too fast. We finished the Goat Creek camp just a few days before Thanksgiving, and reluctantly headed back to the valley to prepare the lodge for winter.

Normally during the winter I spent most of my time in the mountains, guiding people through our hut system, coming home at the end of a trip for just one night and leaving again the next morning with a new group. In a typical year there would be enough snow on the ground to ski by the first of December, but this year was not typical - it will always be remembered as the winter of no snow. Not a flake fell until late in December, and then we only got five or six inches. There was finally enough snow to ski in March, but it was too late. We had to cancel trips and were only able to take a couple of groups into the mountains, not nearly enough to keep our business going.

Our Shangri-La had been frayed a little, but it was not all bad. I had more time to spend with Jesse and Sheila and on sunny days we would bundle Jesse up in his goose-down bivouac bag and the three of us would go for short hikes. Sometimes, for a change of scenery, we would pack up and hike into one of our camps where we would spend a day, sometimes two.

It was a long, dry winter and we hoped that spring would bring rain along with it. All we needed was a little water in the rivers and our kayaking school could get underway. Jesse would be a year old in May and he was taking his first steps, determined to be off on his own.

I always fancied that I knew something about the secrets of life. I had lived about as close to nature as a modern day man could get and it had given me some insight into life. I believed that all things travel in a circle and move in cycles; a drop of water joins others, creating streams, rivers, and oceans, transforming into vapor and becoming, once again, a drop of water. I believed that no particle, no matter how small or insignificant, ceases to be - it merely changes form, and that human beings, being part of the whole, do not cease with death, but like everything else in the universe, also change form. I believed in God with all my heart, and I considered nature to be one of His expressions - one way to help us understand eternity. Nature had given me confidence in my own immortality and I was living my life in faith, knowing there was no beginning and no ending. My faith and understanding were soon to be tested.

Summer does not usually arrive in the high country until sometime in July. Our kayaking program opened in June, but only the hardy were willing to jump into a cold mountain river when snow was still melting off its banks. My first student that year was a doctor from Utah. He was a good student and took to the kayak like a fish in water.

The days this far north were long and when the sun was shining there was not a better place to be in all the world than in a kayak floating down the river. The sun was setting on the river as we pulled our kayaks out of the water in late afternoon and we headed back up the river to the lodge - we were chilled and were ready to sit in front of a warm fire with a hot cup of coffee.

Sheila and Jesse had left early that morning, driving over Galena Summit to Sun Valley, to buy groceries and take Jesse into the doctor for his baby shots. She had been home just long enough to make sandwiches and coffee for us, knowing we would be cold from the river. She put Jesse down for his nap and joined us while we warmed ourselves, laughing as the doctor described his first day in a kayak. We heard a noise come from Jesse's room and Sheila went to check on him.

In that one single moment our lives were changed forever. It was instantaneous, could not be undone and nothing would ever seem as bright as it had been before. I will never forget how I felt when Sheila called out for me, she sounded far away and her voice was filled with fear. The doctor and I both rushed to the bedroom, recognizing instantly what was wrong; Jesse was having a seizure. Sheila was panicking and trying to help him. The doctor gently moved her away from the crib and did what he could to keep Jesse from hurting himself as he moved through his convulsions.

When he had finally settled, we wrapped him in blankets and readied ourselves for a trip over Galena Summit to the hospital in Sun Valley. The doctor didn't explain much to us as we drove to the hospital, we were in too much shock to ask any questions.

Seizures are dramatic and they leave a lasting imprint on the mind. As we drove over the summit I tried to think of everything I knew about seizures. I knew that they could be controlled with medication, but I was wrong. Several weeks and many tests later we brought Jesse home. We had gone to three different hospitals in Idaho and Utah and had seen the best neurologists they had. None of them could diagnose Jess's condition, or control his seizures with medication. He was semi-conscious and unable to move - the prognosis was that he would not live for more than a few weeks. It was impossible to believe that our child, who just a few weeks ago had been so healthy and so happy to be alive, was dying, and that we were helpless to do anything about it.

As the weeks passed Sheila and I spent a lot of time praying - every day we prayed for God to spare our child. Our friends prayed, groups in Stanley and neighboring cities prayed, people we did not know prayed, yet there was no improvement in Jess's condition - in all those weeks he had not moved. Occasionally his eyes would open and he would swallow liquids given him with a spoon. His clear blue eyes had gown dull and he did not seem to recognize anyone, not even his mother. We were in agony, helplessly watching as Jess's life slowly ebbed away, and as he grew weaker we grew weaker.

We tried to keep our business going, smiling to our guests, hiding our devastation. Early one morning I was up before sunrise getting ready for a trip I was guiding into the White Cloud Mountains. The sunrise was beautiful, the mountains were brilliant, ablaze with alpine glow. I realized I had not been seeing the world around me anymore - all of the marvelous beauty that I lived in was passing me by. It was as if I had been living in darkness and for the first time since Jesse became ill I made an attempt to see again. I walked up the river bank and silently watched as the warm sun burned the alpine glow away, and then I turned to the river. In the past, when I was depressed or confused, I would go to the river and sit, listening to its message of eternity. The message was still there but I was incapable of hearing it. My attempt had been futile, I felt detached, insensitive to everything, and wondered if I would ever be able to feel again.

I wandered back to the lodge and into Jess's room. He was lying on his back with his head turned slightly to the side. He was asleep, his face as fair as ever. My eyes filled with tears and my heart cried out for my child who was suffering so. I reached down and brushed the side of his face with the back of my hand, my mind and heart filled with love. Through my tears I saw his eye lashes flicker - his eyes opened, and like a flower unfolding, he slowly turned his head and looked at me. Suddenly he smiled and the room filled with light, as though the sun itself was contained in that little bedroom on the Salmon River. He knew I was there and had recognized me.

It seemed that our prayers had been answered. Jess's ordeal had set him back several months, but he was regaining lost ground rapidly. The medication he was taking to control his seizures tired him, but we were confident that he would soon be back to normal, and held the hope that the medication could be stopped. Later in the fall his improvement slowed some and his seizures continued, but we remained optimistic. A person learns to be patient when living in the mountains - time moves slowly and everything has its season. We were prepared to let Jesse heal in his own time. Each difficult step he took forward was greeted by us with thankfulness.

I put the ski huts in myself that year, neither Jesse nor Sheila were there to help me. For the first time I felt lonely in the camps, I missed my family and their laughter, missed working with Sheila. I would hike out of the mountains often for another load of equipment and to be with Sheila and Jesse for a time. I didn't want to miss out on any of his new achievements. He had not started walking yet, a triumph for him that I was determined to witness.

* * *

The previous winter had been brutal on the small businesses that relied on snow and Idaho had fallen into the disaster category. The government was loaning money to businesses and farmers, who were fighting to keep their doors open, hoping it would keep the economy of Idaho afloat. Reluctantly, I borrowed twenty thousand dollars, which would tide us over until snow arrived and we would have paying guests again. It was a godsend and relieved us of financial concerns - we knew with a good winter we would survive and be able to pay back the loan we had been reluctant to take.

David Ayer booked a ski trip with us, and would be flying into Sun Valley in December. He was from Boston and this would be his first venture into the mountains of Idaho. He arrived and I knew, the moment I met him, that we were kindred spirits. One of those rare moments in life when you know you are right where you should be. He was an interesting, but quiet person. Unlike me, he held his words close to the chest. I felt that somehow this trip was a kind of pilgrimage for him, somehow a statement of having the courage to look further into life hoping to find something more meaningful and fulfilling.

David may have been quiet, but he didn't miss a thing that took place around him. He loved the trip, he loved the mountains, he loved the lodge and he loved how he felt when he was in Idaho, away from the pressures of his current life. I enjoyed skiing with him and after the shell had been broken, we talked and laughed as if we had known each other all our lives. He told us he would be back, and I hoped it would be true.

He *did* come back, and when he returned to Boston he returned as a partner in Leonard Expeditions. David had fallen under the spell of the Sawtooth Mountains and the skiing business. He believed in the business and could see we were struggling, not only financially, but emotionally. Jesse was better, but something just wasn't right. The doctor and hospital bills were mounting, bills that wouldn't be paid until years later; we had no insurance. When David offered to become a partner, it was as if all was made whole again. Not only did I *want* David as a partner, the financial support would give Sheila and I some reprieve from our burdens.

We changed the name of our company from Leonard Expeditions to Leonard Ayer Expeditions. With David's help for the first time we were able to advertise, create a beautiful brochure, and replace worn out equipment. We built yurts to replace the wall tents we had been using for our huts, and bought new rental skis and boots. His enthusiasm became our own and his belief in Leonard-Ayer Expeditions made us more determined than ever to make it successful, for him as much as for us.

Jesse was still not walking by Christmas, but he was trying. That Christmas the snow was abundant, and so were the presents under the tree. Sheila insisted that we must have the finest, the most beautiful tree in the world; I protested. I felt we should leave the most beautiful tree in the world where it stood so its beauty would gladden the hearts of those fortunate enough to find it. She argued that the most splendid of trees were happiest when they were selected to become Christmas trees because it was their divine destiny to inspire people to celebrate the birth of Christ. And so we searched the woods until we found the most splendid tree in the world and our guests helped us celebrate the most wonderful Christmas of our lives. We had so much to be thankful for, ample snow for our skiers, enough reservations to make the winter prosperous, David had joined hands with us, and a new year was coming, overflowing with hope for Jessie's health; paradise was being reborn.

But spring came with a cloud hovering on the horizon. It came hard and fast. Jesse was not well, paradise could not exist on earth for long. Early in May his seizures returned in fury. The medication that had been controlling them no longer worked - he had suffered a relapse. The doctors still had no idea what the cause was and did everything in their power to control his seizures. They changed medication time and time again, they increased and decreased dosages, but it was all in vain. His seizures had become uncontrollable and he lapsed back into a semi-coma.

We started to pray once again. The wonderful and thoughtful people of Stanley put on a benefit for Jessie to help cover the medical expenses. Friends and family came from everywhere to do what they could to help. It was a touching tribute to our son that so many people loved him.

Jesse was unresponsive and suffering - Sheila and I were waiting for the inevitable to come. The doctors had given up and told us that we could continue experimenting with the medications, or stop giving them and see what would happen.

It was as if the days just kept passing, but we were not present in them. Sheila had drawn into darkness and it was all she could do to move through the motions of everyday life. She tried so hard, smiled or laughed when it was required, but her heart was not there. A decision had to be made and I made the most difficult decision I had ever been faced with in my life, one that would stay with me forever. I took Jesse off his medication.

The only thing I was certain of was that if I were in Jess's place I would not want to go on. I believed that if he were meant to live, he would live with or without the medication, and believed also that if it was time for him to go, we had to let him go freely. I believed that 'God's will be done' and had myself experienced the power of prayer. I could only hope that our prayers would be heard and that Jesse would recover.

* * *

One evening while sitting in the lodge I was thinking about my belief in the power of prayer and recalled an experience I once had:

The year was 1967. At the time I was meditating religiously and was attending a study group that was interested in the readings of Edgar Cayce, the man who had written *There is a River*. I owned two acres of land in the foothills of Boise and I wanted to build a house on it. Leonard Koch, who was a friend of mine and was also involved with the study group, needed building material to add an addition to his small home.

I had met a woman who owned some land in the suburbs of Boise, with a large barn and two-story house, both part of the original homestead. She wanted to build an apartment house on the property, but couldn't begin until the old buildings were removed. She called me one day and asked if I would be interested in the lumber. "You can have all the lumber Joe, if you take down the buildings and haul it all away." I told her I would do it.

I called Leonard and told him about the buildings offering him half the lumber if he would help me take them down. He was happy to join me and soon after we started to take the buildings apart. We had the buildings dismantled, but had not put much thought into how we would transport all the wood to our building sites.

Leonard looked at me and said, "Lets pray about it, Joe." I thought that was an excellent idea and we climbed on top of one of the piles of lumber and prayed, telling God that we had a problem and asking Him for help. While we were praying we heard a car drive up. We said "Amen" and opened our eyes. The vehicle we heard was a small pickup truck driven by a woman. "Have you got any hardwood flooring that you would sell me?"

I looked at her with a smile and said "No, but we would trade you some hardwood for the use of your truck." She agreed and we filled her truck with hardwood and took it to her home. Her truck was too small to carry the long beams and lumber and after some discussion I suggested that we try praying again. We climbed back on the woodpile and started praying, this time we were a little more specific. "God thank you for the answer to our prayers, but we need a bigger truck." *Once again*, during the prayer, we heard a loud engine turn into the drive way. We opened our eyes and a man driving a big two-ton truck stopped and got out. "It looks to me like you boys need some help."

From that moment on, *I believed in the power of prayer.*

* * *

After he was taken off his medication Jesse became alert again. The seizures continued but he regained consciousness and seemed to recognize us. I prayed as never before, for Jess's recovery, and for myself, and the burden I carried when I made the decision to take him off his medication. I put a gun to my heart and made a bargain with God - if he would heal Jesse I would never take another drink, I would even join a monastery if that was what was necessary. The gun exploded, its aim sure and swift - guilt lodged deeply in my heart, a deep wound that I carried with me every second of every day, for years. Jesse lived only a few weeks longer and on a dark day in June the clouds descended. Jesse Joe left his beautiful mountain valley forever, and the shadow of his passing remained behind.

For a long time Sheila and I attempted to lose ourselves by staying busy with our business. It helped dull the cutting edge of our grief, but the pain continued as a blunt pervasive force, wedging itself in our minds, penetrating our very being. The way fear penetrates the night, our grief would come with the least provocation and once it surfaced it would linger, stripping away all other emotions. I started drinking heavily and eventually my ulcers returned. Even our home had lost its brilliance and the business we had spent so many years developing wasn't enjoyable anymore.

The lodge held too many memories and we were continually reminded of Jesse. About a year after his death we sold the lodge, paid back our government loan, and paid the bank the money we had borrowed to build it. Another year went by, and still the pain of Jesse's death was eating away at us. The grief of our loss was shredding our lives and throwing us into the abyss, and then into the abyss of the abyss.

I believed that I was no longer worthy and it was my fault, not Gods, that my prayers had not been answered. I could not doubt God, but I could doubt myself. I was filled with guilt and recrimination. It had been my decision to take Jesse off his medication, it was my decision alone. I became more and more depressed and began to blame myself for his death. I was self-destructing.

Our love had been born and had grown during times of happiness, now it seemed that all we had to share was sadness, and our love was not able to overcome it. We decided that it was best if we lived apart for awhile and Sheila left and I stayed on to run the business. Separated and alone with our thoughts, we finally realized that without each other we had nothing. Living without one another had not made life easier, it made it unbearable. Alone, we were like birds who had forgotten to go south in the winter. Life had no meaning.

Sheila came home again and we tried desperately to understand what had befallen us, and how to find some kind of happiness again. We both were reluctant to seek therapeutic help so we faced our demons alone. I began again, after months of leaving it behind, reading *The Course in Miracles,* which was the most important thing I could ever have done. It forced us to keep looking inward, deeper and deeper.

Our problems were not with each other, but were to be found within ourselves. We put forth as much effort as we were capable of, trying to rebuild our lives, but we did not fully appreciate the fact that what we thought we were, we were. We thought we were miserable and so we were. Not understanding the cause of our depression, we decided that a change, if only for the sake of change, would make our lives better again and in desperation we closed our business.

Then we had nothing.

Jesse was gone and we no longer had a home or business. We had nothing but our memories and our love of the mountains that bound us to our sacred valley. We were drained, living in a vacuum, and were totally lost. When we closed our guiding business we hoped to replace it with something meaningful, and if not, at least we would find escape. We soon realized there was no escaping a problem created by hopelessness, but understanding the problem and knowing what to do about it are entirely different things. We were unable to let Jesse go and were throwing our lives away in our desperation, and the desperation was creating chaos. It was born of our own self-pity, destroying our confidence and well being. Our minds were seated habitually in their misery producing state, our bad attitudes tenaciously directing our thoughts.

It took days, months, and years for us to regain our lives again, but we did it, *The Course in Miracles* playing no small part. When Jesse died, a part of each of us had died with him, but we had not lost everything. We determined to find meaning in our lives again, and with patience and love we began the slow climb out of our self-imposed darkness. Something we could never have accomplished without faith, belief in destiny, and belief in God.

We had suffered, but had come to understand ourselves and life as we never had before. Losing a child is hard. The pain never goes away, but it can be something you learn to live with. Jess's life had been a gift, and we learned more from him in his short life than we would have learned in a lifetime without him. We were beginning to live in light again and the doors of understanding we had securely locked when Jesse died were slowly opening. We were learning to love again, with a deeper appreciation of each other than we had ever had before, and I returned again to another passion - photography, a passion almost as close to my heart as guiding had been.

Life would go on, however, destiny would have to show me the way.

ZIMBABWE, AFRICA

Leaving dark times,
hoping to find light
in a dark continent.

In 1964 I was asked if I would be interested in photographing a hunting safari in Kenya, Africa. Because of my environmental beliefs I had turned the offer down and had evermore regretted my decision.

It was now 1980 and a friend, Hans Borbonas, had offered me a second chance. Hans was a hunter and was heading to Africa seeking a trophy elephant, lion, and Cape buffalo. I thought about the offer I had passed by in '64 and realized I would most likely never be offered such an opportunity again, and wondered if I was being sent for some reason I was unable to comprehend. I was under no illusions about what I was going to be involved in, but remembering that old lame cliché 'If I don't do it someone else will' I set my beliefs aside and accepted.

We would be traveling to the Wankie Game Reserve in Zimbabwe, which shortly before our arrival had been known as the land of Rhodesia. Mugabe and his people had just won their war and the country had settled into a disturbed peace. The moment we left the plane I could feel the tension in the air; dark and hovering aftereffects from war. Zimbabwe was in a state of chaos. Over the past few months many of the white people who had lived in Rhodesia all their lives had fled the country - they had lost their war and were fleeing from an unknown future.

The airport was in total disarray. Hans mentioned the last time he was in Rhodesia all the airport employees were white. Noticeably, now all of the people working at the airport were native Africans who were not yet familiar with its workings, except for the baggage handlers who were efficient. They delivered our luggage, guns and cameras in good time and we passed through the airport terminal to meet Geoff, the owner and guide of the company Hans had hired. Going through customs was a tedious and lengthy process, but we were finally approved and boarded Geoff's Cessna that would take us to his lodge located on the border of the Wankie Reserve. He flew us over a section of the refuge before landing at his lodge and the landscape was mesmerizing, I felt as if I were in a dream and was anxious to feel the African soil under my feet.

We landed several hundred yards from the lodge, on Geoff's small dirt runway. Out of the plane window I could see several African porters waiting for us, running to the plane when the engine died, to remove our luggage. My cameras and luggage were lying on the ground and as I reached down to pick them up, Geoff gruffly told me, "Leave it, the nigs will get it." It was startling to hear the dispassion and hardness in his voice. The derogatory term rolled off his tongue like water.

He led us to a Land Rover that was parked to the side of the runway, as we walked he looked back over his shoulder and said, "It's tea time, let's go on to the lodge where we can relax and talk about the hunt." I climbed into the back of the Rover and Hans took the passenger's seat next to Geoff. As we drove away I noticed the porters had picked up our luggage and were slowly walking after us. I wondered why our gear hadn't been loaded into the back of the Land Rover, there was plenty of room for it.

We were sitting at a table under the long veranda that covered the face of the lodge. The furniture had a rustic, but sophisticated look about it. Trees grew in abundance shading the whole of the veranda, plants and flowers in every color cascaded from the roof filling the air with exotic fragrance.

Servants brought cake, fruit and drink to the table, all served on very fine china. It all had a surreal feel about it, as if it were a scene taken from a movie.

It wasn't long before the first of the porters arrived carrying our luggage, all but mine. I looked back down the path and saw a middle-aged black woman struggling to carry my heavy camera gear and suitcase. I stood up and walked to her taking my gear, relieving her of the heavy burden. She didn't smile, she didn't even acknowledge my presence. It seemed she didn't want my help. She couldn't understand my language when I told her I would carry the luggage the rest of the way, but reluctantly allowed me to take her heavy load. Nothing was said when I returned to the table to join Goeff and Hans, but I saw in Goeff's eyes the same hardness and dispassion he had exhibited when he told me "the nigs will get it."

I sat silently listening to Goeff tell Hans how the safari would proceed, where they would be hunting, and who would be joining in the hunt. His manner of speaking was crude and vulgar. It was the first time I had heard someone speak about the African people in such a vicious and deprecating manner.

I lay on my cot that night, surrounded by mosquito netting, listening to the night songs of Africa. It was for this I had come on this venture, to see the land, the wildlife, to hear the music of the animals, and learn as much as could of the African people. I had felt a distancing from Geoff after I took my luggage from the African woman and wondered how it would play out during the hunt.

Early the next morning we were joined by the Africans we were to spend the next month with. Skorks, our tracker, was a bushman. He was a little over five feet tall but filled with deceiving strength for one of his stature. Sylvester, one of the porters, was a school teacher and would be our translator. Charlie was another of our porters and I would find him to be the fastest runner I had ever met. Geoff was the white hunter and was our official hunting guide. And, finally there was Anderson. He had been a gardener all his life, but had lost his job with a wealthy English family when they fled the country after the white people of Rhodesia lost their war. Most of the porters were barefoot which concerned me, until I looked closer - their feet were protected by huge thick callouses.

Not many people ventured into Wankie during the war, and in consequence the park was left in relative peace. The wildlife was healthy and abundant. The biggest threat the animals faced were the poachers who killed them in brutal numbers for ivory. As we walked across the land we were told to watch out for ground mines that had been set in the recent war – a constant reminder of the strife the country had lately suffered – and thankfully, we never ran across one. We were entering a comparatively pristine wilderness and it was hard to believe that I was finally in Africa after dreaming about it for so many years.

We had been in the park for ten days when our tracker, Skorks, located a huge bull elephant. He was an amazing tracker - he could track an animal over solid rock, through thickets so dense you couldn't see five feet in front of you. As we hiked through the land, I looked intently for even the smallest sign of a passing animal, but could not see what Skorks saw. He found the tracks of a large elephant with no trouble and at once we were on the hunt.

It was the time of the dry season and most of the foliage had lost its leaves. The elephant grass was taller than the average human, and we moved through it like ants crawling about through the brush. We tracked the elephant through this surreal terrain for several days, emerging from it early one morning as we followed Skorks up a barren hill. He reached the top of the mound before we did and waved to us, gesturing that we should get close to the ground and crawl the rest of the way to the top. When I reached the top of the mound, lying on my belly, I was left speechless at the sight. The valley below was filled with elephants, eland, kudu, zebra, Cape buffalo, wildebeest, and gazelle – thousands of animals, stretched out like a carpet on the plain. Skorks pointed into the far distance where we saw, in its glory, the bull elephant we had been tracking for so many days. He was magnificent. His trunk was raised high in the air, trying to catch any scent that was out of the ordinary – it was as if he understood we were tracking him. I did not know a lot about elephants, but I did know they did not see well, and that, to make up for this shortfall, their ability to smell was remarkable. I gazed at him in wonder and sadly accepted the fact that he might become Hans' trophy elephant.

We could not, from our spot on the mound, begin our trek to the huge elephant. We would only scatter the thousands of animals grazing below on the plain, and our quarry would doubtless escape in the ensuing chaos. We returned to the tall elephant grass, and once more began hacking our way through its denseness.

Skorks, who was always a ways out in the lead, suddenly came sprinting back towards us gesturing wildly and yelling. Not far behind him was a charging female lion. I saw Skorks leap into a tree, pulling himself higher and higher. Everyone else tried frantically but with less catlike success, to follow his example. I picked a tree that seemed it could sustain my weight and started climbing as fast as I was able, stopping when I reached the last branch I was confident would hold me. When I looked around every tree had a person hanging on a limb, they were all pointing at me, laughing and yelling "You are the highest climber of anybody else!" Sylvester called. "That is because you are the most frightened person of all!"

"That means that I'm the best climber of all!" I shot back. Sylvester translated, and their laughter filled the dry forest.

It seemed Skorks had stumbled into a lioness with her cubs and she was only trying to protect her young. Sylvester later told me that if the lion had been hungry she would have waited patiently under one of the trees we were clinging to until someone would fall - than she would have her dinner. He also told me they were impressed at how fast I had climbed the tree. "We usually like having a white man with us," he laughed at me.

"Why is that?" I asked

"Because we have never met a white man that we couldn't outrun. The slow man dies first."

"So why does Anderson stay so far behind the rest of us?" I asked.

"He is afraid," answered Sylvester, smiling broadly. "This is his first time in the bush. He has been a gardener all of his life. He lost his job when the war ended. The white people he worked for were afraid and moved to South Africa."

When Geoff chose the spot for our camp at the end of the day, the Africans set up a large tent, installed sleeping cots and laid out the table with four chairs, for the four white men; they would eat and sleep under the stars. All the equipment had been brought in by one of Geoff's assistants in a Land Rover. After everything was in order and the camp was completed, the porters brought a bottle of fine whiskey and set it, with four crystal glasses, on the table. They left the tent and began preparing dinner.

I had come to Africa as a guest and employee of Hans. I did not know Geoff, nothing of his history nor his life, nor was I certain whether Hans would approve of what I was about to say. I had only been in Africa a few weeks, but the racial prejudice was as thick as the air about us, so strong I could not hold my tongue. I could no longer sit quietly, my conscience would not allow it.

I questioned Goeff about the way the white Rhodesians treated the native Africans. His lack of civility and open hostility was obvious. I questioned the derogatory names he used; nigs, niggers, black devils, worthless animals, names that were as much a part of the vocabulary as were elephants, lions or bush. I asked if he wasn't concerned about the possibility that when Mugabe's army arrived there might be retaliation. At this last question the table went silent. Finally Geoff spoke, he was angry, "You know nothing about these niggers, and you never will because you don't live with them. Until you understand what we put up with every day keep your opinions to yourself."

I had gone too far, and all this before I had even seen first blood. My line had been cast. I left the table soon after dinner and repaired to my cot, laying in the dark and listening to the sounds of the bush. Hyenas put on a lovely show, laughing for hours. I wondered if they were laughing at me. Occasionally a lion could be heard in the distant night. The sounds were not threatening, they were the sounds of a primitive world, the sounds of my ancient heritage.

We tracked the elephant for several days. Skorks said that we were getting closer; the tracks were much fresher. He said that the wind was in our favor and the elephant couldn't smell us, and that with luck it would relax and slow its pace. The countryside was changing as we moved on - the elephant grasses dwindled and the land emptied.

Wankie is rolling country, and it is old. The mountains have been worn down over millions of years - the rocks are smooth and the country is open. We followed the terrain as we found it, now rising, now descending, and now pursuing the flat plain. We climbed another hill and again, Skorks motioned for us to get down. This time I saw no wildlife from the top of the hill - just a sort of vale extending below, filled with dense brush, trees and pools of water. But Skorks assured us that the elephant was there, waiting for us, in the heavy bush, by a watering hole.

It was decided that the two white hunters – Geoff and Hans – would go ahead alone. Because the rest of us had no guns, we were to stay where we were until needed. We found a comfortable place on the side of the hill and waited, passing the time with stories and jests. An hour had gone by when I heard the first shot. I looked at Sylvester, "Did you hear that shot?"

"Two shots!" he said, his eyes flashing to where the sound had come from. He was suddenly alert and very worried. "One shot is good, two shots is bad! Two shots means that the elephant could be wounded!" His big black eyes were wide open as he explained that the elephant was considered the most dangerous of all the animals in the bush - particularly a wounded elephant. We waited a while longer, silent now and tense. Skorks finally stood and said that we should go to find out what had happened, that the white hunters might need our help.

We started down the slope following a game trail, which widened as it approached the bottom. As if to signal the danger we were in, Charlie, ever the fastest man, was now leading and was well ahead of the rest of us. Anderson, as was his custom, stayed about fifty feet behind. The difference said everything: Charlie was confident in his abilities, Anderson was fearful and apprehensive. We had walked less than a mile and I could still see Charlie several hundred feet ahead. Without warning he suddenly turned around, flying back toward us. We froze in our tracks, straining to see what he was running from. From around the corner and behind him roared a huge bull elephant, his trunk high in the air, and running faster than could be imagined for an animal his size.

Skorks and Sylvester spun around and began racing away. I caught up with them, keeping closely at their heels. After watching each of the men on the trip over the past days I had decided that if anyone knew how to survive in the bush it was Skorks. I would stay as near to him as I could, and do whatever he did. Charley sped by us like he was on a bicycle, leaving us in the dust as bait, and passing Anderson like he was standing still. We too were running fast and soon caught up with Anderson. He could hear us on his heels and turned his head to see who was catching up - he saw me, and I could see the terror on his face when he realized that, *the white man*, was going to pass him. He immediately panicked and ran off the trail into the bush. Sylvester had decided, as I had, to stay with Skorks. The moment Anderson left the trail, Skorks turned in the opposite direction and fled onto a slope thick with trees, and Sylvester and I went with him. I was having no trouble keeping up with Skorks and followed as he wove his way through and behind the trees and brush as he ran.

We must have run for more than a mile, and none of us, not once, looked back to see how close the elephant might be. We stopped on top of a knoll in a clearing to catch our breath, relatively assured that we had evaded the rampaging beast below. Skorks and Sylvester started speaking rapidly, gesturing wildly. When they finally took a breath, I asked Sylvester what was happening. He responded, "We reckon that Anderson is dead."

I was stunned. "What makes you think so?"

Sylvester gestured toward the sky. "He ran into the wind. "

I had been right to rely on Skork's judgments - he was a bushman, and they are known to be the best, most knowledgeable, and most experienced guides in Africa. He was aware all the time which way the wind was blowing and he had led us downwind. If the elephant was looking for someone to beat against a tree it would be the slow and foolish whom he caught. I was trying to catch my breath and calm myself with the news about Anderson, when suddenly Skorks began laughing and slapping his thighs, pointing to the top of a hill on the other side of the canyon. I looked in the direction he pointed and there stood Anderson, alive and apparently well, waving to us against the horizon.

I learned later that when a bull elephant grows old and loses his strength, he acquires a young bull elephant for protection. It is the responsibility of the young elephant to watch for danger while the elder feeds and rests. It happened that the young bull elephant that was to have been protecting the elder bull (the bull we had been tracking) had failed in his responsibilities. The old bull had been shot, and the young one abandoned the old bull and fled. We happened to be on the trail he had chosen for his escape route, and he, like us, was running for his life. It was this and this alone that saved Anderson's life.

We soon found Hans and Geoff, standing triumphantly by the carcass of the old bull. It had, indeed, taken two shots to bring him down.

Charlie was dispatched to run to the nearby village and bring back its people. They would dress out the huge carcass and in return were given the meat. The hunters were interested only in the skin and the tusks. The meat would feed the people of the village for some time to come. This was the arrangement that had held for years between the people of the local villages and the hunters who came to win themselves trophies.

The people of the village arrived with knives of poor quality, sharpened on rocks, and some even had sharpened butter knives; but despite the poverty of their tools, it was remarkable how fast they worked. The meat was laid out on a large rock and the women beat it with another, tenderizing it. While some of the villagers were busy butchering the meat from the carcass, others had already started a fire and set to cooking.

Having taken part in the destruction of this magnificent animal, I felt the need to honor him, and I asked Sylvester if he would take me to the cooking fire so that I could join the people as they ate the meat of this mighty elephant, and in so doing honor his life. A woman from the village handed me a piece of juicy meat, her face smiling, and her eyes filled with delight. I had treated the African people with respect – respect for their knowledge and for the difficulty of their existence. I admired their dignity. They had come to accept me, not as a white man, nor as a member of their tribe, but as someone who accepted them for who they were and who acknowledged them as equals.

My trip to Africa was a watershed moment in my life. If I had refused this opportunity on account of my environmental philosophies, I would have missed seeing the beautiful country and the abundance and diversity of the wildlife. I feel honored to have witnessed the wilderness of those days. As time has gone on the wildlife of Africa has been decimated, mostly by poachers and the greed of people desiring ivory at any cost. It has been at a great cost indeed: it has brought the tragic decline of elephants and rhinoceros, and the scattering of the abundant wildlife that had so stunned my eyes as we crouched in the bush that memorable day, overlooking the plains of Africa.

If I had closed myself to the hunt, I would never have seen those things, would perhaps never have awakened from the depression and sleep in which I had been living in late years. And, most importantly, I would have missed the experience of sharing a small part of the culture with the native people of

Africa, which is also being lost to history. It was an exceptional experience, one which I cherish and will continue to cherish.

ADVENTURES IN COSTA RICA

Healing

The river rolls on.

Because of our outdoor experience and my success in producing multi-media programs for environmental causes, Spencer Beebe of the Nature Conservancy International Program asked if we would be willing to photograph the National Parks of Costa Rica and produce a multi-media program. It would be used to raise money for the Costa Rican Park's Foundation and would help finance the acquisition of private lands that still existed within the boundaries of the twenty-one national parks, and to purchase lands adjoining the parks that were needed to protect wildlife habitat.

It was exactly what we needed to take us away from our memories. The change took our minds off ourselves and our personal suffering and we were working at something that was close to our hearts: conservation. We were involved again, and we were helping future generations – the generation Jesse would have belonged too. We were excited and optimistic about the future, and happier than we had been in years.

Our adventure began in 1982. Spencer had planned on hiring a Spanish interpreter to travel with me through Costa Rica since I spoke no Spanish, and I told them that Sheila spoke Spanish fluently and would be a great asset for me on the trip. We were soon preparing for a trip that would last three months traveling through the parks of Costa Rica.

We had spent many years working in the wilderness, and I had photographed places in Africa where guns and revolution were part of the scene. We were uncertain what we might be confronted with in Costa Rica. In short time we discovered that although Central America was one of the hot-spots in the world, Costa Rica was one of the most peaceful. If we stayed clear of the Nicaraguan border we would have little reason to fear any danger - at least from human beings. As for the local fauna, the park lands were filled with different varieties of poisonous snakes, spiders as big around as your hand, crocodiles, and wild boar that ranged through the thick undergrowth of the forest. Sheila was game, which was fortunate, because my vocabulary in Spanish was limited to *"Adios"* and *"No dinero."* She was not even in the least bit doubtful about the prospect of sleeping for ninety days in her sleeping bag in unknown country.

We arrived in San Jose, the capital of Costa Rica, early in November, with forty pounds of camera gear, our packs, tent, sleeping bags, and camping equipment. San Jose was a clean, modern city nestled at five-thousand feet on the slopes of two volcanoes – Poas, which was still quite active, and Irazu, which was sleeping, or maybe just taking a nap. Both volcanoes are national parks, and we would visit them at some point during our photographic tour. We found the people of Costa Rica to be friendly, honest, and peaceful, unlike other countries existing in that turbulent time in Central America.

The people loved their country and were willing to make the sacrifices necessary to preserve the diversity of their beautiful land and to protect its wildlife. They had managed to dedicate twenty-five percent of their country to parks, wildlife refuges, national monuments, archeological sites, and forest reserves. Parks and biological reserves alone encompassed eight per-cent of the land mass. Costa Rica is only two hundred miles long, and the shortest distance between the Atlantic and the Pacific Oceans is a mere seventy-five miles. If you want to see the sun rise over the Atlantic Ocean and set on the Pacific Ocean all you have to do is climb 12,532 feet to the top of the volcano Chirripó. If you like variety, you could spend the day sweating in a jungle at sea-level, and the night on top of Chirripó watching the ice form in your cooking pot, wishing you had known enough to bring a sleeping bag. The diversity of the Costa Rican lands, forests, jungles, and wildlife is unbelievable. We photographed sixteen parks and no two were alike.

The first park we visited was Santa Rosa, which lies on the Pacific coast. Santa Rosa consists mostly of dry forests in which most of the trees lose their leaves during the dry season. This park has over two-hundred species of birds, several species of cats (including jaguar), tapir, deer, coyote, armadillo, hog-nosed skunks, coatimundis (an inquisitive cross between a teddy-bear and a large raccoon), peccary (an animal which looks like a wild pig, but isn't), and several species of monkeys, not to mention a plentiful assortment of snakes, lizards, crocodiles bats, and insects.

We decided to visit Santa Rosa first because it was the season for the sea turtles to come ashore and lay their eggs. We were to share this extraordinary phenomenon with several biologists who were counting and tagging them. The biologists were trying to understand where the turtles go, how often they return, and why, thankfully, they return to Santa Rosa in such great numbers every year.

We were lucky in our timing. The night we arrived, forty-thousand Pacific Ridley turtles poured from the Pacific Ocean to perform their ritual. It was estimated that they laid four-million eggs, but because of all the difficulties encountered by both adults and young, only about eight-thousand baby turtles would return to the sea. Santa Rosa is also the nesting ground for the Green Turtle, which are about the same size as the Pacific Ridley, and for the giant Leather-Back Turtle, which can weigh as much as fifteen-hundred pounds.

One of their nesting grounds is a lovely white-sand beach named Nancite. This beach is about two kilometers long with a gentle slope that climbs from the ocean to meet the mangrove trees and the swamps behind them. Behind the high-tide mark and the mangrove swamp is a narrow corridor that provides the nesting ground. The sand there is the perfect temperature to incubate the eggs until the young hatch.

Just before dusk, we moved onto the beach to await the coming of the Pacific Ridley turtles. Gradually the sky changed from intense blue to yellow, from orange to red to indigo. Just before dark it turned violet and darkness followed quickly. There was no moon that night - the only light aside from the stars came from the biologists' head lamps, but the sky was clear and the stars were so bright we could easily see shadows on the white sands of the beach.

It was well after dark before the ghost-like turtles began to emerge from the sea. In the beginning, only a few struggled out of the water and with tremendous will they over-came their newly-acquired weight, and with gasping moans, they painfully dragged themselves forward, their great bulk bulldozing the sand out of their way. Soon they were arriving by the thousands, deposited by the waves at the edge of the beach. The sound of their groaning could be heard everywhere, and the ordeal caused tears to fall from their eyes. With every passing moment the beach grew darker, the white sand disappearing under the bodies of turtles. The sand was black with their shadows, but each shadow was filled with a sparkling light - the huge beasts emerged from the water adorned with phosphorescent organisms that the turbulent ocean had dredged from its floor. They were covered with shining blue and green jewels, as if they were coming out of the depth of the sea, not only to give birth, but also to celebrate the sacred occasion. The waves also honored this moment. As they exploded toward the shore they caught the phosphorescence and brilliance emanated from them, as though the full moon had fallen from the sky and now lay just below the surface of the ocean.

I walked down the beach to photograph a large Leather-Back turtle as she came through the last wave. I turned around noticed glowing foot prints in the sand - they were my own and I felt I was experiencing a Biblical moment.

As more and more turtles arrived, the beach became chaotic. Soon the turtles that were struggling from the ocean were colliding with those that had completed their mission and were returning to the ocean. Turtles were crawling everywhere - some were digging up the freshly laid eggs of those that had come before. A few, who were tired or injured, dug their nests below the high-water line, where the eggs would perish, never having hatched. Others, perhaps out of desire for respite from all the confusion, went too far and fell into the lagoons behind the beach, where crocodiles patiently awaited them.

In the midst of all this turmoil we found three newborn turtles, no bigger than a baby's hand. Fifty days ago their mother had left her eggs buried in their nest of sand and for all those days they were hidden from their enemies. The beach was constantly scoured by bands of coatimundi, raccoons, and vultures all sniffing and pawing the earth, hungry for the sweet taste of turtle eggs. The newborns had chosen this inopportune moment to hatch, and in all the confusion they were attempting to find their way through the battleground that lay between them and the ocean, their salvation. It was a hopeless task. These were the only baby turtles we found - their brothers and sisters lay crushed and buried in the turmoil below. Compassionately, perhaps because we remembered our own hunger for survival, we picked up the little ones and carried them gently to the bosom of the sea, the only mother they would ever know.

Inland from Santa Rosa, in the Guanacaste Mountains, is the park called Rincon de la Vieja. Few people had seen this park in 1982, for it was closed to the public. It is as Yellowstone was before the white man arrived. The geysers are not so dramatic, and there are no buffalo, but it is as unusual as any place on earth. Flowing through the park is a large stream, the temperature of bathwater, and soaking in it was a delightful and sensuous experience. The cold water of the stream was warmed by a boiling pond. The pond was eerie, the water below the surface was milky white, and at the surface it was a deep blue. The boiling of the water mixed the colors as if someone were stirring two different colors of paint. Standing at the edge of the pond was like standing on the edge of a steep cliff. The boiling water was not far below us, but the fear of falling into that caldron was overwhelming, and we had an uncontrollable desire to hang onto something.

The sounds at Rincon de la Vieja are like nothing else on earth - a combination of howling winds, song birds, hot bubbling mud pots, geysers, steam escaping from the earth through cracks in stone, and howler monkeys that roar like lions. The park is a Garden of Eden. All the plants that we Americans surround ourselves with and care for so lovingly grow wild there. Most of them are too big to fit into a house, let alone a pot. They grow on the banks of clear fresh streams and over waterfalls that cascade down rocky cliffs, while monkeys swing from their branches.

Every paradise contains some evil and the devil in Rincon de la Vieja is a snake called the terciopelo or (*fer-de-lance*). This snake is not only extremely poisonous, but is also mean and aggressive, and during its mating season it is particularly dangerous. At that time, for reasons unknown, it likes to chase people with every intention of biting them. The natives carry machetes to fend them off. Sheila and I carried anti-venom, since we weren't convinced that we could stop running long enough to kill one with a machete.

Then there was the wind. In the jungle we were protected from it, but we could hear it roaring in the canopies overhead. It blew continuously and violently, trying to penetrate into the jungle. It sounded powerful and angry as though seeking to destroy everything in its path. It made for a disquieting sleep and we never really felt rested when the morning light filtered through the jungle greenery.

High above us was an active volcano. Its lands were desolate, and nothing bigger than grass and stunted bushes grew in that tormented environment. For the sake of photography we left the sanctuary of the trees, and sought the summit. Once out of the jungle we made our way up the volcano with difficulty, bending into the wind, our heads down, our eyes staring at the earth - intimidated by its intensity and its relentless onslaught. As the ridge narrowed we were forced at times to crawl, grasping at every available bush and handful of grass. During the ascent dark clouds and heavy windblown rains enveloped us, and when we finally arrived at the crater we couldn't see anything - the world was a soup bowl of gray fog. All we received for our effort was the smell of rot and vomit coming from the bowels of the earth, and humbly, we retreated to the protection of the jungle, where we could pitch our tent out of the wrath of the windstorm.

In 1982 the Park Service did not allow people to visit Barra Honda, a park of limestone caves, without a guide. Our guides were park service employees who were very personable and took their jobs quite seriously. They brought along a rope one-inch in diameter that would have stretched from the Pacific to the Atlantic Ocean if laid out end to end - it was so long and heavy that the guides brought a horse to carry it. The length of the rope made Sheila nervous. She knew we were going to descend into several of the caves, but the huge coil of rope convinced her that we were going on a journey to the center of the earth. The rope was to be used for our descent into the caves, but we would use no more than 70 feet - its great length was needed by more serious explorers than we.

The caves are located in the driest part of Costa Rica. Traveling above ground was not as difficult there as it was in most areas of the country, where there were thick jungles and forests. While hiking to the caves we began to hear the soft sounds of drumbeats and had the sense they were following us wherever we hiked. They were deep hollow sounds that took me back to my kayaking trip down the Salmon River during the flood of 1974. I found myself wondering if we were being pursued by wild men with painted faces and spears in their hands, with shrunken heads dangling from their belts.

Our guides watched us as we became quiet with looks of bewilderment on our faces. They couldn't contain themselves for long, and trying to control their laughter, they explained that the ground beneath us was hollow. The drumming noise was the sound of our own horse's hooves striking the earth. They pointed to holes in the ground; they were everywhere and the surface of earth was but a thin roof over the hundreds of caves below. It was not a place to go with your sweetheart for a moonlit stroll. Some of the holes were so small that you could get only your arm into them, others were big enough that a body could fall into them, and many were big enough to drive a car into. The holes were created by earthquakes and heavy animals that had walked over weak spots causing the thin layer of earth and rock to give way. We prudently stayed far behind the horse and the heavy rope he carried.

We made one descent into a cave called Terciopelo, which was named by the first person to explore the cave. When he descended into this first cave, he found a fer-de-lance lying on the floor of the cave under the end of his rope. The story has it that he was given quite a scare - I know it would make my mouth dry to be hanging on a rope 70 feet down with a poisonous snake in the only place I could land my feet. Fortunately for the explorer, the snake had fallen from the top of the cave to its death, never to chase another human.

The inside of the cave was a dark wilderness and so quiet you could hear your heart beat. I had expected it to be a place without light, where nothing grew or lived. There was black beyond imagining, but when we turned on our headlamps it was blackness full of life. Thousands of bats, crickets, beetles, and snails lived in this unworldly place. There were huge spiders with eyes on the end of long slender stalks that protruded out of their heads, and salamanders with little eyes that could not see.

Terciopelo was filled with limestone statues carved by nature and encrusted with flakes of crystal that sparkled like diamonds under the glow of our head lamps. One of the sculptures was called the organ, and when thumped it produced a deep rich tone that echoed from wall to wall and down through its cavities. The creation of the cave began in the Paleocene age, about seventy-million years ago, and is still evolving.

When I took photographs the light from the flash on my camera would be absorbed by the crystal in the stone, and for a few moments the cave would glow, trying desperately to hold the light, only to grudgingly release it. I felt as if the cave had a soul which had been deprived of the sun for millions of years. The light, I imagined, reminded the cave of ages long past when it still knew daylight, and now awakened, it longed to once more feel the warm light of day. As we left Barra Honda and its strange and quiet world, we spoke with each other, still in the undertones that the cave seemed to impose on us, whispering to each other in amazement that life could exist in such darkness.

The rainiest place in Costa Rica is a park on the Atlantic side called Tortuguero. There the only practical form of travel is on its miles of canals, which are full of turtles, manatee and various kinds of fish - tarpon and mojarra and grunt. Even though the waters of Tortuguero are warm, the canals are not a pleasant place for swimming. In the dark waters lurk snake eels, moray eels, shark, crocodile, and the carnivorous gar that can grow to two meters in length, with strong jaws and long sharp teeth.

The Park Service was providing us boat transportation into the interior of the jungle - all we had to do was meet one of the park employees at a dock in a town called Moin. They asked us to be there early in the morning because it was too dangerous to travel the canals at night. It was over fifty miles to the headquarters, where we would spend our first night, and we had to arrive before dark set in.

We found the dock by nine in the morning, but the park employee who would transport us to our destination did not arrive until about eleven. We had to wait, he said, while his people bought provisions. They were already shopping and would return soon - then we could leave. At two in the afternoon our small, over-loaded boat got under way with its supply of provisions, the captain, Sheila, I, and three other passengers. The boat was deep in the water and crowded when we finally got underway. In the beginning it was a pleasant journey. On the bank of the canal the limbs of the trees were heavy and noisy with birds and the jungle was filled with sloths, spider monkeys, and howler monkeys.

Soon, it grew dark, and we were still miles from camp. The sky turned the color of the water, and the canal became narrow, with vines and limbs overhanging it. I dug my flashlight out of my pack and used it as a beacon to light our way, but the captain wordlessly confiscated it, handing it to one of his crew who held the light off the port side at the bank of the canal, while another crew member shined his light towards the starboard bank. Apparently this maneuver allowed the captain to see that he was guiding the boat down the middle of the channel and away from dropping trees and branches that lined the sides of the banks.

Since he was the captain, my complaints about the dark void in front of us went unheard. The only natural light came from the sky, which was one shade lighter than the jungle and two shades lighter than the water. The sky provided a trail and as I looked up I watched the jungle closing in on us as the waterway narrowed. As we continued deeper into the park, the trail in the sky became a narrow slit and we were continually being slapped and whipped by the invisible limbs and vines that overhung the water. The captain was going too fast, I thought, and we were all forced to keep our heads down to protect ourselves from being thrashed by the vegetation. The captain knew the canal well - he was careful not to be misled into following one of the many tributaries that joined the main canal, but it was impossible for him to see every piece of floating debris and the canal was full of drifting trees and broken snags. It was inevitable that sooner or later we would hit something.

The sounds of the crash were a horrifying blend of the racing engine wildly howling as it left the water, the gasping moans that came from the throats of the passengers, the crunching sound of aluminum being crushed, and the screams of one woman passenger who cried out with fear and raged at the unjust God who was about to take her life.

The boat had struck a log, and to the horror of all those on board, was climbing out of the water and starting a slow motion roll, up and over. The boat was heaviest on the port side, and it started to tip over while it was in the air. Sheila grabbed the camera gear to protect it from the water. Thanks to years of boating experience on white water, both Sheila and I instinctively threw our bodies at the high side of the boat, praying we would not arrive too late - we had both feared and expected such a possibility.

As I came down hard against the rising part of the boat, a terrible vision flashed through my mind of the moment we would be thrown into the dark murky waters, full of snakes and crocodiles, just waiting for a good meal. But, just as fast as the boat had run into the tree and started to flip over, it landed flat once again on the water and right-side up, as if acrobatics were a just a normal part of the trip. The small boat had not suffered any leaks, or major damage, but it no longer rushed to its destination. The captain of the boat handed me my flashlight asking me to hold it straight ahead and the passengers in our little boat settled once again into their seats in quiet contemplation. Sheila and I were preoccupied with the taste of being alive.

The largest park in the country is La Amistad, or Friendship Park, on the border of Panama. An effort was under way in Panama to contribute Panamanian lands that bordered La Amistad in Costa Rica, creating a national park that would allow the animals of both countries to migrate during hard times when food was scarce - insuring the survival of the tapir and large cats.

At the end of a very long dirt road that stopped at the border of La Amistad lived a man named Solomon. He was part-Indian and proud of it. In Costa Rica there are few Indians left; most of them were killed when the white man came, and Solomon was amongst the few remaining. "I would rather be a poor man living in the mountains than a poor man living in the city," he said. "In the city a poor man is a beggar, but in the mountains he has dignity."

Solomon lived in a one-room shack made of hand hued oak lumber. The windows, also of oak, were simple shutters that could be opened on rainy days, but they were left closed on sunny days because of the insects. Solomon had wisdom in his eyes, but no sorrow. The sorrow belonged to his wife. She had grown old at thirty from doing laundry on rocks in the creek, from years of child-bearing, and struggling from the creek to the cabin with buckets of water for drinking and cooking. Her life had been hard, but now, in her old age, things were a bit better - some of her ten children were old enough to help with the chores, and she had time to sit on the steps of their little shack and dream of how things might have been if she had lived in the city.

Palo Verde is a bird refuge located in a wetland that is so large birds from all over the western hemisphere come to it for their wintering grounds. Much of the wetland was lost to a banana company and more was lost to rice paddies. The government created a wildlife refuge on the remaining wetland. Until we arrived at the company town, where the employees who worked on the banana plantation and in the rice paddies lived, we hadn't yet experienced hostility from the people of Costa Rica.

When we drove into the town, we noticed that the houses were all built in rows with common walls. The walls between occupants consisted of a one-inch-thick oak board - it must have been impossible to get a good night's rest. Whether from these miserable living conditions or for some reason unknown, the people of the village were unfriendly. When we asked directions, we were ignored. The people would simply walk away.

There was only one dirt road through town, with the town on one side and a river on the other. Near the bridge that spanned the river we found the company store and went in to pick up a few provisions and to ask for directions again. We paid for our cans of beans and rice and asked the clerk if she could tell us the way to the bird refuge. She didn't answer but simply pointed at the bridge. The people living here obviously had a strong dislike for foreigners - they were suspicious, like the people in the small mountain towns of the Western United States. Maybe they had been taken advantage of once too often.

We drove across the bridge and were stopped by a large fence and gate with a guard house just inside. We waited in our diesel Toyota for a few minutes, and when nothing happened I honked my horn. The guard, a big man who looked like he got out of the wrong side of the bed, walked up to his side of the gate. In Spanish he asked what we wanted. Sheila explained that we needed to get to the wildlife refuge. He responded loudly that this was private property and we were not allowed to trespass. We asked if there was another way to the refuge. He shook his head no and turned back to the guard house. We sat in the car, somewhat intimidated, trying to decide what to do. We *had* to film this park - it was one of the most important parks in the country, and if this was the only way in, then this was the way we would have to go. We had been given a letter from the Costa Rican government that we could use in situations like this. It simply stated that we were working with the government and that we should be given every courtesy.

I honked the horn again and both Sheila and I got out of the car and walked up to the gate. The guard came out of the shack, now looking quite hostile. He was growling something that would have been unintelligible, even had I spoken Spanish. Sheila understood and became noticeably angry. She started waving the letter from the government and vociferously explained that he had better let us through or there would be consequences. When he was close enough, she handed him the letter - I hoped he could read. When he looked at us anger flashed through his eyes, but he reluctantly returned the letter and opened the gate, waving us through.

As we drove up the bank out of the river, we saw rice paddies that stretched away as far as the eye could see. The road was raised a few feet above the paddies and was in good condition. We followed it, and we followed it - there seemed to be no end. There were many side-roads as well, but they seemed less used, some of them even dropping off into the paddies, so we continued on the main road for several more miles. In the distance we could see raised land; there was, after all, an end to the paddies. As we came closer to the tree-covered area we could see what appeared to be a large lake - and the road we were on seemed to head straight into it...

We stopped, perplexed, sure that we must be mistaken, but looking around us, we could see no alternative route. There was no way around it. Our road disappeared into the lake. The lake itself looked to be almost a mile wide and we could see across to the other side, where the road came out of the water and climbed the bank. We sat in our diesel four-wheel-drive Toyota and looked at the far bank. We were both wondering and worrying how deep the lake was, and how full of mud. We had already come many miles from the lonely guard-house and its aggressive guard. Neither of us knew how long we would have to wander before encountering some friendly face. It was going to take a lot of courage to drive into this lake.

"I think it's time for lunch, don't you?" I asked Sheila.

She didn't reply. She simply reached into the back and brought out the food bag. We thought while we ate, both silently wondering what to do next. Finally, I suggested that she drive while I wade ahead to check the depth and try to determine how solid the base was.

"What about crocodiles?" she asked worriedly. She was right to worry - we had already seen crocodiles in almost every body of water we had encountered.

While I was searching the lake for any sign of crocodiles, I was remembering the small ponds in Africa where they lurked, waiting for an animal or a human to come for a drink. When the unsuspecting creature bent down for a drink the crock would lunge out of the water and drag its dinner into the pond by its head to drown it. I told myself this was not the time for those memories, but they came unbidden.

Lunch was finished and it was time for a decision. I began taking off my shoes and removing my socks when I noticed in the distance a cloud of dust. Someone was coming our way, and they were coming fast! Sheila and I looked at each other, reading each other's minds. Here we were alone in the middle of hostile country. We certainly had not made any friends and had no place to run or hide. We would have to wait here and let what was going to happen, happen. There was barely enough space on the side of the road to move the Toyota, allowing room for the vehicle to pass, so I parked the car as far off as possible. As the vehicle came closer we could see it was a large truck and it had a number of people riding in the back. We watched their approach uneasily, praying that all would be well. As they got closer they slowed down to a crawl and stopped beside us. I smiled.

The man in the front seat stuck his hand out his window and said in Spanish, "Follow us," and drove into the lake. We followed. The water was soon deep enough that it was filling the floorboard of the Toyota, but the diesel engine didn't flinch. It surged ahead, plowing through the lake like this was not at all an unusual requirement. We safely reached the far side of the lake and drove up the bank with water flowing out our doors. The driver of the truck we had been following pulled to the side of the road and let us pass. The passengers had smiles on their faces and waved as we passed them by.

After traveling for some time, we found the caretakers of the park at last. They showed us a place to camp and introduced us to the outdoor shower, which made Sheila's day. They said they were happy to have company and invited us to dinner. We had a wonderful shower – something that we didn't experience often, since usually we had only a stream to freshen up in. That evening at dinner we discussed how I would photograph the refuge. The refuge itself was about five miles away from our camp. The caretakers told us they would take us there on horseback and return later for us.

We spent several wonderful days photographing the birds and wildlife that lived in the refuge. The beauty that was all around us was magnificent. All day long the flamingos would turn the sky pink like a glorious sunset. So much diversity, so many migratory birds, waiting to return to their nesting grounds in the north. We even had the rare opportunity of photographing the Jabaru stork, a large black and white bird with a red ring around its neck, whose species was near extinction, like so many life forms struggling to survive the encroachment of humans whose values are not in tune with Mother Earth.

Time and space don't allow me to share memories of all the parks we visited. At Braulio Carrillo I remember the giant blue wings of the Morpho butterfly that never stops to rest, and flies only to share its beauty. In Cahuita, a park on the Atlantic with lovely coral reefs, I recall butterflies with transparent wings floating beneath the trees, where the white-faced monkeys peered out at us, not knowing that we could see their white faces. In Palo Verde we saw migratory birds of every color imaginable, waiting for warmth to return to their nesting grounds in the north. In Corcovado, the Jesus Christ lizards walked on water to prove that nothing is impossible. In Monteverdi we photographed the golden toad. Those photographs may be among the last ever taken of this rare creature, for soon after they were determined to be extinct.

Every park was magnificent and had its own wonders; each was filled with beauty and mystery.

As we few out of the airport in San Jose I thought to myself that it would be good to be home in time for spring. We didn't own a house anymore, so we set up one of our yurts, making it home. Inside the yurt Sheila had created a masterpiece of warmth and comfort. It was situated on a rise overlooking a meadow, at times filled with groups of dancing Sandhill Crane. The meadow was resplendent. It was a shining carpet, a breathtaking array of wild flowers, and the blue sky was filled with bluebirds and blue butterflies and growing everywhere were butter cups and shooting stars and elephant heads and rising above this splendor were magnificent jagged peaks crowned with snow that soared into the heavens. No one on earth lived more simply, yet as magnificently as we.

* * *

In all that tranquility it was unimaginable that I could still have an ulcer, but I did, and in June it started bleeding and I ended up in the hospital. Not only would the doctors operate, but they had discovered a tumor on one of my lungs which they believed was malignant. Neither operation could wait for long. It seemed as though it was our destiny to have these tremendous contrasts in our existence; a time for paradise and beauty, a time for tragedy and misfortune.

Nature has its attraction for the soul. During the operation on my stomach I have vivid recall of being in a divine country. I had no sense of my physical body but was very present in my spiritual being. Beautiful music was playing and I was surrounded by fields of flowers, I felt happiness and contentment, in that moment I was supremely alive, I was free. The moment was broken by a painful and moaning sound. I looked down, through a shrouded mist, and saw my body on an operating table. It was laying in fetal position, arms wrapped around its stomach, rocking back and forth in pain.

"I am not going back to that!" I said aloud. In that instant I *was* back in my body. I was moaning, my arms wrapped around my body, and I was rocking back and forth in excruciating pain. I remembered only a moment ago I had been in wild flower garden, full of joy and contentment. In an instant I fully understood that physical existence was not a choice, it was a requirement.

My stomach operation was a success and surgery on my lung confirmed that the growth was not a tumor at all, but a fungus that I had picked up on one of my journeys - I had a habit of sniffing things.

* * *

Soon after my operations one of the greatest moments in my life passed. Jesse came to me in a dream. He was walking toward me and I bent down to pick him up. I was overwhelmed with love and happiness. When he got near enough to me he reached out with his little hand and touched the middle of my forehead with a finger. The touch sent a beautiful bright white light surging through me, it was vibrant and alive. He smiled at me with his gentle and beautiful smile and said, "*I love you.*"

It was a blessing beyond description. In one powerful instant the guilt that had plagued me with Jess's death was gone and I felt a lightness I had not felt in years.

The rest of our summer passed as a dream. It was a time for healing and spiritual growth. It was a time for long talks and for holding hands. It was a time for love to grow again. It was a time to sort the glory and wonders of life from its disappointments and tragedies. Most of all it was a time for planning the future – the time had come to decide if we should try, once again, to bring another child into our lives.

That decision was hard, a question that had to be faced in reality. Nobody would ever know what caused Jess's life to be so tragic and short. We had spent the last five years agonizing over all the possibilities. To continue suffering from our loss had become a tragedy in itself. Through our long struggle to find solutions we had always looked outside of ourselves. But the answers were not there, all that time they were within us, they were found in faith, and in hope, and in the power of love. It was a time to live in faith again, to look forward to the future with confidence and joy. We bought a small log cabin on Crooked Creek, we had a beautiful view of McGowan Peak out our kitchen window. We resurrected our hut system and I started guiding again.

THE HAND OF GOD

Why
do we
consider
miracles
so
miraculous
when we are
surrounded
by them.

By the 1980's back-country skiing had caught on nationwide, there were new hut systems cropping up all over the west. Many had also discovered yurts, and no wonder - they were portable, comfortable and could support a lot of snow. Dean Conger of National Geographic had skied with us in the early seventies when we were using wall tents for our huts. He had traveled in Mongolia and was very impressed by their yurts - and, thinking they would be perfect for our huts, he sent us specifications on how to construct them. Kirk Bachman, who guided for us at the time, had heard about yurts and helped us build them for our hut system - I believe we were the first to use them in the United States.

Our skiing business was at somewhat of a disadvantage - we were a long way from anywhere. Sun Valley, Idaho, was the nearest ski resort and we were sixty miles away and over Galena Summit. Our biggest handicap was also our biggest advantage - we had lots of powder and mountains that hadn't been skied by anyone.

Time Magazine wrote about our business in an article on back-country skiing and we began to attract the vertical crowd - "How much vertical can we expect?" became the mantra. In

January of that year we received a call from a group of skiers and they booked a trip - they were excited to be skiing virgin mountain slopes. I was beginning to miss the skiers who wanted to explore the beauty of back-country in the winter, where skiing was a part of the journey and not the ultimate goal. But at the same time, business was business.

A group of men, interested in how many vertical feet they would be skiing, arrived in late January, as did the January thaw. The group was on time; the thaw was late. The thaw was almost always guaranteed to arrive in mid-January, usually followed by a period of very cold temperatures. During the thaw we could get everything from rain to heavy wet snow - it was not the best time for skiing. The cold weather following the thaw usually set perfect conditions for a good base to ski on. Cold storms would deposit some of the famous Idaho powder and skiing would be at its best. The thaw in '86 started out with a lot of very wet snow. A big storm had come through the mountains, gradually cooling down, leaving a layer of wet snow under several feet of drier snow. The wet layer hadn't had a chance to bond with the other layers and avalanche danger was extreme.

I explained the situation to our new skiers and told them that the avalanche conditions were so dangerous that we would be confined to protected slopes less than thirty degrees. We would have to wait until the avalanche danger was diminished to ski the steeper terrain. It was a six day trip and I told them I was confident that as things settled we would get some steep skiing in. They were disappointed but decided to continue on with the trip as planned.

We left Stanley early the next morning and arrived at our highest hut, Marshal Lake, before dark.

We had an early breakfast and were on the slopes at first light. The skies had been cloudy since the thaw - we needed clear, cold nights to remove the warmth from the snow in order to stabilize the pack. I dug a pit in the snow to check the layering and indicators that would determine the potential danger of an avalanche, and found, about two feet below the surface, a wet layer of snow that was very unstable. I climbed out of my hole and informed the group that we wouldn't be skiing anything steeper than thirty degrees that day. Needless to say, they were disappointed - every day missed was a day that their vertical count was not going to improve. They told me that evening that they all had personal license plates that advertised the number of vertical feet they had skied. Their numbers didn't improve much that day, or the next. In fact, I wouldn't let them ski the slopes they were interested in for the next four days.

At first they were discontent, spending their nights restlessly dreaming of their license plates. As the days passed on, their discontent turned to anger, until finally, they began to doubt my judgment and accused me of being too cautious. The responsibility of guiding people into the mountains was immense for me and I always erred on the side of caution. I had not lost a skier yet and I did not want this to be the first time.

Two nights before their trip was to end the sky was clear and full of stars. The next morning I dug a new pit and discovered that the wet layer had finally started to bond with the rest of the snow pack. It wasn't bonded as well as I would have liked, but I was under great pressure to get them on some steeper slopes. I explained the conditions and told them we would climb a ridge that led to the summit of Thompson Peak and that we would ski the upper middle of the slope. I told them that we would ski it one person at a time, so that in the event of a slide there would only be one person in the danger zone.

We were all wearing avalanche transmitters, which was a device that was worn around the neck and was set to transmit a beeping signal. In the event the mountain slid and someone was buried beneath the snow, the beeping signal would be picked up by the other transmitters making it possible to locate them under the snow. I checked to make certain all our transmitters were set properly and we began our climb up the ridge. I instructed them once again, to ski one person at a time down the slope, and that if an avalanche should break loose they were to ski to the nearest tree at the edge of the ridge, get behind it and hang on for their lives.

When we reached the point where we would begin our downhill descent, I repeated once again - "*Remember*, only *one* person at a time. I will go first. I want all of you to stay to the left of my tracks. The next person will follow *only* after I have skied beyond the first tree at the base of the ridge." I wanted to make certain the slope was stable and I wanted them to stay to the left of my tracks - the right was more exposed and much steeper. I planned to stop at a tree I had already picked out, just under the ridge, where I could watch each of them ski the slope. The responsibility of guiding these men on the slope was weighing heavily, and as I started downhill I yelled once more, "Stay to the left of my tracks and only one at a time!"

The skiing was superb - the powder was almost a foot deep, and the base seemed solid. I hadn't thought to check my bindings before starting down the slope and one of my boots popped out of its binding releasing my ski. I watched as it sped down the mountain, leaving me behind. It hadn't gone far before it flipped over and stuck in the snow.

I turned to a stop on my remaining ski and looked back up the slope. I watched, in horror, as all four of the skiers start down the slope at the same time, each taking a different path.

They thought that because I had made it down the slope, it was safe. There was nothing I could do but watch - and pray.

They were all whooping and yelling as they careened down the mountain. The moment they had been waiting for had arrived and they were ecstatic to finally ski the slopes they had dreamed of. I watched, praying that the mountain would not slide - but my prayer was not heard. One of the skiers fell.

It was Cliff, and all two-hundred pounds of him hit the snow hard. I felt the snow collapse under me, looked up the face of the mountain and saw, over a thousand feet above me, the snow separate from its anchor point at the ridge line and explode. My worst nightmare had become reality, a reality more terrible than I could ever have imagined – we were in an avalanche, an avalanche bigger than any I had encountered in all of my years of skiing. I watched, stunned, as the fracture line shot across the face of the mountain and spread in both directions, as far as my eyes could see.

I screamed at them, *"Avalanche!"* but they couldn't hear me. I screamed louder, *"Avalanche!"* This time they heard me. All turned to a stop and looked down the slope towards me. I pointed up the mountain and as loud as I could, I screamed again, "A*v-a- lanche!"* At last, they looked up and saw the snow plume - well over a hundred feet high flying right at them, like a tidal wave.

Cliff was still fighting the snow, trying to get his skis under him so he could stand up. He was finally standing upright and was able to look up the mountain - what he saw was a cloud of snow, filled with cartwheeling trees, exploding down the slope and heading directly towards him with terrifying speed. He panicked and too quickly he turned to start down the slope and fell over backwards. He found himself again fighting the snow, trying desperately to get his skis under him.

The tree line at that latitude ended at about nine-thousand feet. The fracture line started well above that, and within seconds the avalanche hit the tree line, tearing trees out like daisies, as it rushed on down the slope. As the initial shock of what was happening took hold, I instinctively calmed myself and assumed my role and responsibility as guide. I noted the exact position of each person on the slope and where they might end up if they were overtaken by the avalanche and buried. If someone was buried under the snow they had to be found quickly - it would be a matter of life or death.

I was shocked to see three of the skiers, contrary to both my instructions and to common sense, ski into the middle of the slope, as if they hoped to outrun the maelstrom behind them. I watched until they dropped out of sight. I had only an idea of the direction they had skied, and it would be hard to find any of them quickly. Cliff was still trying to master his balance. He was an expert skier, but in his panic, he made the mistake of trying to stand on his skis while they were pointed downhill and his skis slipped, leaving him once again fighting to stand. I watched him struggle until he disappeared into the wind-driven snow, the forerunner of the avalanche.

When I was able to move my focus from him I watched as the snow and debris raced towards me, as if it were all part of a giant explosion. There were trees standing on end, flying sideways and rolling over and over in the avalanche of snow - all of this happening just above me and moving like a jet airplane. I turned and pointed my single ski downhill and kicked off with all my strength. I reached the nearest tree and turned behind it. Grabbing hold of it, I spun around, wrapped my arms around the trunk, pushing the side of my body against the backside, and held on for dear life.

The wind from the avalanche hit me first. I was hammered by a tremendous blast of wind-driven snow, filled with branches and debris. Powdered snow filled my eyes and mouth and I prepared myself for the tons of snow that would soon wrap around me from all sides and above. I bent my knees and crouched down hoping I would be able to force my way up through the snow of the avalanche before it had a chance to solidify. And, I braced myself.

And then - *nothing*. I waited, eyes shut tight, but nothing happened. The wind abated and the branches above me grew quiet. In bewilderment I peeked timidly around the tree. There was nothing but complete silence - no wind, nothing but tranquility. I looked up the mountain and saw, less than one-hundred feet above me, a giant wall of snow with broken tree trunks and branches protruding out of it. All was dead still - it seemed impossible, but I knew there wasn't a moment to spare. I gathered myself together and moved rapidly into rescue mode.

I was quite certain that at least one of my guests was buried, probably more, quite possibly all. While struggling with only one ski towards the huge pile of compacted snow and debris the avalanche had deposited I turned my transmitter to receive. I put the microphone in my ear but could hear nothing. I had to get closer but the wall of snow and debris in front of me was like a cliff. I released the toe clip from my remaining ski and used the shattered tree trunks and branches to climb as rapidly as I could to the top of the mass, and when I reached the top I called out, "Yell if you can hear me!" I heard a voice, and I turned around to find Cliff standing on the slope below me. The relief I felt at that moment was overwhelming - I thought he had been the first to be buried, I had seen it happen. Then, over Cliff's shoulder I saw the other three - they had made it to the bottom. We were all alive - and, what was even more miraculous, all unburied.

* * *

I have never fully understood what happened that day. There has never been an adequate explanation for why the snow, against all probability, against its own momentum and vastness and violence, stopped dead in the middle of the slope. Perhaps all the trees created a log jam, but the slope itself was clear, and there was nothing there that would impede the snows forward motion. Perhaps trees were driven into the snow at such an angle that they slowed the forward motion of the avalanche. But it was traveling at tremendous speed, and it was only seconds before it fell from the top of the mountain and reached us. I had experienced the sensation of time slowing down. I have no idea of how long the event actually lasted, but it couldn't have been more than mere seconds.

One thing was certain. If my boot hadn't slipped from the binding I wouldn't have stopped and looked back up the mountain seeing the snow fracture line break above us, so I wouldn't have been able to warn my guests of the avalanche. Some of them would probably have been caught up in it, and perhaps some would have died. Cliff's life had been saved because his skis were pointed downhill. When he struggled to stand up the wind blast had pushed him ahead of the avalanche.

I have believed for years that nothing happens by chance - it has been proven to me many times - over and over again.

A SAWTOOTH MOUNTAIN RESCUE

There is
no
magic in
miracles.

Snow caves are a good alternative to tents; you don't have to carry them on your back, they are warmer, and best of all, they are totally wind resistant. I will regress here to share a story about a snow cave we built in the Sawtooth Mountains.

In 1971 when Dean Conger of National Geographic came west to write about and photograph Idaho, he contacted us and asked if we would be interested in guiding him - he was interested in back-country skiing and climbing. We set about planning the itinerary and decided we would first climb Mt. Regan in the Sawtooth Mountains, and then, because he had heard about the big Molybdenum mine in White Clouds, we would ski him into the White Cloud Mountains where he could photograph Castle Peak. Norm and I were hoping it would help stop any plans the mining company had of destroying that magnificent mountain.

We wanted to make Dean's trip extraordinary - it was a great honor to be guiding National Geographic. Our goal was to have snow caves ready and waiting - camp one at the base of Mt. Regan and camp two located halfway up the mountain, that we could use in event of bad weather. We set off to make all ready and two days later had completed the caves. We returned to base camp looking forward to a good-night's sleep, planning to return to Stanley the next day.

Snug in our cozy cave of snow we were totally unaware of a blizzard that had arrived sometime in the night, depositing four to five feet of snow atop our cave. Next morning we found the door to the cave had been snowed in. We burrowed through the new-fallen snow and finally came to its end - the world was white and the blizzard was still raging. We searched for our buried skis that we had stuck into the snow the night before, dug them out and once again retreated into our snow cave to wait the storm out.

Ten days later the storm finally moved on, but we had not been idle. We continued carving out our snow cave and had created a mansion, two stories high, with a spiral staircase leading to the second floor. We carved four bedrooms upstairs, downstairs a kitchen, and a room large enough for all of us to gather for conversations and stories.

Dean never got to see the snow caves. I fell ill the night before our scheduled trip and was unable to guide. He couldn't change his schedule and would not go without me as lead guide - the climbing trip was canceled. While he was in Stanley he took a photo of the infamous Stanley Stomp, which graced the cover of the National Geographic issue written on Idaho in 1972.

Ten years later the Stanley Stomp would become infamous, because of a journey two young ladies undertook to join in the fun.

* * *

It was February 1982 in Boise, Idaho, when one Friday afternoon after work two young ladies got in their car and headed for Stanley, Idaho. They were going to take part in what would become the infamous "Stanley Stomp" - a time of great fun, where anything goes and folks come from miles around just to cut loose and shake a leg. They had no idea they were soon to become the main characters in a classic tale of survival.

The young ladies left dressed in their party clothes: blue jeans, cowboy boots, and light weight blue-jean coats and began the mountainous drive on Highway 21 towards Stanley. Part of the highway ran deep, through a steep and narrow canyon, and each year as winter descended, the Department of Highways would close that section of road when they determined it was too dangerous to drive.

When the girls arrived in the small mountain town of Lowman, snow had been falling hard for some time and the highway department had erected a "road closed" sign and set up their barrier for the winter. When the young women arrived at the road barrier they made a perilous and puzzling decision. After some moments of debate and standing in the swirling snow, they leaped back into their car, drove around the barrier and into the dark of Highway 21 - they weren't about to miss their date with Stanley. Up the winding highway they drove, higher and higher, all the while with snow accumulating at over a foot per hour. They managed to drive almost twenty miles when, inevitably, their car could no longer push the heavy snow and got stuck.

They then made their next mistake - another desperate and dangerous decision – they decided they would walk the rest of the way to Stanley, a mere thirty snowy miles away. Apparently, one of their boyfriends told them if they didn't arrive in Stanley by dark on Friday night he would come looking for them on his snowmobile. The girls walked for miles following the path of the highway as the blackness of night descended around them. Finally, terrified and exhausted from fighting the snowy blizzard, for by now four feet of snow had fallen. They sat down in the middle of the road and huddled together for warmth. They sat there surrounded by wailing winds and biting snow, and awaited their rescuer.

He never came.

The folks in Stanley had no knowledge of the folly of these young women until four days later. It was the following

Tuesday when the Sheriff in Lowman called the Sheriff in Stanley, explaining that two young ladies had been reported missing. They hadn't shown up for work Monday morning, or Tuesday, and their families hadn't heard word from them.

The Lowman Sheriff said he had talked to one of the girl's workmates and she remembered over-hearing a phone conversation Friday last, mentioning something about the Stanley Stomp. He had also spoken with someone in Lowman who noticed a car late Friday, after dark, passing through the barrier and heading up the highway towards Stanley.

Continuing on with his story, he said that on Monday afternoon a rescue group from Lowman had attempted to snowmobile up the highway towards Stanley to see if they could find the girls, or at least their car, but by that time five or six feet of snow had fallen and large avalanches were rushing down the mountainsides onto the road. The avalanche activity had become too dangerous for the searchers to continue on. It was still snowing as he finished his story.

The Stanley Sheriff relayed the message to my friend David Kimpton, who was the Sawtooth Forest Ranger at that time. David gathered up a group of people with snowmobiles, a Thycol snow-crawler that belonged to the Harrah Company, and because I was experienced with avalanche, he asked me to join the rescue mission.

At that time I owned a Larven. The Larven was made in Sweden and was similar to a snowmobile but much lighter and had no runners to turn with, the rider wore his skis using them as leverage to turn the machine. The group gathered on Highway 21, just down the road from my cabin, about 12:30 in the afternoon on Tuesday, and, because the Larven was slower than the snowmobiles we lifted it onto the bed of the Thycol. We all packed up and started down the highway, hoping to find the young women who had been missing for four days and nights. Between Friday, when the girls started on their trek to Stanley, and Tuesday afternoon, the storm had laid down about eight feet of snow.

Snowmobiles are very efficient in snow, unless there is a lot of it. The Thycol, on the other hand, has no problem plowing through deep snow, but top speed is only about seven miles per hour. The snow was deep for the snowmobiles so they tried following the Thycol, running in its tracks, but at the speed of the Thycol, the snowmobiles all started overheating. The drivers revved their machines and flew past the Thycol one behind the other, attempting to stay on top of the snow, but they didn't get far before the first machine buried itself deep in the snow and was stuck. One machine after another would take the lead only to be buried, as the machine before had been, until all were stuck deep in the snow.

We had no time to lose, so we unloaded the Larven and I went ahead to see what I could find. The Larven was so light it was floating on top of the snow and I was making good time. I went over Blind Summit and started down the road to Lowman where it wanders through a canyon with steep slopes on both sides of the road. It was not long before I came to the first of many avalanches that had piled up on the highway. My Larven had served me well for shuttling food into the ski huts, and it proved as worthy in this snow-laden canyon. It easily climbed over the debris and piles of snow, and I continued on. Watching constantly for any sign of avalanche, I found myself in an area with a steep slope high above the highway that hadn't slid yet. It was too dangerous to drive the Larven under the potential slide area because I was alone, and if I was caught in an avalanche the rescuers wouldn't even know where to begin looking.

Frustrated, I turned around and rode back to find Kimpton and Steve Cole - they had made good time in the Thycol and weren't far behind. I told them about the slide area that I would have to cross, turned a Peeps on, explained how to use it, and handed it to them. I went on ahead crossing the avalanche area safely, and continued down the highway on my Larven. The storm had passed and the temperatures were dropping rapidly - it was going to get really, really cold. If these young women were still alive, they had to be found soon.

I was looking for a large mound of snow on the highway, big enough to look like a car buried under the snow. A short time later, in the middle of the road, I passed a hole in the snow with an opening about two feet in circumference. I was going quite fast because the sky was getting dark, and the situation desperate. I managed to stop about 20 feet beyond the hole, got off the machine and skied back. I had seen holes similar to this in snow before, at the den of a hibernating bear, and also a squirrel that was nesting. I knew before I looked what I would see deep down at the bottom. I could only hope that I would find the two women alive and conscious. I bent down on my knees and looked into the darkness of the cave and there they were - two young ladies sitting on wet pavement six feet down.

They were alive.

"Are you OK?" I yelled. They looked up at me and I could see relief flood through them - after four days of being trapped in their cave they had given up hope of being saved. They stood up, frantically trying to climb out of the snow that had formed round them, but it was far too deep. I reached down and pulled them out.

Later, I learned that they had walked through snow that was waist deep until they were so exhausted they could go no further and they sat down hugging each other sharing what little body heat they could. It was snowing so hard and heavily they were covered with snow almost at once. Their body heat had melted the snow that fell on them, forming a snow cave around them, at once their prison and their salvation. The snow had saved their lives.

When I managed to pull them up out of the snow cave they, and their clothes, were soaking wet from melted snow. They were dazed and suffering from hypothermia. Having no spare clothes with me, I gave them my coat and wind pants, trying to warm them as best I could. Fortunately, at that moment I saw Kimpton and Steve making their way down the road in the Thycol. It had a heater inside and we were able, between the three of us, to get them out of their wet clothes and dry them out. We wrapped them in wool blankets, radioed for an ambulance to meet us in Stanley, and started back with two very lucky young women. They had survived.

They had frost bite on their feet and elsewhere on their bodies, but considering the length of their ordeal, physically they were in fair condition. The mental trauma they had gone through, on the other hand, was intense, and that took time to over-come. It is hard to imagine these two young women and what they suffered in those terrible days and nights. Over the years when I have thought on this story I have wondered from where they pulled their strength to endure.

They had been saved by the snow which had protected and isolated them from the wind and cold temperatures outside of the cave. If it hadn't snowed so much, so quickly, they would not have survived the first night. The snow cave was a gift - it was their savior, and had kept them alive for four days and four nights

If we hadn't found them when we did they wouldn't have survived the fifth night - that night the temperature dropped to fifteen degrees. If we hadn't had the Thycol and the Larven they wouldn't have survived, for snowmobiles were unable to break through the deep snow to find them.

Is all of this coincidence? I don't think so.

I have it from a good source that "He watches over the lost and wandering."

"GOD'S DOG"

Courage
opens doors
that might
otherwise
never
open.

David Kimpton, who was the leader of the rescue of the two young women who went missing on their way to the Stanley Stomp, had been my friend 'forever'. I remember well the first time we met in this life. It was at the Rod and Gun Club in Stanley, Idaho, the year was 1970. I walked into the club for a beer and David was sitting at the bar. I sat down beside him. "Can I buy you a drink?" I asked.

"Does a bear shit in the woods?" he laughed. I laughed too - it was the first time I had heard that reply and I liked him instantly, his laugh was infectious. In those days I was looking for a friend who wasn't associated with Robinson Bar Ranch. I had plenty of friends at the ranch, but none that I could discuss my favorite subject with. In those days spiritual conversations were rare, even taboo in some circles. With Kimpton I discovered I was talking to a kindred spirit.

"How do you like your new job?" I asked.

"I love it - Stanley is the most beautiful place in the world," he replied.

"You must have good karma." Karma was my key word. Some people didn't know anything about karma, some thought it was funny - but there were those rare moments you would meet someone who would instantly relate. Such was the case with David, and we instantly became life-long friends, again.

He raised an eyebrow - "Must be. What about you, do you love it here too?" We spent the rest of the evening talking, and over the years we had many wonderful conversations, mostly about how to find God, and the discussions were always enhanced by a half-gallon of wine. When the spiritual conversation lagged, we shared experiences that had occurred in our lives. Both of us loved a good story.

God's Dog is David's story. It's about his adventure with a coyote during his time with the Forest Service in Mountain City, Nevada. I believe what he achieved there should be ranked up there with a solo attempt of Mt. Everest. What he accomplished goes well beyond what would enter the mind of most people. David reached into a new dimension, he reached down into his soul and found a power that is available to everyone and brought it into reality.

I have taken some liberties with his story. I attempt to tell it from the point of view of the coyote as well as trying to get into the mind of Ranger Dave. As the story will prove, David doesn't think like most people. But I have known him forever and if I miss the mark on what he thought and accomplished, I know he will understand, and I have been told that the coyote loves his story.

I wish I had been there. I wonder if I would have had the courage to do what David did - I would like to think so.

* * *

He could smell the spoiled meat from a great distance. The air was pure and fresh, and strong odors travel far in the heat of the desert. He lived in the high deserts of Nevada, a desolate country, with hot windy days and icy cold nights, where food was not scarce but it was hard to find, and harder to catch. The desert doesn't relinquish its food easily, and he had eaten only mice in the last few days - he had used a lot of energy finding

310

his food and was hungrier than he had been in a long time. He not only had to provide for himself, but back in his den a family of five patiently awaited his return and the food he would be bringing them.

Turning into the wind he followed the scent and soon came to its source - it was a piece of meat covered with dirt and flies. He circled the meat several times sniffing the earth, determining whether it was safe. He had learned to be careful as he was constantly being hunted. He had been shot at more than once and was suspicious of anything that could be achieved easily. Satisfied that no humans had been, or presently were in the area, he hesitantly reached out with his paw to touch the rancid meat and drag it closer. His first tentative move was not enough and he grew bolder pawing harder at the meat. Instantly the ground exploded violently. In terror he sprang attempting to run away, but was abruptly thrown to the ground on his back with a searing pain spreading through his leg. With all his strength he fought frantically to get away - he jumped in every direction, only to have his body thrown over and over again onto the ground.

He had been caught in the steel teeth of a deadly coyote trap. The trap was fastened to a chain that connected to an iron bar which had been driven deep into the ground. His desperate efforts only caused the trap to cut deeper into his flesh, tearing muscles and ligaments. Soon the trap had cut to the bone. The pain was unbearable and feeling a sense of defeat, the coyote spent the rest of the hot, dry day worrying the ground around the stake that held the trap. The stake had been driven two feet into the ground with a splitting ax and he could not make it budge. Digging down two feet with only one paw was an impossible task and he soon grew weak and helpless from the ordeal. He thought of his mate and his pups who were awaiting his return - he thought of how the pups would leap and jump licking his face and tugging at whatever tender meat he carried in his mouth. He desperately wanted that thought to become his reality.

Coyotes mate for life. He and his mate had found each other last fall and hunting together made life easier. They spent the winter living off mice and rabbit and when they were lucky, which was wasn't often, they caught a larger animal. It had been a hard winter - the snow came early and didn't leave until mid-April just before their pups were born. The pups were eight-weeks old now and big enough to have a ravenous appetite, he and his mate spent all their time hunting to keep them fed. A coyote will eat anything. Their diet consists mostly of rabbit, prairie dog, and mice, but they will supplement with birds, grasshoppers, snakes, frogs, sheep, lame or sick cows and fruit if they can find it. Occasionally, when joined with others of their kind, they will hunt larger game and might catch a deer, usually selecting the old or injured, or a fawn. Life is not easy on a coyote and once they become adults they spend most of their time searching for food.

Yet life is good to them in many other ways - they are free to hunt and roam at will and they have learned how to survive by working together. They are an extremely intelligent animal and they live their lives with dignity and are respected by most humans for their cunning. The Indians called the coyote God's Dog, sometimes the Song Dog, and revered him as such. They believed that the moon rose from the earth and only God's Dog could call it forth, with his song.

When her mate hadn't returned by dark she left the pups in their den and climbed a ridge to call him. She stood there for a few minutes sniffing the air hoping to catch his scent and when she couldn't she gave out a mournful wail. No creature on earth can compare with the 'song dog' and their ability to sing of the injustice that exists in the world. She was several miles from him but he recognized her voice and he returned the call. Earlier he had been afraid of making a sound for fear of drawing attention to himself, but now that it was dark he yelped and howled without reluctance. His voice told her something was wrong, and she moved swiftly toward the sound of his call, but not in a straight line, she circled and came downwind checking for danger as she went to him.

As she drew close she hesitated, sniffing the air to be certain that he was alone, and continued on. She found him pinned to the ground and in so much pain that he had quit struggling and had quit digging in the rocky soil. He was overjoyed to see her and she greeted him with a wet tongue encouraging him to follow her, but he was unable - he could struggle no longer that day. He couldn't go and she couldn't stay. She was worried about her pups - her first responsibility even over her own life was to them, and she had to return to the den. She came to him for one final touch, nuzzling him and licking his eyes, staying by his side as long as she could. Then with whimpers of sorrow, with her tail between her legs and her head down, she left.

The eagle, the cougar, the wolf and the coyote, which have lost their mate, all die, it is said - of a broken heart.

Her parting from him was like the last breath of his life going out, and he had no power left to bring it back. He lay there waiting for death. As the cold of evening came and found him alone, helpless, and in terrifying pain, his throat as dry as desert sand, he gave himself up, waiting for the painfully slow darkness of death to take him. If he were lucky the trapper would come soon and put an end to his suffering.

The trapper was experienced at his trade - he had to be to catch a coyote. The coyote is the smartest of all predators, they have attained such a status because they have been harassed and persecuted since man first started competing with them for space. The trapper had cleverly dug a shallow hole just big enough for the trap. He had taken great care to hide his human odor, covering his boots and clothes and much of himself with the blood and guts of a cow that had been butchered for food. He carefully baited the trap with raw meat and covered it with a very thin layer of fine loose dirt and grass. To hide the last traces of his human smell he poured blood on everything he had touched, including the ground he had walked on. He had done a good job - the coyote was caught. Now all he had to do was return to the trap, shoot the coyote, skin him and collect the bounty. But this trapper was an insensitive and lazy human who didn't check his traps until he got around to it.

It was a weekend and David Kimpton, the Forest Service Ranger out of Mountain City Nevada at that time, had filled his old World War II Jeep with gas and headed to the mountains, intent on spending the day exploring the back country. The country was not only desolate, it was barren of people - few found it worth their attention. Those who spent time there were either prospectors looking to get rich, hunters looking to get fed, or trappers looking to make a sparse living. The country is filled mostly with sagebrush, jackrabbits, rattlesnakes and lizards. Some of the visitors would see the subtle beauty of the desert - hear the doleful wailing of the coyote and, if lucky might even see one off in the distance.

Ranger Dave was more sensitive than the average person. He probably got that way because he spent most of his life in wild places, some desolate, others spectacular. David loved the desert and not only worked in it, five days a week, but spent his free time just enjoying its quiet and solemn beauty. The longer he lived in the desert of Nevada the more he had grown to love it. It must have been destiny that brought the ranger and the coyote together. In all those thousands of square miles of wilderness David came walking down the very ridge that the coyote lay suffering on.

The coyote was aware of David long before David knew the coyote was there. When he first smelled the dreaded human scent he had lain there tense and quiet, not moving, trying to become one with the brush and dry grass around him. But as the scent grew stronger so did his fear, until finally he could stay still no longer, and renewed his futile attempts for freedom. He lunged and fought with the last of his strength, strength that was created by love - love brought by memories of running free through desert flowers and rainbows with his mate at his side, enjoying life only as the wild creatures can.

The coyote's jumps and leaps caught David's eye - he wasn't certain if he had really seen something or if the shadow that ran across his eye was only in his mind. The coyote lay just behind a low rise on the ridge and all that David had seen was the flash of the coyote's body as he jumped in the air and reached the apex of the jump. As he grew nearer the site and the frantic leaping continued, he could tell it was an animal but he couldn't begin to comprehend what was happening. When he cleared the rise he was no more than fifteen feet from the helpless animal. The sight stunned him and a sweeping revulsion crept through him like a cold winter wind - the cold wind blew on the embers of his anger and blew the anger into a fury.

When the coyote saw David come over the ridge he quit his useless struggle and lay down to await his fate. As David got closer to the coyote, he could tell by the scat and the swollen and torn leg that the coyote had been there for three or four days and his fury fueled to rage. David believed in the brotherhood of all things, and because of his feelings, the sight of the helpless and suffering creature created a combination of compassion and disgust in him. Compassion for his animal brother, and disgust for his human brother who had so little respect for life. It was beyond his understanding that a human would not only take a life but would rob it of all dignity, leaving it to lie in its own scat and urine to die from thirst and infection, shock and pain. The first thought that crossed his mind was how he could put the poor wretched beast out of its misery. He had no weapon and he was physically powerless to kill it.

The solution came from deep down, deep within his heart. Filled with emotion he decided he would find a way to set the coyote free. It seemed impossible, but that was what he was going to do - he felt it his duty and with passion he tended his thoughts on how to achieve his goal. He was *committed.*

If he were going to accomplish this feat he knew he would have to think like an animal - he would have to use his intuition, he would have to tap all the power that he had within himself. He would have to be more than human, he would have to draw on his inner self, and he would have to communicate with the animal using the language of nature, the language of the universe.

He started by talking to the coyote, not the way he would talk to a fellow human but the way he would talk to the sun, or a tree. He talked quietly and gently, he talked with the breath of a gentle wind. He looked deep into the golden eyes of God's Dog and told him that he was there to save him. He had come to set him free, free to be wild, free to hunt for his family, free to call the moon from its sleeping place beneath the earth. As he whispered to the coyote he moved closer, but his movement was imperceptible. He moved slowly like grass growing. He moved breathing their oneness, acknowledging their brotherhood. It took him almost an hour to travel the fifteen feet that separated them - it was an eternity before he was close enough to touch the animal. In all that time the coyote had remained motionless, never taking his eyes off David. He had lain like a rock patiently awaiting the centuries to pass.

The trap was a double-sided spring loaded affair and was covered with blood and rust. The springs were in the handles, one on each side of the jaws. To set it a man had to compress both sides. Usually he held one side down with his knee and the other with one hand, then he would carefully reach into its mouth with the other and set the hair trigger - a feat that required skill and care. David had never set a trap and only had a basic understanding of how they worked, but he knew he had to apply a great deal of pressure to the spring to get it to open. What he didn't know was that in order for the trap to open completely he must apply pressure on both springs. He stood there for an eternity studying the situation, trying to decide how to best accomplish the miracle he had set for himself. He was pleased that he had gotten this close to the animal without it going crazy with fear. He looked into the coyote's eyes, trying to read what emotions the animal felt - trying to determine if he would cooperate and not attack him when he attempted to open the trap.

Very slowly, like the stars move across the sky, he lifted his left foot above the left spring of the trap and lowered it onto the spring. He shifted his weight to the spring handle and gratefully felt the tension in the jaws relax. When he transferred his full weight to the spring he expected it to open, but realized too late that to fully open it he had to squeeze both sides down. He found he was unable to move his right foot because he was off balance. In order to move he would have to remove his foot entirely and start over from a different position.

The coyote had felt the pressure being released from his paw, but he had never taken his eyes off David. He heard his soothing words and had grown accustomed to his slow movements. However, as David slowly shifted his weight off the spring he felt the pressure increase and the searing pain returned with a rush. The coyote jumped into the air trying to rid himself of the whole horrifying situation. When he jumped David jumped with him - the coyote jumped up and David jumped back - he started running and didn't stop running until he was on top of the ridge again. He stopped and spun around hoping to see the coyote gone and the ordeal finished, but it was not to be - the coyote was still there. The getting-acquainted half of the relationship had gone on for more than an hour, but the separation happened like a lightning bolt and he hoped it was not permanent.

Again, with his patience renewed, David started over. This time he moved a bit faster, and he moved with more confidence. When he was about five feet from the coyote he sat down, trying to reestablish their rapport. He told the coyote about humans - he told him that there were many people who were good and loved all living beings. He told him that the Indians called him the Song Dog, God's Dog, and he had heard their stories of how the coyote created all the tribes of Indians who live on the earth. He told him that many people tried to protect coyotes. He told him that others were aware of their kinship and cherished it as something sacred. He told him he was one of those people and he wanted to set him free to roam and sing - to set him free so that people could hear him sing to the sky, so that men and women would be inspired to live free themselves.

After David's wild flight, the coyote had lain back down with his uninjured paw lying across the trapped one, and he was resting his head on top of his crossed legs. This time David moved in close - close enough that he could put one foot at a time on both sides of the trap. Again in cautious slow motion he put his left foot on the left spring and felt the tension released, then with care not to lose his balance, he placed his right foot on the other spring and applied his weight to it. The trap opened - the coyote was free to jump and run - but he didn't move, he lay there between David's feet, his paw in the trap.

David stood in confusion. Now what? He couldn't stay there forever, and he couldn't let the trap close on the paw again.

What David did next took tremendous courage, but his compassion pushed his fear from his mind. He reached down and gently placed his fingers under the powerful jaw, and slowly lifted the coyote's head off his paw. The coyote didn't resist. He placed the coyote's head on his boot and removed his hands from under the coyote's jaw. Again he expected the coyote to bolt, but again he didn't move, except to raise his eyelids and look up into David's eyes. David took a deep breath, reached down and carefully lifted the good paw off the other and placed it to the side. There was still no resistance and again the coyote was content to lay there, his head resting on David's boot, his paw in the trap. The paw in the trap was ugly - festered and helpless. It was a horrible sight - covered with dirt, dried blood and freshly bleeding blood from the latest struggle.

What the hell am I doing here? David asked himself. It's the question asked by a climber who finds himself on a rock face with nowhere to go and his legs turned into sewing machines. Just like the climber has no choice but to move, or fall, David had no choice but to make the next decision. He was afraid if he touched the wounded paw, the coyote, out of pain, would attack him and the best he would come out with was a lacerated hand, maybe even scars on his face to remind him of the time he was crazy enough to try to rescue a coyote. He was also afraid if the coyote snapped at him he would instinctively jump and the powerful jaws of the trap would snap shut on the paw again. He steeled himself - he was determined to remove the paw and not panic, no matter what happened.

He had come this far and he knew if he failed now he would not get another chance. Cautiously he bent down, slowly he slid his hand under the damaged paw and with great care started to lift it out of the trap.

The coyote turned his head and followed the hand with his sad golden eyes - he watched as the hand lifted his mangled paw and lay it aside. David had accomplished what he had set out to do - the coyote was free. He was free but he remained motionless, he lay there staring at the empty trap. David didn't move either - the coyote's head was still lying on his boot where he had placed it. They stayed in that position for several minutes, neither of them understanding what had happened, both wondering what would happen next.

David was the first to move. He calmly lifted the head with the long ears and golden eyes off his boot - this time the coyote held his head up. David took his weight off the trap and let it close. He stepped back and sat down again. Their eyes met - they looked deeply within each other, both trying to understand the other, trying to understand the relationship they had established. They sat there, the coyote and the ranger, sharing a bond that seldom happens between the wild ones and man. They were still close enough to touch, and David moved his hand to the coyote's head and caressed it. He felt the soft long hair - it was as soft as down and the colors of fall. It was yellow and brown, mixed with white, gold and red, tipped with black. He caressed the tawny ears. He was overwhelmed by the trust the animal displayed. They stayed together like that, touching with hand and eye, sharing feelings that sprang from their souls.

David was the first to leave. He rose from the ground quietly and slowly backed away, unwilling to break the bond that they shared. Nothing in this world lasts forever, and he turned and walked away. When he reached the top of the rise he looked for a last good-bye. The coyote still had not moved.

The Indians tell of animals giving themselves up. They claim that an animal knows when it is his time to die, and because of their noble spirit they accept death as part of living. Before David had arrived, the coyote had given himself up and had waited for death. Now that he was free he still wasn't certain that he wanted to live. But memories of his life came back, and thoughts of his mate and family crowded out all thoughts of death. As David watched from the top of the knoll the coyote lifted himself up and limped away. The coyote had gone some distance before he stopped and looked back. Perhaps it was his way of saying thanks, or perhaps he felt hope for the creatures that walk upright. One of them at least knew the order of things, one knew about the oneness of the universe. If there was One, maybe there was hope.

On a ridge in the distance a coyote called - it was his mate. David could see her silhouetted against the sky. The coyote lifted his head high - he could feel life return again and with his useless paw hanging at his side, he limped into the future and the promises the ranger had made. He was free again and going home to the healing warmth of his den - going home to be greeted by his pups and the love of his mate.

* * *

David couldn't help but think about the events that occurred that day. His anger toward the trapper had mellowed a little - after all, the incredible event would not have happened if it weren't for the trapper. Setting the coyote free had been a water-shed event but he still wanted to teach the insensitive trapper a lesson.

David has a sense of humor unlike anybody I have ever known. His humor returned and in it was a diabolical solution. He scrambled around the north side of the ridge until he found the trunk of an ancient tree that looked like it had been hit by lightening, or been in a fire. He picked up a splinter of the tree that was fire charred - it was about ten inches long and five inches wide. He sanded it against a granite rock until it was smooth, flat and white. He reached into his pocket and retrieved his pocket knife and carved a message to the trapper.

He went back to the trap and again he opened it and he placed the wood in the jaws of the trap and closed the teeth on the wood - the message rose above the trap and would be painfully clear when the trapper read it. David looked at his handy work, and he was well pleased. As he left he brushed away all sign of his ever being there. He turned and as he walked off the ridge I could hear him laughing. I can still hear him laughing. He was laughing because of the message he left behind:

DO NOT MESS
WITH MY DOG!

GOD

He laughed again when he wondered if, like Moses, the trapper would carry the tablet off the mountain, and share it with other trappers down below.

That evening, if you listened very carefully, you could hear the coyote calling the moon from beneath the earth.

PART THREE

THE VEIL OF TIME

TRANSITIONS

*Chasing the
Elusive Summits.*

Life can be extreme. Leaving the world of constant adrenalin for a life of quiet contemplation makes for an enormous change, and it is hard. There is so much one must be willing to give up. Yet at some point even the most energetic person gets older, and there is no choice but to face this change, and try as best as one can to embrace it. The question basically becomes *what* to replace the hunger for adventure *with*. Distraction and ever-diminishing pleasures are one possible road. The other is to take all that one has acquired over the years, all the experiences and setbacks and achievements, all the heaven and all the hell, and to extract from this undifferentiated mass of raw *life,* the lessons it has to teach.

Everything that passed before in my own life had led me to this moment, driving me inward. The time had come for me to make sense of it all – everything that I had seen, had lived, had been. The awareness of something greater than myself had been sleeping silently in the background and was forcing itself to wakefulness. I was facing the highest mountain I would attempt to climb, and truth be known, it was the most difficult obstacle I had ever faced – that of my own ego. It had been born through a need to survive, a desperate will to continue and preserve itself. Desertion, self-preservation, vanity and death had been its sires, and it had clung to its very existence with pitiful and frantic fear.

I once read a story about a team of courageous young men who set themselves to climb Hkakabo Razi, thought to be Southeast Asia's tallest mountain. Mark Jenkins, one of those young men, said something that was quite stunning, and I instantly recognized myself in his words:

"All serious mountaineers have big egos. You cannot take on risks and constant suffering of big mountains without one. We may talk like Buddhists, but don't be fooled, we're hard-driving narcissists."

Up to this point my life had been one physical exertion after another, but I was aging and my body could no longer endure the extreme measure that I exacted from it. It was time for acceptance. It seemed that destiny was playing its hand yet again, and my inward search for true meaning found fertile ground.

"Our greatness lies not so much
 in being able to remake the world,
 as in being able to remake our selves."
Gandhi

But how does one transition from self-love to an inclusive love that concerns all of life? In the search for the answer to this question, my life continued to unfold, as it always had, and always will.

The change *was* great, but I discovered new passions and rekindled old ones. I became involved in environmental issues, pursued photography, and chose to spend my time in service, helping others and sharing my expertise when asked for. What I found was renewed joy, purpose, and awareness.

I read books, and then more books, on spiritual growth and awareness - and I still do. *The Course in Miracles* has claimed my mornings and sets my course for the day. I have studied it with the same fervor and persistence in which I have climbed my mountains. I still falter, but always come back to my belief in *Oneness*, and I try to live by that standard. There is no moment in my past I would change, nothing I would take back. These moments are, after all, my reason for *being*. I can only hope that I have lived, and that I am living, in such a way as to be worthy of this gift of life.

PEOPLE OF THE SIERRA MADRE, MEXICO

Simple folk
have problems
that
they solve in
their own
mystical ways.

I remember awaking one night in a snow cave that I had built for our guests, high in the Sawtooths. We often built such snow caves as temporary way-stations between one hut and another, and sometimes we would spend the night in them. They keep their temperature remarkably well, and are, in the right conditions, comfortable homes for the dark hours. Once we built a snow cave into an enormous snow drift that had gathered against a rock wall. The drift stood some forty-feet high and by the time we had finished our cave it had become a veritable ice hotel, three stories high and with a spiral staircase going from each floor to the next.

On this night the snow cave in question was much more modest. It had been built to accommodate just a few people. It was part of my responsibility to wake each night and to check the ceilings of these caves, to make sure that the heat of the sleepers and the warmth and humidity of their breath was not causing the cave to slump. I would awake some four or five times each night, lift my hand into the pure blackness above me, and seek the ceiling. And so I lifted my hand above my face - and felt just inches from my nose the ceiling of the cave. I would have to rise now, and wake our guests; it was necessary to dig everything out once again. And I thought to myself, I'm not having any fun...

That was the end of my guiding career.

In 1987 Sheila and I made the decision that it was, once again, time to move on. We sold our cabin on Crooked Creek, and closed our business. We began spending our winters in Alamos, Sonora, Mexico, in the foothills of the Sierra Madre Mountains, where Sheila's parents owned a beautiful orange grove in the countryside. I took to my cameras, intent on filming the people of the Sierra Madre. I hired Manuel Sanchez, a friend of the family, as a guide and interpreter to lead me into the mountains. He spoke good English and knew all the roads that led into the back-country and into the villages. During the three winters that we traveled together he became invaluable, particularly in helping me avoid the marijuana growers, who had little use for gringos stumbling unknowingly through their territory.

Each winter Manuel led me deep into the mountains and explained to me the history of the Mayo Indian, whose lives were changing rapidly, and whose native language was disappearing. He patiently convinced the Mayo Indians to let me take their photographs - no easy task, as some of them believed that a photograph would steal their soul. We would drive for hours on rugged back-roads to reach a village, where I would take hundreds of photographs of the people and then return to our casita in Alamos, sometimes very late into the night. I would then spend a week developing 8x10 black and white photographs and return to the village giving each family, or person, their own photograph, in some small way to repay them for the kindness and generosity they had shown me.

Word had passed around the villages about the gringo with his camera. When Manuel and I drove into a village the whole population would come to meet us. It was always a thrill for them to receive a photograph of themselves or their children, but not as great as the gift was to me. I always let Manuel distribute the photographs so I could watch their faces as they received their treasures, for some the photos were the first they had ever seen of themselves.

We returned one day to a very remote village we had visited some weeks before. There was a beautiful young woman I had photographed and I watched as Manuel handed her picture. She looked at it expressionless, neither a smile nor frown on her face. She turned it upside down and then sideways, then she turned it over and looked at the blank back of it. When this happened I asked Manuel what she was looking for. He shrugged his shoulders and said, "*No se*, maybe she don't like it." All the people in the village gathered round trying to see the photograph, they all seemed as perplexed as she was. Suddenly, one of the villagers exclaimed, "Mira! Mira!" One by one a look of wonder fell on their faces and they began to yell incomprehensible words, laughing and grinning as they pointed at the photograph. I didn't know what to make of it, I couldn't tell if they liked it or not.

When we returned to the States that spring, I was telling an anthropologist the story about the strange behavior of these mountain people, and he explained that if you have never seen a black and white photograph, at first glance all you see are shades of gray. It takes a few minutes to actually see the image on paper. These events left me to ponder, and I have asked myself many times since: is it possible that awareness is required, to see reality through the shades of gray surrounding us? We are all so accustomed to these things that we have lost the wonder of them; but there, in Mexico, even a simple black and white image could be the source of marveling. I believe that we all can find the marvelous in the simple things in life, if we seek to return to a basic and truthful perception of them.

I distributed literally hundreds of photographs through the mountains in my years there, and have often wondered if they still hang in their little adobe homes. I like to think that some record of my time there remains still, a humble adornment for a humble people.

The Indians in the small mountain communities were an extremely self-sufficient and generous people. If you were invited into their home they always asked you to sit with them for a meal, or cup of coffee. As poor as many of them were they would, without exception, serve tortillas, beans, coffee, goat cheese, and dried meat if there was any to be had.

In the 1980's, in this part of Mexico, most of the homes in the villages had no electricity, but there was always a small store on the road leading into the village that had access to electricity where you could purchase basic items. You could usually find a refrigerator filled with cool Coca-Cola and *cerveza*. Their homes were very small, had no windows, and were made of adobe with earthen floors. Their cooking stoves, were usually built outside the house under a veranda, they were crude constructions made of adobe. The local mesquite wood provided fuel for cooking and warmth on cold winter mornings. A strong smell of mesquite permeated the air, a smell that can never be forgotten. They planted fields of corn and bean, enough for the whole village, and small gardens provided them with vegetables, some of which they sold in the nearest markets. They raised goats and butchered them, cutting the meat into thin slices where they hung from the kitchen ceiling to be dried.

They were happy people and seemed content with the simplicity of their lives. They loved their children and sent them off each day to school, all dressed in their best clothes, clean white crisp shirts on the boys and colored day dresses on the girls. I remember, one day, watching a young boy pushing his brother to school in a wheelbarrow. Later I learned that the boy in the wheelbarrow had deformed legs and could not walk. His brother pushed him each day to school so he would not miss out on the education they were all given. They all worked together as one, accepting their lot, finding joy in their community.

One day we drove down a rise into one of the tiny villages. The smoke from mesquite hung in the air like fog and I could see a crowd hovering around the door of one of the small adobe homes, everyone struggling to look through its small door. The family had recently placed winning numbers on their lottery ticket and with their new found fortune had purchased a generator, satellite and brand new television set. All were there to see, many for the first time, what the world had to offer outside of their beautiful mountain village. I felt unsettled at the sight and could not help but question the changes this new technology would bring to the people living in their quite simplicity, and if it would be the beginning of the end of their beautiful and peaceful lives. These questions became more pressing the more that I saw of their customs and traditional ways.

Manuel and I were once invited to a family reunion. We started into the mountains early one morning, winding through the valleys planted with ajonjoli and beans, driving through river beds that flooded with summer rains, and passing old haciendas falling in disrepair, their dreams abandoned. When we arrived at the home where the reunion was being held, it was bustling with activity. Manuel told me that in the early morning hours before sun-up the pig had been put to roast on a spit and had been cooking throughout the day. They had prepared it well in advance of the celebration, feeding it with a special food they said would make it fat and juicy.

I was invited to sit with the men in a large circle and because I was the guest of honor I was seated next to the patriarch. The men were telling stories from the good old days and drinking cold *cervezas*. From where I was seated I could watch the preparation of the banquet and finally, after what had seemed hours, the first course was served by a beautiful *señorita*. With a silver platter, held high over her head, she carried the hors d'oeuvres, presenting them with pride. She reminded me of a waitress in an elegant French restaurant in New York City where I had once eaten years ago.

They were a humble people, proud of their country and their village and they wanted to share it with this strange gringo who took pictures. Following their traditions, as the guest of honor, I was the first to be served. As the lovely *señorita* lowered the platter for me to select my choice of meat, I could see that the beautiful silver platter had magically turned into a Chevrolet hubcap. The meat selections consisted of pig intestines cut into lengths, each about ten inches long. As hungry as I was it was all I could do to look at the lengths of hard red intestines, much less eat them. Manuel had trained me well and I knew that I could not refuse their gift, because in so doing I would have lost their respect and my position as the guest of honor.

Accepting my status, I slowly selected a piece from the top of the pile and tried to break it in half. It was like trying to break a bicycle tire in half and I struggled, striving to turn ten inches of pig intestine into five inches. I heard my host clear his throat and there was silence around the table. I looked over my shoulder at him and watched as his finger pointed to the sky, slowly moving it back and forth. There was no question about his meaning so I took possession of all ten inches of my little piece of heaven, and bit off the end. It was, without doubt, the worst tasting thing I had ever put in my mouth. I felt sick to my stomach and cringed at the thought that there were still nine inches left to go.

"How you like it?" my host asked in broken English.

"Bueno, muy bueno, perfecto!" I replied, trying not to gag. The taste seemed to improve as I continued to choke the pig intestines down, no doubt, because of the ice cold *cerveza* that appeared in my hand as if by magic, one bottle after another. The *cerveza* was as plentiful as the pile of pig intestine that had been served by the beautiful senorita on her beautiful silver platter.

Later that same year one of the wealthy families living in the mountains said their daughter was going to be married in a few days and they asked Manuel if I would be willing to photograph the wedding. Manuel took me aside and asked if I wanted to take pictures of the wedding.

"Sì, I would like to."

"The family is wealthy, it could be bad not to accept," Manuel replied, with a strange expression on his face.

"Why bad?" I asked.

He hesitated before he answered, "La familia grow mari-wana."

I thought about this and asked, "Would it be dangerous?"

"Sì, muy pelegroso say *no*, better say *sì*."

I had trusted Manuel for three years, he had never let me down.

I said "Si," without hesitation.

We returned to the casita where Sheila and I lived in her parent's orange grove, and I asked her if she wanted to go to the wedding with us. She was delighted and said she would love to go. The next day when Manuel stopped by I asked him if he thought it would be dangerous for Sheila to come with us. I watched his face as he pondered my question, "No problema, las mujeres at the wedding, they make her safe."

The day of the wedding I grabbed my camera equipment and the three of us headed into the mountains to the wedding that awaited us. We waved at our friends as we passed through the small village, driving on to the casa of the bride to be.

The mother of the bride met us on the veranda, introducing herself as Maria. She seemed overjoyed to see us. She took Sheila by the arm and introduced her to the ladies of the family and to the other female guests, insisting that Sheila accompany her as she sauntered through the crowd who had come to share in her happiness.

The father of the bride came out of the house followed closely by a servant with a tray of beer. He introduced himself as Carlos and greeted Manuel with a bear hug while the servant handed each of us an iced beer.

We drank and listened as Carlos gave us a brief history of his family. When his story ended, he took us by the arm and gave us a guided tour of his house and property. Carlos came from a wealthy family and his home had been passed down from son to son. It was an old, old hacienda, one of the most coveted properties for miles around and he carried his pride, as a peacock does its feathers.

He started with the barn, obviously proud of the status it brought to him. He had six beautiful horses in his barn, all were dancing horses, a prized procession in Mexico. I found myself thinking: Yes, he is right to be proud - having this many beautiful, well-cared for and well-trained horses says a thing about a man.

His house was built entirely from adobe. Arch after arch surrounded the inner courtyard, the walls had matching arches, each leading into large beautiful rooms. The inner courtyard was vivid with bougainvillea, pink, red, purple, and white. Huge pots sat in the shadows overflowing with ferns. The rooms were sparsely decorated, but held a sense of antiquity and carried echoes from parties, long ago held, in the days of the Spanish conquerors.

The guests kept arriving - they came in cars, on horseback, some riding mules and many families on foot. The Mariachi band arrived with their instruments riding in the back of an old truck.

The wedding was to be held under the veranda in the courtyard as there was no church in the small village closest to their hacienda. The courtyard was overflowing with people, young people and children sat on the adobe walls, laughing and watching the antics of their elders. Beer was copious and I never saw a man without one in his hand

All the while I moved as a flashing ghost through the crowd taking photographs.

Minutes before the wedding was to take place a car drove through the crowds and stopped at the entrance to the courtyard. The groom stepped from the back door of the car. He was dressed in a dashing Charro suit, all black with silver buttons running down the side of each leg, silver buttons on his jacket, a silver belt buckle, a white ascot neatly tied round his neck. He stood regally, holding a black hat circled with a silver band, his family following close behind. It was hard to imagine how they had all fit in the small car.

The time had come. The musicians lit up their instruments, cleared their throats and began singing and playing classical Mexican music, the kind of music that makes you want to weep upon hearing it, even if you are not of that disposition. The father and his daughter entered the courtyard through one of the arched doorways arm in arm. The bride was hidden behind her veil, a chimaera of beauty. She was dressed in a white gown with fresh flowers woven through her hair, a lovely bouquet in her hand. Her father walked with her, proud and noble, as if he were delivering her to a king.

The darkest of night had fallen as the car arrived to take the newlyweds away. I took pictures of the bride, tears glistening in her eyes, as she walked from the home of her parents for the last time, into the star-lit night. The inexplicable joy of the Mexican people, their romantic and sorrowful music, their mythical religion, and their old-fashioned ways had set the stage for one of the most elegant weddings I had ever attended.

I couldn't get the beautiful hacienda out of my mind and wanted to learn how the people had constructed their earth dwellings, buildings that obviously lasted for decades. One day I stood in the sun and watched as a whole village turned out to help one of the families, who had outgrown their living space, add a bedroom onto their home. Manuel explained to the villagers that I was interested in the techniques of building with earth and would welcome any information they wanted to share with me. They immediately had me join in the project and graciously taught me how to make adobe blocks, how to lay them, and how to apply the final plaster on the walls. And, later, they shared with me the secret ingredient for hardening adobe floors: blood from the animals they had killed for food.

In later years, some of the more prosperous families started building with fired brick. They said it was the new way to build, that it would save time and they would no longer have to patch the plaster on their homes after the monsoon season. It was more modern and they would not be left behind. Many of the villagers who could not afford to build with bricks became jealous of their wealthier neighbors, but soon discovered there was no reason for their jealousy. The thick adobe walls in their small *casitas* were much more efficient and comfortable - warmer in the winter and cooler in the summer. Those who lived in the brick homes were frozen to ice in the winter months and melted like honey in the summer months.

It was during my time in Mexico that I decided the next house I would build for my family would be more sustainable, and built of earth. Once again, my path had been laid down for me.

A LOOK AT THE EARTH IN A SPIRITUAL LIGHT

The fate of our mother
Earth
is in our hands.
Alas,
shepherds
are rare.

I had guided and explored many of rivers and national parks in the western part of the United States, and also into the Arctic. I had fished for salmon in the ocean off Kodiak Island in Alaska and photographed the national parks in Costa Rica and Africa. I had traveled the back-roads of Canada and Mexico and sailed through the Aleutian Islands into the Alaskan Peninsula. I was an environmentalist, and I was distraught with what I saw happening to our planet.

Edward Abbey was alive and well in the minds of all environmentalists, fighting to preserve the natural wonders of the world with stories filled to the brim with anarchy. I fought the only way I knew how, through sharing the natural world with all who would join me on rivers and mountains, and through speaking to audiences who wanted to hear my stories and philosophy about the natural wonders of our world, in both public and corporate venues. I created multi-media programs for The Nature Conservancy, Bureau of Land Management, and my own personal tribute to Idaho, *A Journey into the Sawtooth Wilderness,* which was shown throughout the country.

In 1982 I was asked to speak for the Idaho Conservation League, who is still valiantly fighting to keep Idaho's pristine rivers and lands intact. I kept that speech and will share a few excerpts of it now. It is over thirty years later and my words are as relevant today as they were then. I smile at the memory of my intensity at the time - not that I have changed in my thinking, but that I *attempt* to watch more as a witness now, believing in full faith that all is at it should be, that there is a reason behind the chaos, and that all will be right in the end. Yet, sometime soon, I hope that we will become aware that our quality of life will only get better when we are willing to include all life, not human life alone.

A Look at the Earth in a Spiritual Light – 1982

"The thoughts you will hear tonight are thoughts that come from my heart and the heart of others who have been fortunate enough to see the earth in a spiritual light, and because of that light have come to a deeper understanding of the spiritual power the earth offers to all mankind.

Chief Luther Standing Bear of the Lakota Sioux spoke of his peoples' feelings for the earth:

'He loved the earth and all things of the earth, the attachment growing with age. The old people came literally to love the soil and they sat or reclined on the ground with a feeling of being close to a mothering power. It was good for the skin to touch the earth and the old people liked to remove their moccasins and walk with bare feet on the sacred earth. Their tipis were built upon the earth and their alters were made of earth. The birds that flew in the air came to rest upon the earth and it was the final abiding place of all things that lived and grew. The soil was soothing, cleansing, and healing. That is why the old Indian still sits upon the earth instead of propping himself up and away from its life giving forces. For him to sit or lie upon the ground is to be able to think more deeply and to feel more keenly. He can see more clearly into the mysteries of life and come closer in kinship to other lives about him. The old Lakota was wise. He knew that man's heart away from nature becomes hard; he knew that lack of respect for growing, living things soon led to lack of respect for humans too. So he kept his youth close to its softening influence.'

For millions of years planet earth has been providing for the myriad life forms it holds. In the last 100 years, or a fraction of a second in earth time, man has managed to rip, dig, blast, and tear the earth, pollute the water and air. He has created acid rain, he destroys over 28 million acres of priceless rain forests each year. He has managed to alter the weather and has the power to destroy every living thing that exists, and for the sake of self and greed he might just do it. Many are in denial. They can't foresee the results of what they have wrought.

Our loss of awareness is the manifestation of our separation from earth. The earth is the great teacher. It can teach us about ourselves. Nature can touch your heart and mind and in its touch it can tell you where you have come from and where you are going. It will teach you that life is continuous, that you have no beginning, you have no end. All you have to do is turn your mind to it, to be still and listen.

If you are quiet and listen, the river will tell you that you are part of the universe, the whole. If you take a cup of water from the river and return it, the water will not be identifiable from the whole. It will tell you that even if you drink it or pour it on the ground, it remains as it always has been, part of the river, a part of creation. It will tell you that life is an endless circle and that your body is not separate from the earth. It will tell you that your spirit is part of the universe like the river is part of the sky. That your spirit is eternal.

Those of us that share this philosophy hold the earth sacred far above mans futile striving for material wealth. The economic problems of today would not exist if we understood that an earth undamaged by greed would provide us the necessities of life in abundance. And the necessities of life not only include food, clothing, and shelter, but freedom, joyful living, and a basic understanding of our own continuous existence. These basic God given rights are slipping through our fingers because for generation after generation we have allowed ourselves to become cuckolds of people who only care about money and power. These people continuously tell us that what we need are more gadgets, more toys. They tell us to work harder so we can spend more to keep the good life going. They tell us that we must give up more of the earth's bounty and beauty in order to maintain our way of life.

We don't really want more gadgets and toys. Most of us don't want this way of life, at least not deep down. What we want is more time to experience the beauty of nature, more time with the ones we love, less financial dependency, more free space, and more freedom to enjoy that space. We want to breathe fresh air, to drink pure water, and to feel that we are one with the wildlife and wild places that are left.

As we come to understand that these precious gifts are gifts to be cherished and to hold sacred, all of us will develop a bond with nature and the earth that no advertising gimmick or smooth talking politician can take away.

We are as a group strong. We must overcome the insensitivity, the contempt for nature that is all about us destroying it even as I speak. We must stand united in that responsibility.

The earth is alive, it has its own spirit, and you are one with that spirit."

* * *

My guiding years had come to an end, but my conviction that we could all lead a more sustainable life was strong. I wanted to be involved with like-minded people and knew that with patience something would come along, somewhere I could put my knowledge to good use. The people of the Sierra Madre had pointed me in the direction I was to follow, but I still lacked the occasion to fully realize what they had indicated. But then, as had happened before in life, I found myself in the unlikeliest of places, and working with people that were open to whatever idea I could bring to life, as long as it was sustainable.

5000 YOUNG WOMEN

I will always buy
my share
of Girl Scout cookies
when I can find them.

In 1992 I was hired by the Sahuaro Girl Scout Council in Tucson, Arizona. They needed a Site Manager for their summer camp on Mt. Lemmon, and I fit the bill. Gail Gurney was the director of the Council at that time, a woman of vision and courage, and she was totally dedicated to the young women who participated in Girl Scouts. The camp was nestled in a forest of ancient ponderosa pines and sat at 8,000 feet above sea level.

Sheila, our son, John, and I moved into the camp and set to work. We cleaned and painted buildings, cleaned and burned slash piles, and most importantly, replaced five old and smelly outhouses with five composting toilets. At that time Clivus Multrins were something almost unheard of for use in public facilities, but the Council had committed themselves to all things sustainable, and installed them in every necessary place throughout the camp. The girls wrote and sang songs about how to take care of them. Best of all, the composters worked like magic and we had people from other organizations come to see how they worked and how they might use them in their own camps and public buildings.

They were good years. Our son John went to school in the one-room schoolhouse on Mt. Lemmon and Sheila commuted to Tucson where she worked in Superior Court. The commute was difficult, a climb of 7,500 ft. in a mere 25 miles, and John's school only went only as far as grade five. We loved it on the mountain but knew it was inevitable that we would have to move again, because there were no schools beyond fifth grade there. Not really wanting to leave the Girl Scouts, I decided to share an idea with Gail Gurney that I had been thinking about for quite some time.

During my time in Tucson I had met a gentleman named Motts Myhrman. He told me that he had built a small straw bale house for his mother to live in, small enough that he was able to build it without a permit. It was the first time I had heard of building with straw bale and was intrigued by it. He explained how comfortable it was, cool in the summer and warm in the winter. I had developed a passion for alternative dwellings after living in a yurt and I couldn't help but light up as he talked about the wonders of building with straw bale. Seeing my interest piqued he offered to show it to me. It was small and beautiful. My imagination ran wild.

The Council owned a beautiful piece of property on Sabino Canyon Road; seventeen acres of prime real estate, undeveloped but for one building and a couple of ramadas. On occasion the Girl Scouts would use it for special events, but it sat empty most of the time. Sometimes I was called upon to repair plumbing or electrical problems in the aging building and would walk the property, seeing its potential and imagining what could be created on this unique property. I thought it would be the ideal location for an Environmental Center where the Girl Scouts could learn about their environment, learn how to live sustainably, and take part in the construction of a straw bale building where the site manager would live. They could give tours of the facilities and the Girl Scouts would be recognized for their contributions to the sustainable world.

Gail, as always, was open to anything as long as it would enrich the lives of the Girl Scouts. She approached the Board of Directors with our idea and they wholeheartedly approved it. With the help from Girl Scouts of all ages we built the first permitted straw bale house in Tucson and started improving the property. The building was beautiful when completed and people came from all over to visit it, wanting to learn all they could about how to build a straw bale home of their own.

There was an old shallow well on the property that was badly polluted, so we installed solar panels and a solar pump which sent the well water to a pond and wetland we had built. We filled the wetland with cattails, bulrush and pickerel weed to clean the polluted water. In no time at all the wetlands were attracting all sorts of wildlife - great blue heron, doves, wrens, and ducks; frogs and toads, snakes, and lizards; rabbits and gophers. It was the perfect habitat for dragon flies and damsel flies which took care of the mosquito population. It was magical watching the evolution of habitat occur so rapidly, and most importantly, the girls took great pride in their accomplishments.

In the straw bale house and around the flourishing wetlands, we built furniture out of sandbags, fence posts out of milk bottles, and courtyard walls filled with unwanted trash - old televisions, office equipment, anything that wouldn't rot away, and covered it all with cement stucco.

It is still there and thriving after twenty years. Over the years the Council has continued improving the property as a showpiece for sustainability. It is now home to a new kind of school – a high school for environmental studies, a Sonoran oasis in the midst of suburbia. The Sahuaro Girl Scout Council can forever be proud of the example they set, and I hope that there might be at least one young woman who has been able to fulfill her dream of someday living in a straw bale house of her own.

The years I spent with the Sahuaro Girl Scout Council, the dedicated staff, Girl Scout counselors, and the Girl Scouts themselves, were some of the most enjoyable in my life. I will always be grateful for the trust they put in me, their willingness to listen to new ideas, and for the endless energy and enthusiasm they shared in the creation of them.

When the time was right for it, we moved on, holding fast to our dream of one day building our own straw bale house.

BUILDING WITH EARTH AND STRAW

Our Mother is being
destroyed.
Saving Her is necessary
to save ourselves
through living right
living sustainably.
The time to change
is now,
here, where
we find ourselves.

In 1997 David and Lexa Ayer gifted us twenty acres on the Snake River. Because of their generosity our dream of building a straw bale home for ourselves became a reality. We moved from Arizona back to Idaho and began building our dream home.

Fittingly enough, Bliss was the name of the tiny town nearest our property, and the clay found along the banks of the Snake River was perfect, it was called Yahoo Clay. We chose not to use cement stucco, preferring earth plaster instead, both inside and out. We used recycled wood, doors, and windows, galvanized tin for the ceilings, outdoor pavers for the floors, and installed an old restored claw-foot tub in the bathroom. The house looked as if it had been there for years. Looking at it you could imagine it had been the original homestead. It was a joy to build and a delight to live in and we were honored when PBS Outdoor Idaho filmed our home as part of its program on The Architecture of Idaho.

Getting approval for permission to build a straw bale house in those days was nearly impossible, but I found a way around the roadblocks that were presented and ended up working with the supervisor of the County Inspection offices. He was skeptical, and with good right. There had been a couple of straw bale homes started in the county and never completed, which left him reluctant to risk giving us a permit. He insisted that he would be the inspector of our project and hold us to the highest of standards. We were determined to show him that a straw bale house was not only a valid way to build, but a necessary one; that to build sustainably was essential to the well-being of the planet. He followed us each step of the way, sometimes watching our work over our shoulders.

When the project was finished he was impressed with our home and everything it represented. The last thing he said to us when he signed the permit that allowed us to occupy the house was that he was going to build one for his family and would invite us to see it when it was finished.

We had irrigation rights to the water from the Snake River and we planted over a thousand trees on land that had grown only sagebrush and weeds. The trees were a species of willow that grew over 12 feet a year in the fertile waters of the Snake River. Our neighbors, Christopher and LuAnne Hormel, gave us branches from their willows which we planted in the ground and watered like mad - in four years the first of our plantings had grown over thirty-feet tall. They created a micro-climate, shading us from the hot summer sun and protecting us from the strong Snake River winds.

The only thing we hadn't accomplished was to own our home free and clear - no mortgage, no payments, no debt. It was a goal we had never let go of, but one we did not speak of often because if we really meant to reach that goal we would have to sell our home, and build again. It was something John was too young to understand completely, but he was old enough to know we suffered with it.

One day I got a telephone call from the Girl Scouts in New Mexico asking for advice about how to install a composting toilet in their facility. I volunteered to help them out and made arrangements to visit their camp just outside of Angel Fire. Since I would be driving through Taos, I planned to visit the Taos Pueblo which I had heard so much about. It was the oldest and longest-lived-in dwelling in North America. The building was five stories high and completely made of adobe mud and grass, the floors were made of earth and its roofs made of earth and branches. It had been home to the Pueblo Indians since AD 1350 and was still inhabited. I wanted to see their work and hoped to learn something from them.

I was enchanted, as are many who visit this historical site, and remember thinking to myself: I could live here. I loved the architecture and the country was beautiful. I also remember telling myself that I had to be careful about thinking too hard about such thoughts - that I was prone to try to make my dreams become reality. I blamed the affliction on my private tutor, Olive Suprell, and once again recalled her exact words to me:

"Do you daydream, Joe?" she once asked me.

"Sometimes I do," I replied.

She shook her head disapprovingly. "Daydreaming is a bad habit, Joe. Never daydream unless you mean to make it come true."

That advice has stuck with me forever - for better or worse.

* * *

John was attending St. John's College in Santa Fe and fall term had ended. Sheila and I decided to drive to New Mexico and bring him home for the Christmas holidays. We passed through Taos on our way home and I told them about the

Pueblo, its history, construction and its people. Sheila loved the story, John was pretty quiet. Sheila had told him the story about Olive Suprell and he had a premonition of what was to come.

John had been involved in building sustainable buildings since he was nine years old, first at the Environmental Center in Tucson, and later building our house in Idaho. He knew what kind of labor was involved in earth and straw construction, especially the way his dad did it - like the Mexicans, spending as little money as possible, and scorning all heavy equipment like the devil himself had created them.

We drove west out of Taos on Highway 64, stopping to look off the Gorge Bridge into the depths of the Rio Grande Canyon and watched the water flow slowly down its course. About ten miles farther on we saw a sign at the beginning of a dirt road that said "Cielito Lindo - Sustainable Community" and I suggested we drive in and take a look. We drove down the road for a couple of miles seeing only a few homes, spread well apart, surrounded by a sea of sage. We turned back to the highway and headed home, but the idea had taken root. One of the first things we did when we got back to Idaho was search for Cielito Lindo on our computer and read everything we could find about Cielito Lindo and Taos.

The land was situated on a mesa that got little rain, had numerous rattlesnakes, tarantulas and rabbits, and was subject to frequent wind and lightning-storms; but the sunsets, the rainbows, and mountain bluebirds were plentiful and beautiful. There was no electricity available, no utilities at all. All of your water would be provided by rain and snow, all your energy needs by the sun. It was my dream come true - totally sustainable and environmentally correct.

Olive Suprell's words had come to life once more and we put our house on the market for sale.

We had our doubts about selling a straw bale house that had been plastered with mud both inside and out. Straw bale houses were unique and rare. When people came to see our house they sometimes referred to the Three Little Pigs, "ha, ha." When they weren't laughing they were intimidated at the work involved. Straw bale houses with clay plaster can be beautiful and inexpensive to build, but the amount of work it takes to construct one by hand is not for the faint of heart. I knew whoever bought our house would be wealthy and would want it for a show piece, something unique that no one else had. I also knew financing a straw bale house would be very difficult and we would have to find a cash buyer.

Our house remained on the market for more than a year. We had plenty of lookers, but as I had feared they were mostly curious and wanted to see a straw bale house, not to purchase one to live in.

It was late in August - the country was dry and the fire danger was extreme. It was early morning and our neighbor decided to burn some weeds, wanting to get it done before the winds picked up. It only took one stray gust and the fire blazoned out of control. The flames obediently followed the course the winds set. The whole river canyon was soon aflame, and the inferno of it was heading our direction.

It wasn't long before the BLM firefighters were on the scene with their tanker trucks, a large back-up crew, and helicopter support. They parked in our driveway and readied themselves to protect our home from the on-coming torrent. The helicopters were flying to the river, scooping water into their huge buckets and dumping the water on the leading edge of the fire. They were slowing it down, but the brush and weeds were very dry, plentiful and volatile - the fire would not cease without a fight.

It was complete havoc, fire fighters racing everywhere, helicopters racing loudly through the air, smoke so thick that you couldn't see more than five-hundred feet in any direction. I went out into our field with a machete and took to frantically laying low anything that looked like it might carry the fire too near.

In the midst of this chaos, with absolutely perfect timing, a woman arrived who wanted to see the house.

She was a tall woman, and she was beautiful. She walked and moved like clear water flowing over white sand. Her silk dress gently rippled as she walked, as if she had grown up carrying water buckets on her head. I would learn later that she had been born in Sri Lanka and had been raised in a mud house. She wanted to see something that would remind her of her childhood and the home she had left behind. Driving in she had seen our "For Sale: Please Contact Joe Leonard" sign through the billowing smoke and the ash falling from the sky.

She looked at me through the smoke as I stood sweating in the field, machete in hand, and said, quite calmly, "Mr. Leonard, is your home for sale?"

I had to wait for the noise to subside before I could answer her - helicopters were flitting overhead, firefighters were pumping water out of our pond spraying the grass and trees down, and people all around were yelling. I was worried about the rapidly approaching fire and fearing for my property, but I stopped worrying long enough to realize that if I sold the house in the next twenty minutes, I could gather up my photographs, some mementos and make a run for it.

"Yes, it is," I responded, smiling invitingly.

"Can I see the inside?" She seemed totally oblivious to the chaos surrounding us.

"Certainly, it would be my pleasure." And it would be. I couldn't wait to get away from the noise, and to get my potential client out of sight of the madness that was so implacably approaching.

We walked her through the house. She looked in wonder as she toured its rooms, her mouth open.

"How much are you asking?" she asked me.

"Today?" I replied, glancing out the window at a firefighter dodging a spurt of red flame.

She only smiled and nodded. "Today."

As I told her the price I felt almost faint, not believing what was happening.

"I will buy your home, Mr. Leonard, it is beautiful," she said as she rubbed her soft hands on the velvet smoothness of the clay. "It reminds me of my home in Sri Lanka. I just sold my home in Seattle and I got more than I asked. I was wondering what to do with the extra money, but the moment I saw your house, I knew."

And so we sold our home. She asked Sheila and me if we would like to stay on and be the caretakers. "You can live in the house. You can build another one down on the river for me and my family, and you could build a barn for our horses over by the corral. You could help with the landscaping and help entertain my friends when they come to visit."

We told her we would think about her offer, but we already knew the response. We had been in this position more than once and understood what we could expect. But beyond all such concerns, there was something deeper that made us turn her offer down. We wanted a home of our own - a totally sustainable home, in which we could live our own lives, simply and peacefully.

John's suspicions had been well-founded indeed. We ended up putting a deposit on twenty acres of sagebrush in Cielito Lindo, with not a tree in sight, save for a few scraggly juniper on a distant hill. It was the first time we had ever made such a huge decision without John's approval. He hadn't even seen the piece of land we were buying, but we also knew that it was getting close to the time in his life when he would be leaving home to find his own place in the world.

We stayed on in Bliss through January drawing plans for our next home and learning what we could about solar power, water catchment and how to compost all our waste. It was an exciting project and with the sale of our house we had just about enough money to accomplish my dream, thinking, not for the first time, that it would be my last. And, not for the first time, I would be wrong.

STRAW BALE AND EARTH HOUSE, NEW MEXICO

Sun
sustains us
water
nourishes us
life is an
impossibility
without them.

We left Idaho on a cold and windy day in February. We rented a U-Haul truck and loaded it with all the necessities; a wall tent, a wood stove, sleeping bags, and all the tools necessary for construction, which consisted mostly of trowels, shovels, a wheel-barrow, and various tools. The weather in Taos when we arrived was beautiful - tee shirt days and sweaters at night. I remember promising Sheila it would be our last big straw bale project and that if she would live in a wall tent while we built, I would make her coffee every morning and serve it to her in her sleeping bag. She made me promise twice.

The first people we met were Nakeesha and Ivy, who had built their house some years earlier and had arrived much the same as we had - in a Toyota 4Runner, just like ours, and a U-Haul filled with tools and necessities. They had lived in a dome structure while building their home. They were gracious from the first and invited us to dinner as soon as we got settled in. Ivy is a successful contractor and has taken straw bale construction to a new level, his houses are beautiful and excellently built, built to stand forever.

John had a short break from his studies and he came to help get us started. Our first project was to put in the road leading to our construction site. John, knowing I would never hire a road grader, bent for his pick and shovel and we began cutting our road through the sagebrush and clearing a space for the tent platform. I selected a spot near the arroyo for our tent. It wasn't a large arroyo, it was in fact quite modest, only about three feet deep in places, and I had plans for capturing its waters during spring runoff.

As I began clearing the space for our tent John looked at me and remarked, "Dad, it looks like it could flood here..." "Not a chance," I responded, referring to my superior wisdom in matters of a Biblical nature. "We only get twelve inches of rain a year, and it would have to rain half that much in one day to flood the arroyo."

Alas - God decided this would be just the opportunity to teach me a lesson in humility. In August of that year a storm of biblical proportions came, thunder and lightning so bright and loud you had to cover your eyes and ears, the sky split open like a water melon and it rained six inches in thirty minutes. The arroyo rapidly became a river, thirty feet in width, and flooded our tent with three feet of water, carrying pots, pans, and anything that would float towards the Rio Grande. It scattered these things all across God's countryside, leaving them as providential gifts for whoever might discover them. I supposed that I had lost some credibility with John on Biblical matters after that.

But, all of this was to pass many weeks into the future, at present we had not even set up our tents. Three days after we had finished the road, all was sunny. We had raised our tent up on its platform and we had our toilet facility built. Inside the twelve-by-fourteen tent we had a kitchen, bunks for two, and plenty of firewood (sagebrush) for the stove. It had been sunny and warm every day since our arrival and I worked in short-sleeved shirts and short pants. Our tent was up and we were ready to begin building our dream. John returned to the world of academia and life was good.

Then it began to snow, and it didn't stop.

John came to visit again from Santa Fe – it was spring break and he was bringing a friend, Kristen, to visit. Our tent was not big enough for all of us so we bought a cheap Coleman tent that would suffice for our guest cabin. It had loads of room, you could even stand up in it. With a good sleeping bag Kristen would be warm and comfortable. They arrived in early March, John prepared for roughing it, and Kristen wearing high heels, wondering how she could maneuver through the snow to reach the tent. John and I set their tent up and fastened it tightly to the ground as the winds whirled round. It looked like it would be comfortable and Sheila and I thought they would be just fine. It hadn't been very cold at night - about eight degrees - and their bags were rated to twenty below zero. What could go wrong?

We went to bed exhausted from getting things as comfortable as we could and listened as the wind blew in fury. It blew from dusk to dawn, both tents were being whipped and pounded. Kristen and John didn't sleep much the first night, perhaps they didn't sleep at all. The next day it got really cold. The wind didn't let up and it started snowing so we all went to bed early.

It was in the dark of early morning when the Coleman tent began to shred in the wind, with John and Kristen in it. She cried, John grew concerned, and the next day they took a motel room in Taos. The next night the wind blew harder than ever. It blew the outhouse away, it sucked the chimney through the roof of the wall tent like a rocket blasting off, and John's tent went completely missing. Kristen was ready to go. She left with a smile, and never returned. John later told us that she wrote a college term paper about her experience on the mesa. I wish I could have read it.

It required a month and more to install the solar system. John and Sheila worked like slaves on raising the straw bale walls. John had been our saving grace, there was so much we couldn't have done without him. He never once asked what we had been thinking when we sold our beautiful home on the Snake River in Idaho, never once questioned our dream. He supported us with determination and grace. He brought three friends to help during part of their summer vacation from school: Sonia, Jarvis, and Mark. They were there during the hardest part of the construction and we will never be able to thank them enough for their help. We could only hope that they, too, took something from the experience.

We had the roof on the house before John returned to St. John's that fall. The hardest part left was to put up the large windows, which would heat the inside of the house with the abundant sunshine of the mesa during the winter months. We didn't know how we could raise the windows alone, they weighed a ton. I would lie in my sleeping bag at night trying to design some kind of pulley system that Sheila and I could operate ourselves without damaging ourselves or the windows.

Ivy dropped by on occasion to see how we were coming along on the house and mentioned one day that we should be closed in by Halloween, it was then the weather would change and get really cold. He worried over us and one day in late October he drove into our house, bringing his crew to help us hang our big windows. The generosity of our new neighbors, many of whom helped us on the house, reminded me of my time in the mountain villages in Mexico where the entire community was always ready to help when one of its members was in need, a thing that has become too rare in our country. Indeed, it was only with help from our new friends and neighbors that we made it into our house on time, and were not left to suffer another miserable winter in our tent. We moved in on the first day of November, just as Ivy told us we should, and it wasn't a moment too soon.

The following summer John returned home ready to build his own casita out of rammed earth and straw. It was his first home and it was beautiful, filled with all of his books and his great energy. It felt very empty when he was away.

And thus the dream of sustainable living had become a reality for each of us. We lived a simple life, doing as little harm to the planet as possible, and learned to live with the sun and waters of the seasons - our water coming from the rain and snow, most of our heat and all of our power from the sun. We composted all of our waste and from it were able to grow small lovely gardens in the desert. Much of our furniture was built out of earth, hardened like our earthen floors. It was an enriching life, full of sky, sun, and vast horizon and quiet.

STRAW BALE HOUSE, SARDINIA, ITALY

Roots grown
deep in
fertile soil
resist
movement.

After graduating from college John moved to Florence, Italy, where he taught English as a second language. He had fallen in love with the country, the people, the art and the history. Sheila and I were not surprised - it always seemed to us that he belonged in that old and ancient world. His depth of thought and even his demeanor placed him there. We believed it to be a most natural place for him - his reincarnation to be lived again.

As destiny would have it, one day while listening to a singer in Piazza Santa Croce he met Silvia. She was a beautiful young woman from Sardinia, an island in the Mediterranean off the west coast of Italy. They fell in love and decided to leave Florence, to make their home in Sardinia. They were married in the small town of Dolianova in July of 2012. Sheila and I attended the wedding, along with some of Sheila's family. We met Silvia's delightful family for the first time, and her parents, Bruno and Lucia, graciously shared the beauty of their homeland with us. We enjoyed the quaint villages, the narrow streets, old buildings, and most of all, the people of this beautiful, peaceful island.

We returned to Taos filled with happiness for John and Silvia, but we both felt a sense of emptiness at home. Sardinia was far, far away and we knew we would not be seeing John and Silvia often. The distance was too great.

Our plans had always been to leave a legacy, a sustainable house and land with no mortgage, to John. He had worked hard on all of our houses over the years, and in quiet dignity had moved from one to the next. His plans for us were that we would have a comfortable home where we could enjoy our older years.

We skyped John and Silvia every couple of weeks, but it wasn't the same as sitting together in a room and sharing life's stories. One day they called us and asked if we would consider moving to Sardinia. They had checked with the local officials and it seemed they would welcome a sustainable home built with straw bale on the island. Another path, another choice - and not an easy one to make.

It was not hard for us to imagine living in Sardinia, but it was hard to think about selling our beautiful home in Taos. I was 72-years old and Sheila 60. It was hard, dirty and heavy work, and we were not sure we were physically capable of completing such a project. As we sat one morning gazing at the expansive mesa from our porch, I looked at Sheila and said, "But why not - what else would we do? Sit in our rocking chairs and fade away? When would we see John and Silvia again?"

And with that, we called a realtor and asked if he would be interested in listing our house on the mesa. We set an appointment and awaited his arrival.

It couldn't have been a worse time to put our house on the market. The real estate market had collapsed and houses were not being sold anywhere in the U.S. Many people would negatively perceive the things we thought of as being essential in a healthy home; a composting toilet, water catchment, and electricity that was totally solar generated. Also financing would be difficult, if not impossible. Most banks would not finance earth and straw bale houses and definitely would not finance one without a septic system or well. We didn't expect to sell within the near future. Not only would we have to find someone who was interested in a sustainable dwelling, but that someone would have to be, once again, a cash buyer. The chances were slim to none.

The realtor arrived and was impressed with our mesa home. He told us he would love to list it and we determined an asking price, telling him we would not accept a penny less than the amount we had listed it for. He left, assuring us he would be by with the listing agreement in the next few days. In the afternoon of that very day he called and said he had a prospect who would like to see the house.

They arrived soon after and we were introduced to his client. She was a retired marine - tough, strong and capable. She wanted to look at the house without a guide, so I took a few minutes to explain the drawbacks, in the interest of clarity; a composting toilet, no sewer system, rattlesnakes and tarantulas, and all the projects that would have to be completed before we sold it. I explained that we would be moving to Italy and the sale of the property would include all the furniture; kitchen utensils and dishes, construction tools, bicycles, skis - everything that was attached or not attached. The only exclusions would be John's library, which filled one wall of the casita, and our dog Sam; he was going with us and so was the library. She listened to me, somewhat impatiently, before hurrying through the house and John's casita, both inside and out. She spent all of thirty minutes and was gone. So much for that client.

Later that day our realtor called and asked if we were available to sign the listing agreement later in the evening. I said we would be home and would look forward to seeing him. He arrived with the listing, all was as expected and we signed the forms. After the signatures were completed, he looked at us, smiling. He reached into his brief case and withdrew a contract, a full cash offer. Absolutely stunned, we immediately accepted. We set to work on the house and completed all the requests that were listed in our contract, and two months later we were on our way to Italy.

We flew into Rome where we spent hours getting Sam out of customs, only managing it with the help of our taxi driver, who fortunately spoke English. Our driver then drove us to the terminal and we boarded the ferry that would carry us over the Mediterranean Sea to Cagliari, the capitol of our new home. Silvia, Bruno, and John were awaiting our arrival and we packed all our bags, John's guitar, and Sammy into Bruno's van, leaving the ferry behind.

We were a bit dazed from our long trip and everything seemed surreal. They pointed out landmark after landmark as we drove on to Dolianova, where they had rented us a house that we would live in while we were building our own. It was a colossal three-story house made of pure cement, as are most of the homes here. It was a house full of history, but a house that motivated us to complete our straw bale home as soon as possible, for it was frigid in the winter and humid and hot in the summer. But I had promised Sheila she would never have to live in a tent again.

We have learned true patience here in Sardinia. Life does not move rapidly and the bureaucracy boggles the mind. It is not what one would call "a well oiled machine," but when all is said and done, it is a glorious place filled with extraordinary history and people. The people are determined to keep as much of their little island as untouched as possible and protect their agricultural lands. They care for them in the old ways, rarely using the new equipment and technologies that have destroyed the small farms in the United States. They still harvest the foods that grow naturally in the wild and seldom do you drive down a road that someone is not picking something from the earth to take home for their meal.

John and Silvia found a beautiful property with an olive grove of 190 trees, most over 100-years old, and the land is blessed with a strong flowing artisan well. We have built our home with the clay that we dug from our foundation, and straw bales that we purchased from a farmer nearby. We have constructed a black-water wetland filled with water plants, and a separate pond that has taken on a life of its own with fish, frogs, dragonflies and cattails. The artisan well is like gold and John and Silvia have planted fruit trees and are planning on starting an apple orchard, which is rare on the island. Sheila and I have started a small vineyard and have planted lemon trees, apricots trees and nectarine trees – our flower gardens are beautiful and we eat the figs and almonds from trees that have grown on this land forever.

The village of Serdiana, full of friendly Sardinians, is about a mile away - close enough that we can ride our bicycles there to shop for groceries. The markets remind me of my childhood, small but with all the necessities. The little meat market is filled with quality fresh meats, sliced by the butcher while you watch; bakeries full of oven-fresh bread and pastries; vegetable markets overflowing with fresh fruit and vegetables grown by the local farmers.

The Mediterranean Sea is but a short drive away. There is no obvious poverty on the island, there are no homeless people sleeping on the streets, and few beggars. Guns are outlawed here, but for hunting in season, and the people live in peace. They have free health care and the poor are provided housing. The people seem secure, happy and free to complain about their government, which they do with animation. The country has its problems, but where in this world today is there a country without them?

It is early morning and I am sitting on the porch of our new straw bale home watching the sun rise. As I look around me and at all we have accomplished over the past three years, I feel a deep contentment. I still have my moments of wander lust, but I am happy. My days are filled with labor, some I like, some I don't. Sheila and I have shared our lives for 40 years and my sons are all healthy. I have a beautiful daughter-in-law, Silvia, a delightful Sardinian grandson, Conrad David, and we live in a beautiful and comfortable home built of straw and earth that we have built ourselves. What more could one ask for?

Another Mountain to Climb?

POST SCRIPT

Destiny will
not
be denied.

Throughout my life I have constantly been confronted by mountains, some unyielding and unforgiving, some which have been beyond my recognition and understanding, and many that have seemed unconquerable, but *all* have been of my own creation. I have climbed, or made attempts to climb, each one of them only to discover another, waiting on the horizon, all of them intertwined. While climbing the mountain of judgment I have found myself on the mountain of forgiveness; while climbing the mountain of forgiveness I have found myself on the mountain of defensiveness; mountains of love and loss, mountains of pain and despair, mountains of fear and faith. And so it has continued. With persistence and faith I have reached the summits of some of my mountains and in so doing have been gifted with a deeper understanding of life. I have become one with them, with their steep pitches, overhangs, meadows and lakes. In my mountains I have found my light shining through darkness.

It seems there is no ending to personal and spiritual growth. It is here in Sardinia, of all places, that I have become aware of my need to control. Where better to deal with the challenge! I do not speak the language of the country, cannot read the road signs, and am making a valiant effort to understand a new culture. Long ago I assumed that if I was to be the director of my own movie I would have to take control of my life in order to be successful. I have finally understood that control has been but a stepping stone, and as well as it has served me, it must be left behind. It has been necessary for me to break through the barriers of my ego to find the truth. Understanding this has made all the difference.

I am 76 years old and have lived long enough to see this mountain for what it is. I have only to accept what needs mending, renounce false beliefs and go forth in gratitude and with love; only then can I reach the mountain's summit. Understanding is the journey, and the journey is the path to understanding. This will not be my last discovery, or the end of my story.

The greatest gift given me has been my ability to take risk. When life was not flowing well, or when I reached a crossroad, I was never intimidated. I did not hesitate to choose the path less worn. I took it willingly and with faith, even though I could not see where it would lead. I seized the moment, compelled to experience life to its fullest – to grow and to learn.

The courage to question what life was all about was given me by the little girl with cerebral palsy who I met when I was a young boy. The day she looked into my eyes was the day my spiritual journey began. I was only with her a short while, but when I left her I was filled with questions about her, myself, life, and most importantly, about God. My quest for answers began that day and even though there have been times I have given up, I have always returned, searching for answers and growing with awareness.

My excursions into the mystical; hearing voices, experiencing the power of prayer, or for just an instant experiencing separation of mind from body, is considered by many to be delusional. For me they have all been gifts, given by a greater power, propelling me onward. If I have been delusional, I would rather that than live a life filled with fear, denial, and little hope. I prefer a life filled with wonder, acceptance of the good and the bad of it, and finding meaning and hope in it all.

I have experienced the joy, wonder, and beauty that our natural world holds. Visions and memories of the startling, magnificent moments I have experienced in nature come to mind, but I cannot find the words to do them justice. I have found my home in nature, and no matter how fleeting the moment may have been, I have been humbled and graced with the true meaning of life: *One* with all, *One* with *God.*

John Muir beautifully stated, "Man should stand in nature's temple witnessing the eternal morning of creation occurring all about him." He believed that nature, not man, was the center of the timeless universe.

In his dying hour, Crowfoot of the Blackfoot people, a brave warrior and eloquent spokesman, spoke of life: "What is life? It is the flash of a firefly in the night, it is the breath of a buffalo in the wintertime. It is the little shadow which runs across the grass and loses itself in the sunset."

I may have reached my limits in understanding the process of continuum, but I believe that my final step, in this lifetime, will be well tended. I have no fear of death, because I do not believe in death. It is not the end, nor the beginning, it is but a part of the eternal journey.

Life is a drop of dew on the tip of a blade of grass ... evaporating with the sun's first rays. Not dead, but reborn.

Joe Leonard – 2016

"Yet there are no steps along the road that anyone takes by chance. It has already been taken by him, although he has not yet embarked on it. For time but seems to go in one direction.

We but undertake a journey that is over, yet it seems to have a future still unknown to us.

Time is a trick, a slight of hand, a vast illusion in which the figures come and go as if by magic. Yet there is a plan behind appearances that does not change. The script is written. When experience will come to end, your doubting has been set. For we but see the journey from the point at which it ended, looking back on it, imagining we make it once again: reviewing mentally what has gone by."

A COURSE IN MIRACLES

Thank you all....

My son, Joey, who has ventured on a journey most of us would be unwilling to try. I admire him for his courage. He is definitely climbing his mountains.

My son, Richard, who has been my spiritual adviser and pushed me to continue growing when I was ready to give up. Thanks for your love.

My son Jesse Joe, who spent only three short years with Sheila and I. Jesse taught me to grow beyond suffering and taught me to see a different world - a world full of light. He taught me so much about overcoming fear and death and because of his spirit, I know when I knock at the door to heaven he will be there to greet me.

Bonnie Marx, for her unwavering love and patience for seventeen years.

My son John, who has given me so much joy. He has taken every gift I have given him and given it back a thousand times over. His integrity, intelligence, his music, art, and strength of character is, in the truest sense, awe inspiring. Without his inspiration and encouragement, this book would never have been attempted. Without his editing, my book would have ended up in a box never to have been seen again.

Sheila's family – Bruce, Barbara, Binki, Wug, Brooke, Bruce, Jolene, Roger and Pru, who have been my extended family. I have fond memories of adventure, conversation, inspiration, and love with each one.

David Ayer, my partner in Leonard-Ayer Expeditions, who has been the brother I never had in this life. He has supported me in my madness and made possible many of my life's dreams. His generosity has been boundless. Whatever contribution I have made towards the encouragement of sustainable living, would never have happened without him.

Lexa Ayer, David's lovely wife, who gifted me "A Course in Miracles" in 1979. Through her gift I have found my pathway to the world of true reality - some people call it the path to heaven.

Luann and Christopher Hormel whose love, generosity, and support made it possible to complete our dream on the Island of Sardinia. They literally saved my life once, and had they not, I would never have known these last precious years.

John Zapp, my climbing partner in many of the stories moved to New Zealand in 1970. John never got to the summit of Mt. Regan and I saw him for the last time, in 1990. I hope he has gotten everything out of life that he wished for. He was an inspiration and without him as my mentor, life would have been much different and considerably poorer. I have no doubt he has found other mountains to climb.

David Kimpton, for his great friendship and the many conversations, adventures and stories we shared.

Tom Kovalicky, for all the help in our efforts to climb Mt. Regan, things would have been much different if he hadn't been there.

Norm Garrison, my partner in NJ Ski Tours, we had some great adventures together.

Barb and Bob Michels, Sandy Gebhards, Dan Jordan, Bev Lefler, Fred Brubaker and Steve Gordon, for your friendship and support at Robinson Bar and through the years.

Stacy Gebhards, whose white lightening, and music warmed many a mountain tent on cold winter nights.

Nakeesha, for her wisdom and friendship, and Ivy who was always there when there was need.

Sam and Jim Grossman, two of my first kayaking students. Jim took kayaking into dimensions that I could only dream off.

Steve Mufley, who has been a life-long inspiration.

Dan Blackburn, for his numerous magazine articles, and the book Zen and the Cross Country Skier.

Mary and Wally Smith and their children, Megan, Hillary and Scott, for their participation in Robinson Bar and for all the ski trips we shared together.

Norm and Jean Bishop, for setting the example of good parenting; and their sons, Jayson, Greg, Rand - their outstanding music in needed in our world.

Michael, Teddy, Al, and Paul of White Water, for the many times they came to Robinson Bar Ranch to play for the crew and our guests.

Bob Sevy, who amazes me still.

Bill Hon and Bev Hon, who supported me throughout my years at Robinson Bar and continued supporting me when I left the Ranch.

Nancy Reynolds, for her sensitivity; and her sons, Kurt and Clark, for remembering me.

Kirk Bachman, one of the best guides I ever worked with.

Dean Conger of National Geographic, for introducing me to Mongolian yurts.

Terry Taylor, for his advice and encouragement and for the wonderful books he has written.

Doug and Pat Sterrett and their beautiful family, for all the wonderful memories of camping, skiing, Thanksgiving and friendship.

Jarvis Cline, who has set such a fine example of right living.

The Sahuaro Girl Scouts in Tucson, Gail, Judy, Bonnie, Stephanie, McGyver, and Boo, for their unwavering dedication to the young ladies of the future.

And most of all to Sheila, my wife, companion and fellow traveler for the last 40 years, I am thankful for the love, support, and courage she has shared with me. Without her adventurous spirit and willingness to explore life's possibilities, I would never have lived the life I have. Without her wisdom this book would not be in your hands.

CPSIA information can be obtained
at www.ICGtesting.com
Printed in the USA
BVHW081219060820
585581BV00001B/7